AVATAR AND PHILOSOPHY

The Blackwell Philosophy and Pop Culture Series
Series editor William Irwin

A spoonful of sugar helps the medicine go down, and a healthy helping of popular culture clears the cobwebs from Kant. Philosophy has had a public relations problem for a few centuries now. This series aims to change that, showing that philosophy is relevant to your life—and not just for answering the big questions like "To be or not to be?" but for answering the little questions: "To watch or not to watch *South Park*?" Thinking deeply about TV, movies, and music doesn't make you a "complete idiot." In fact it might make you a philosopher, someone who believes the unexamined life is not worth living and the unexamined cartoon is not worth watching.

Already published in the series:

24 and Philosophy: The World According to Jack
Edited by Jennifer Hart Weed, Richard Brian Davis, and Ronald Weed

30 Rock and Philosophy: We Want to Go to There
Edited by J. Jeremy Wisnewski

Alice in Wonderland and Philosophy: Curiouser and Curiouser
Edited by Richard Brian Davis

Arrested Development and Philosophy: They've Made a Huge Mistake
Edited by Kristopher Phillips and J. Jeremy Wisnewski

Avatar and Philosophy: Learning to See
Edited by George A. Dunn

The Avengers and Philosophy: Earth's Mightiest Thinkers
Edited by Mark D. White

Batman and Philosophy: The Dark Knight of the Soul
Edited by Mark D. White and Robert Arp

Battlestar Galactica and Philosophy: Knowledge Here Begins Out There
Edited by Jason T. Eberl

The Big Bang Theory and Philosophy: Rock, Paper, Scissors, Aristotle, Locke
Edited by Dean Kowalski

The Big Lebowski and Philosophy: Keeping Your Mind Limber with Abiding Wisdom
Edited by Peter S. Fosl

Black Sabbath and Philosophy: Mastering Reality
Edited by William Irwin

The Daily Show and Philosophy: Moments of Zen in the Art of Fake News
Edited by Jason Holt

Downton Abbey and Philosophy: The Truth Is Neither Here Nor There
Edited by Mark D. White

Dungeons & Dragons and Philosophy: Read and Gain Advantage on All Wisdom Checks
Edited by Christopher Robichaud

Ender's Game and Philosophy: The Logic Gate Is Down
Edited by Kevin S. Decker

Family Guy and Philosophy: A Cure for the Petarded
Edited by J. Jeremy Wisnewski

Final Fantasy and Philosophy: The Ultimate Walkthrough
Edited by Jason P. Blahuta and Michel S. Beaulieu

Game of Thrones and Philosophy: Logic Cuts Deeper Than Swords
Edited by Henry Jacoby

The Girl With the Dragon Tattoo and Philosophy: Everything Is Fire
Edited by Eric Bronson

Green Lantern and Philosophy: No Evil Shall Escape This Book
Edited by Jane Dryden and Mark D. White

Heroes and Philosophy: Buy the Book, Save the World
Edited by David Kyle Johnson

The Hobbit and Philosophy: For When You've Lost Your Dwarves, Your Wizard, and Your Way
Edited by Gregory Bassham and Eric Bronson

House and Philosophy: Everybody Lies
Edited by Henry Jacoby

The Hunger Games and Philosophy: A Critique of Pure Treason
Edited by George Dunn and Nicolas Michaud

Inception and Philosophy: Because It's Never Just a Dream
Edited by David Johnson

Iron Man and Philosophy: Facing the Stark Reality
Edited by Mark D. White

Lost and Philosophy: The Island Has Its Reasons
Edited by Sharon M. Kaye

Mad Men and Philosophy: Nothing Is as It Seems
Edited by James South and Rod Carveth

Metallica and Philosophy: A Crash Course in Brain Surgery
Edited by William Irwin

The Office and Philosophy: Scenes from the Unfinished Life
Edited by J. Jeremy Wisnewski

Sons of Anarchy and Philosophy: Brains Before Bullets
Edited by George A. Dunn and Jason T. Eberl

South Park and Philosophy: You Know, I Learned Something Today
Edited by Robert Arp

Spider-Man and Philosophy: The Web of Inquiry
Edited by Jonathan Sanford

Superman and Philosophy: What Would the Man of Steel Do?
Edited by Mark D. White

Supernatural and Philosophy: Metaphysics and Monsters... for Idjits
Edited by Galen Foresman

Terminator and Philosophy: I'll Be Back, Therefore I Am
Edited by Richard Brown and Kevin Decker

True Blood and Philosophy: We Wanna Think Bad Things with You
Edited by George Dunn and Rebecca Housel

Twilight and Philosophy: Vampires, Vegetarians, and the Pursuit of Immortality
Edited by Rebecca Housel and J. Jeremy Wisnewski

The Ultimate Daily Show and Philosophy: More Moments of Zen, More Moments of Indecision Theory
Edited by Jason Holt

The Ultimate Harry Potter and Philosophy: Hogwarts for Muggles
Edited by Gregory Bassham

The Ultimate Lost and Philosophy: Think Together, Die Alone
Edited by Sharon Kaye

The Ultimate South Park and Philosophy: Respect My Philosophah!
Edited by Robert Arp and Kevin S. Decker

The Walking Dead and Philosophy: Shotgun. Machete. Reason.
Edited by Christopher Robichaud

Watchmen and Philosophy: A Rorschach Test
Edited by Mark D. White

Veronica Mars and Philosophy: Investigating the Mysteries of Life (Which Is a Bitch Until You Die)
Edited by George A. Dunn

X-Men and Philosophy: Astonishing Insight and Uncanny Argument in the Mutant X-Verse
Edited by Rebecca Housel and J. Jeremy Wisnewski

AVATAR AND PHILOSOPHY

LEARNING TO SEE

Edited by George A. Dunn

WILEY Blackwell

This edition first published 2014
© 2014 John Wiley & Sons, Inc.

Registered Office
John Wiley & Sons, Ltd, The Atrium, Southern Gate, Chichester, West Sussex, PO19 8SQ, UK

Editorial Offices
350 Main Street, Malden, MA 02148-5020, USA
9600 Garsington Road, Oxford, OX4 2DQ, UK
The Atrium, Southern Gate, Chichester, West Sussex, PO19 8SQ, UK

For details of our global editorial offices, for customer services, and for information about how
to apply for permission to reuse the copyright material in this book please see our website at
www.wiley.com/wiley-blackwell.

The right of George A. Dunn to be identified as the author of the editorial material in this work has
been asserted in accordance with the UK Copyright, Designs and Patents Act 1988.

Library of Congress Cataloging-in-Publication Data

Avatar and philosophy : learning to see / edited by George A. Dunn.
   pages cm
   Includes bibliographical references and index.
   ISBN 978-0-470-94031-0 (cloth)
 1. Avatar (Motion picture : 2009)   I. Dunn, George A., 1957– editor.
   PN1997.2.A94A95 2014
   791.43′72–dc23
                                                            2014016571

A catalogue record for this book is available from the British Library.

Cover image: © Kanuman / Shutterstock.

Set in 10.5/13pt Sabon by SPi Publisher Services, Pondicherry, India

1   2014

Contents

Acknowledgments: I See These People   viii

Introduction: Time to Wake Up   1
George A. Dunn

**Part I Seeing Eywa: "I'm With Her, Jake.
        She's Real!"**   **5**

1 The Silence of Our Mother: Eywa as the Voice of
   Feminine Care Ethics   7
   George A. Dunn and Nicolas Michaud

2 "Eywa Will Provide": Pantheism, Christianity, and
   the Value of Nature   19
   Jason T. Eberl

3 The Tantra of *Avatar*   36
   Asra Q. Nomani

**Part II Seeing the Na'vi: "You Will Teach Him
         Our Ways"**   **49**

4 Learning to *See* the Na'vi   51
   Stephanie Adair

5 It Doesn't Take an Avatar: How to Empathize
   with a Blue-Skinned Alien   62
   Andrew Terjesen

6 "I See You" through a Glass Darkly: *Avatar* and the Limits of Empathy 74
Massimiliano Cappuccio

Part III Seeing Nature: "Try to See the Forest through Her Eyes" 87

7 *Seeing* the Na'vi Way: Respecting Life and Mind in All Organisms 89
Kyle Burchett

8 They're *Not* Just Goddamn Trees: Hegel's Philosophy of Nature and the Avatar of Spirit 104
James Lawler

9 "Everything Is Backwards Now": *Avatar*, Anthropocentrism, and Relational Reason 115
Jeremy David Bendik-Keymer

Part IV Seeing Our Bodies: "They've Got Great Muscle Tone" 125

10 The Identity of Avatars and Na'vi Wisdom 127
Kevin S. Decker

11 "I Got This": Disability, Stigma, and Jake Sully's Rejected Body 139
Ryan Smock

12 "See the World We Come From": Spiritual versus Technological Transcendence in *Avatar* 151
Dan Dinello

Part V Seeing Our Political Communities: "Sky People Cannot See" 165

13 "We Will Fight Terror with Terror": *Avatar* and Just War Theory 167
Joseph J. Foy

14 The Community and the Individual in *Avatar* 180
Dale Murray

15   *Avatar* and Colonialism   190
     Nathan Eckstrand

**Part VI   Seeing Our Ethical Responsibilities:
            "Sometimes Your Entire Life Boils
            Down to One Insane Move"**   **201**

16   "All That Cheddar": Lessons in Business Ethics
     from the RDA Corporation   203
     Matthew Brophy

17   "We Have an Indigenous Population of
     Humanoids Called the Na'vi": Native
     American Philosophy in *Avatar*   215
     Dennis Knepp

18   I See Animals: The Na'vi and Respect for Other
     Creatures   226
     Wayne Yuen

**Part VII   Seeing the Movie: "You Are Not Gonna
             Believe Where I Am"**   **239**

19   The Digital Cabinet of Curiosities: *Avatar* and
     the Phenomenology of 3D Worlds   241
     Robert Furze and Pat Brereton

Notes on Contributors: Our Avatar Drivers   252
Index: My Last Video Log   258

Acknowledgments
I See These People

Many thanks to all the contributors to this volume for the hard work that made this book possible. Their insights have greatly enhanced my own appreciation of the philosophical dimensions of the fantastic world that James Cameron has created and I'm sure that they will do the same for you, our readers. Special thanks to Bill Irwin, the general editor of Blackwell's Philosophy and Pop Culture Series, who shepherded this project from beginning to end, and to everyone at Wiley who worked to bring this project to fruition, including Constance Sanstisteban, Lindsay Bourgeois, Allison Kostka, and Liam Cooper. Nick Michaud, Walter Robinson, and Ariadne Blayde also deserve special mention for their valuable assistance with important aspects of the project. Finally, I would like to thank my friend 毛一琼 (Grace Mao), for her steady encouragement: 加油!

Introduction
Time to Wake Up

Captivating movies are like dreams. They offer a break from our ordinary lives, a release from the stranglehold of mundane concerns, and a passport to fascinating worlds that exist only in imagination. This is all certainly true of James Cameron's spectacular 2009 film *Avatar*. Employing state-of-the-art digital effects, motion-capture photography, and other cutting-edge cinematic technologies, many developed just for this movie, Cameron and his team of artists, designers, and technicians created a lush world of breathtaking beauty, like nothing that had ever been seen on a widescreen before.

Heightening the dreamlike quality of the movie experience was Cameron's revolutionary use of 3D technology and the presentation of *Avatar* on gigantic screens in IMAX theaters – which, much like Jake Sully's avatar, enabled audiences to step outside of themselves and temporarily inhabit the jungles of Pandora. Immersed in this fantastic new world of floating mountains, hexapods, and bioluminescence, we shared Jake's feeling of ever-deepening intimacy with Pandora, curling up alongside him in a Hometree hammock and navigating the skies on the back of a great toruk. The beauty of *Avatar* and of Pandora left many moviegoers shuddering in pure awe. Some viewers even reported that they suffered bouts of depression as they went into Pandora withdrawal. After awakening from such a captivating and realistic dream, our everyday lives can seem grey and dreary by comparison.

Avatar and Philosophy: Learning to See, First Edition. Edited by George A. Dunn.
© 2014 John Wiley & Sons, Inc. Published 2014 by John Wiley & Sons, Inc.

But, as Jake reminds us in the voiceover that accompanies the opening images of the movie, "sooner or later you have to wake up."

More than a dreamlike escape, *Avatar* is also an allegory for events in the real world. Critics and commentators have been drawn into heated debates about the movie's presentation of a wide range of cultural, social, political, and religious themes. *Avatar* is a feast for the eyes, but it also offers much food for thought on issues such as the health of our planet, imperialism, militarism, racism, corporate greed, property rights, the plight of indigenous peoples, and eco-friendly spirituality.

Just as Jake's rendezvous with the Na'vi and his experience of the astonishingly rich panoply of strange biota found on Pandora awaken him to a new view of the world while simultaneously reshaping his loyalties and priorities, so too our experience of *Avatar* can help us to see the real world more truly and perhaps even inspire us to change it for the better. "Everything is backwards now," says Jake at a crucial point in the movie. "Like out there is the true world and in here is the dream." "Out there" is the world of the Na'vi, with their deep reverence for life and their wisdom about how to live sustainably. "In here" is Hell's Gate – the sterile, artificial world fabricated by greedy human beings who have forgotten how to live in harmony with nature. Clearly Cameron is encouraging us to see the environmentally destructive aspects of modern industrial civilization as products of a deluded worldview, a bad dream from which we might be awakened.

Sorting out dreams from reality has long been a preoccupation of philosophers. That's one reason why *Avatar* has generated so much interest among warriors of the "egghead clan," including the contributors to this volume. In the pages that follow, philosophers weigh in on many of the most contentious moral and political issues raised by the movie, addressing topics such as environmental ethics, colonialism, war, and the conduct of corporations. But *Avatar* also provides fodder for reflection on a host of distinctively philosophical questions concerning the relationship between mind and body, personal identity, the possibility of truly knowing an alien civilization, empathy, aesthetics, science, technology, religious attitudes toward nature, and our experience of the world of the movies. Could *tsaheylu* (the bond) really be possible? Is a mind something that can be transferred from one body to another? Are trees really "just goddam trees"? Or might there be more to the world than what we can know through the methods of empirical science?

James Cameron is currently working in New Zealand on three sequels to *Avatar*, which will further explore the Pandoran biosphere and, according to early reports, will introduce a new indigenous undersea culture dwelling in Pandora's oceans. These new films will make use of pioneering methods of underwater motion-capture photography that represent a major leap forward in film technology. Another dreamlike extravaganza – endowed with the power to provoke a response that is at once visceral, emotional, and intellectual – surely awaits. If we only focus on the visual aspect, though, we'll miss more than half the picture. We need to keep our mental muscles in shape to think about the philosophical implications of Pandora. So, while we're waiting for the next installments of James Cameron's epic cinematic wakeup call, let's start reading!

George A. Dunn

Part I

SEEING EYWA
"I'M WITH HER, JAKE.
SHE'S REAL!"

The Silence of Our Mother
Eywa as the Voice of Feminine Care Ethics

George A. Dunn and Nicolas Michaud

"If there is a hell, you might want to go there for some R&R after a tour on Pandora," Colonel Miles Quaritch informs the new arrivals to Hell's Gate. Yet Pandora reveals itself to Jake Sully as an enchanted world of wonder. Can Pandora be both a heaven and a hell?

Quaritch depicts Pandora as a living nightmare, a den of horrors where every conceivable danger lurks. Pointing toward the jungle, he warns the new arrivals: "Out there, beyond that fence, every living thing that crawls, flies, or squats in the mud wants to kill you and eat your eyes for jujubes." To his mind, Pandora is a deadly arena with enemies at every turn. Not only does the planet harbor a race of hostile humanoids with natural endowments and fighting skills that make them "very hard to kill," along with a dizzying assortment of other hostile life forms, but even the atmosphere itself is poisonous. To survive in such an environment, you must harden yourself, so you'll be mentally prepared to do whatever it takes to stay alive. "You're on Pandora, ladies and gentlemen," Quaritch grimly reminds the new arrivals. "Respect that fact, every second of every day." The upshot of his ominous "old school safety brief" is that a healthy dose of fear is an indispensable tool for survival in this pitiless place. Let down your guard and Pandora will "shit you out dead with zero warning."

After listening to Quaritch's description, we might be surprised to learn how very differently the Na'vi view their world. Of course, like Quaritch, they "respect" Pandora, but not as a powerful foe. They

Avatar and Philosophy: Learning to See, First Edition. Edited by George A. Dunn.
© 2014 John Wiley & Sons, Inc. Published 2014 by John Wiley & Sons, Inc.

know the perils of their environment every bit as well as Quaritch does, but fear doesn't define their relationship to their world. Above all, they revere Pandora – and Eywa, the deity who pervades and animates the planet – as a source of life, a nurturing mother, a provider, and a protector. Pandora, for them, is more than just an arena of deadly conflict. It's first and foremost a place of caring.

How Can You See, with Jujubes for Eyes?

That Quaritch and the Na'vi have such divergent views of the natural world may have something to do with the very different *social* worlds in which those worldviews were born. The militarized precinct of Hell's Gate epitomizes the conventional idea of a "man's world" – a place where your status depends on demonstrating courage, strength, and endurance in the face of adversity. It's a contentious world that is forever sorting its denizens into winners and losers. Jake's voiceover at the beginning of the movie nicely sums up the ethos of this place, at the same time as it lays bare his own fiercely competitive tempera-ment: "I became a Marine for the hardship. To be hammered on the anvil of life. I told myself I could pass any test a man can pass." And the world that does the hammering is, according to this hardcore Marine, nothing short of "a cold ass bitch." Of course, to describe Hell's Gate as a "man's world" is not to deny that a tough gal like Trudy Chacón can more than measure up to its demands; but she's clearly in a minority. The military personnel on Pandora is over-whelmingly male. By contrast, the world of the Na'vi is much more feminine. Na'vi women are equal partners with their men and are just as capable as their male counterparts. And as the *tsahìk* (spiritual leader) of the Omaticaya clan, Neytiri's mother Mo'at exercises an unrivalled degree of power and influence due to her ability to inter-pret the will of Eywa, the Na'vi's female deity. With their devotion to Eywa – their "Great Mother," who connects them to each other and to everything else on Pandora – the Na'vi embrace an ethic that is distinctly maternal.

Could differences in male and female temperaments give rise to different ethical outlooks? That was the thesis of psychologist Carol Gilligan in her 1982 book *In a Different Voice*, which has come to be regarded as a watershed in the history of thinking about gender issues.

Whereas men tend to view life as a contest in which individuals constantly attempt to advance themselves at each other's expense, women more typically view themselves as intimately tied to larger interpersonal networks sustained by relationships of care and intimacy. According to Gilligan, these two ways of situating ourselves in relation to the world have given rise to two distinct "voices," masculine and feminine, each of which is associated with a different approach to moral decision making.

The masculine voice puts a premium on *justice* – in particular, on protecting individual rights and on appealing to abstract rules in order to adjudicate conflicts. Principles of justice are important because they allow us to manage our conflicts without having to break out the poison-tipped arrows on a regular basis. We can define justice in many different ways, but in the modern world it has become common to think of justice as consisting in a set of rules or principles that aim to safeguard the rights and to balance the legitimate interests of all people, impartially. One of the most influential theories of justice is known as "contractualism," which likens the demands of justice to the terms of a contract that we have entered into with each other. We all give up our rights to do whatever we please, we agree to live under a set of rules that apply to everyone as free and equal individuals, and we receive the benefits of social cooperation and a guarantee that our rights will be protected just so long as we don't interfere with the rights of others.[1]

The feminine voice, on the other hand, bears a remarkable resemblance to the voice of Eywa, since it focuses not on refereeing disputes, but rather on the *care* that sustains the web of concrete relationships in which people can flourish. "Our Great Mother does not take sides," Neytiri tells Jake. "She protects only the balance of life." We can think of these two voices as belonging, respectively, to the impartial judge and the caring mother. Gilligan argues that men tend to gravitate to the "justice perspective" and women to the "care perspective," though both genders are sufficiently versatile to approach questions of morality from either perspective.

The problem, according to Gilligan and many other feminist critics, is that almost all of the ethical theories that have dominated Western philosophy until quite recently have been one-sidedly masculine: they view conflict as the fundamental fact of society and morality as a way to manage our skirmishes and prevent them from getting too destructive. In short, these "masculine" ethical theories express a view of society not unlike the view of Pandora expressed by Colonel Quaritch. Imagine a different sort of "old school safety brief," one that someone like Quaritch might give not to new arrivals on Pandora, but to individuals on the threshold of adult life in the human world:

> You're not in diapers anymore, ladies and gentlemen. You're in the adult world, where you're just one among many individuals, all fighting to get ahead and prepared to eat your eyes for jujubes if you get in their way.

Truth be told, this isn't a bad description of what we see of life on Earth in the opening sequence of the movie, before Jake leaves for Pandora. And in such a world, where "the strong prey on the weak" and interpersonal conflict is both inevitable and, as Jake's brother Tommy discovered, sometimes deadly, a morality focused on rules that insure fair treatment for all has an obvious appeal. Fairness matters greatly to Jake, as we see when he brings his fists to the defense of a young woman who's being bullied by a man in a bar. As Colonel Quaritch says: "You've got obey the rules." In this case, though, it's not "Pandora rules" but rather the rules of morality that offer us our only hope for survival in "the most hostile environment known to man" – the human social world! However, while conflict may be an undeniable fact of social life – as well as an ineliminable feature of the natural world on both Earth and Pandora, as Jakes discovers in his very first outing beyond Hell's Gate – this is by no means the whole story. Both the Na'vi and the terrestrial proponents of feminine "care ethics" help us see the bigger picture.

The Gifts of Our Mother

"Try to see the forest through her eyes," Grace admonishes Jake. Through Neytiri's eyes Jake will learn to see heaven on Pandora, while the belligerent Quaritch can never see anything but a hellish landscape of danger and strife. Neytiri's more benign vision of Pandora comes into clear focus for Jake at a crucial moment during his training, when the two of them spy on a mother viperwolf playing affectionately with her pups. Previously known to Jake only as a vicious killer, his onetime deadly foe is surprisingly revealed to be a tender caregiver. However, to peer into this corner of the viperwolves' world requires a stealthy approach. Jake and Neytiri must keep a respectful distance so as not to provoke another attack like the one Jake clumsily incited on his first night in the forest; for even the most tender caregiver can turn into a ferocious killer when the welfare of her children is at stake. That's a lesson that Quaritch learns all too well when his assault on Pandora unleashes the fury of Eywa. Quaritch lands on a planet full of life, diversity, and communion, but all he can see is conflict and opportunities for violence. What he never seems to realize is that the violence of Pandora, cruel and merciless though it may be, is in the service of something that his jujube eyes can never see – the tender care that Pandoran creatures extend to each other.

Despite the description that Jake offers early in the movie, Pandora is more than "just another hellhole" where mercenaries and miners do dirty jobs and get handsomely remunerated for their troubles – a world of "hired guns, taking the money, working for the company." Beyond the grubby pursuit of self-interest at Hell's Gate lies another world of breathtaking beauty, where everything is deeply interconnected, each being living from energy that it "borrows" from others and that it is bound in due course to "give it back." The metaphor of borrowing, which Neytiri uses to describe the connection between all living things on Pandora, may sound superficially like the same contractual tit for tat that governs the relationship between the Resources Development Administration (RDA) and its hired guns. That, at least, is an interpretation that fits with the justice perspective, with its focus on fairness and reciprocity. There is, however, a crucial difference between the Na'vi worldview and this contractual model. The Na'vi seem to regard the borrowed energy that nurtures and sustains their existence as a gift of Eywa, their Great Mother. And, ironically enough, the name human beings chose for the Na'vi's world is Pandora, a Greek name meaning "All-Gifts." But the "sky people" seem to lack a full appreciation of the implications of that name, not recognizing that the proper response to a gift is not a jealous sense of entitlement but rather heartfelt gratitude, which is most genuinely expressed as a desire to give back.

Reflecting on mothers and their gifts brings us to the heart of the care perspective. Proponents of care ethics like to remind us that, long before we were in any position to demand justice, insist on our rights, or enter into contracts, we were entirely dependent on the maternal care we received from our mothers or other primary caregivers. As vital to our existence as their relationship with Eywa is to the Na'vi, these caring relationships are not about satisfying the terms of some contract or ensuring that neither party encroaches on the rights of the other. Instead, the hallmark of the caring relationship between a child and her caregiver is the profound bond between two hearts - like *tsaheylu*, but without neural queues - an emotional attachment that makes the parent especially sensitive to her child's needs. Nor is it a freely chosen relationship between equals who have calculated the costs and benefits of cooperation. As the parent opens her heart to the child, she realizes that she can't detach herself from this relationship without damaging her very identity and her integrity as a person. Moreover, she recognizes that being the stronger party in the relationship doesn't necessarily give her the upper hand. It's the needs of her child, the more vulnerable party, that dictate what she must do.

If not for these unchosen bonds of care, the sort of relationships that the justice perspective believes lie at the heart of morality couldn't even get off the ground. Consider Quaritch, who has spent his entire adult life wrangling with powerful opponents and coming out on top through his own ingenuity and strength. Hard as it is to imagine, even this stalwart warrior began life - to quote William Shakespeare (1564–1616) - "mewling and puking in the nurse's arms," only much later becoming "jealous in honor, sudden and quick in quarrel, seeking the bubble reputation, even in the cannon's mouth." Had he survived his final smackdown with Jake, Quaritch might have eventually found himself once again in a state of utter dependency, a physically frail old man, "sans teeth, sans eyes, sans everything."[2] Of course, Quaritch might put it differently. In his own poetic voice, he might say that he entered this world a "Shavetail Louie" and that in the course of time this world will "shit him out dead." But the point is the same: those self-sufficient individuals whom the justice perspective imagines us to be represent at best only one stage of our lives, which is wedged between long periods of dependency. Perhaps Quaritch's contract with the RDA includes provisions for his geriatric care, but the care he received as an infant was presumably not given to satisfy the terms of a contract. If it was like the care most of us received, it was a gift of love.

It's easy for adult men like Quaritch to forget their dependence on the care of others, which may in turn cause them to imagine social reality to be much more conflictual than it really is. As Carol Gilligan observes, "women perceive and construe social reality differently than men."[3]

> Since the reality of connection is experienced by women as given rather than freely contracted, they arrive at an understanding of life that reflects the limits of autonomy and control. As a result women's development delineates the path not only to a less violent life but also to a maturity realized by interdependence and care.[4]

Historically, women are the ones who have had the most intimate experience of care, since they have traditionally been the ones tasked with providing it for children, the sick, the disabled, and the elderly. If the justice perspective was born of the experience of men in the rough and tumble world of "territorial threat displays," where you better "keep your head on a swivel" and keep an eye out for hostiles at every pass, the care perspective reflects an experience of the world much more familiar to women, where nurturing and responsive care, rather than disputatious jousting, are the anchors of daily life.

The Work of Our Mother

Reflecting on how philosophers have traditionally thought about ethics, feminist philosopher Nel Noddings tells us: "One might say that ethics has been discussed largely in the language of the father: in principles and propositions, in terms such as justification, fairness, and justice. The mother's voice has been silent."[5] The Na'vi, though, can hear their mother's voice and so seek to emulate her practice of caring.

The philosopher Sara Ruddick (1935–2011), one of the pioneers of care ethics, identified three activities at the core of what she calls "maternal work": preserving the life of the child, fostering the growth of the child, and training the child for social acceptability.[6] When Neytiri undertakes the work of teaching Jake the ways of the Na'vi and imparting the skills he needs to both survive and flourish in the environment of Pandora, she's engaging in this very same sort of "maternal work" – a fact that's underscored by her initial character-ization of him as "like a child." And, according to Ruddick, this practice of mothering is of singular importance not only because it answers to the vital needs of the child – and childlike adults, such as Jake – but also because it cultivates certain valuable moral and intel-lectual qualities. In particular, the mother must develop a sensitivity and responsiveness to the "nature" of the child, for "children are nothing before they are natural, and their growing is a work of nature. When children thrive, it is nature that thrives."[7] And, through her loving attention to the nature present in the child, the mother may come to acquire an appreciation of nature in general that allows her to see it as something much more than a menacing arena of conflict. As Ruddick explains:

> The settled antagonism of treating "nature" as an enemy is at odds with the engaged, sometimes adversarial, but fundamentally respectful rela-tion to "nature" characteristic of preservative love, even more with the "natural" beneficence underlying growth.[8]

The preservative love that informs maternal work involves taking what is given by nature, safeguarding it, and helping it to realize its full natural potential. For the Na'vi, to engage in the work of nurture and care is to participate in the work of Eywa in her unending effort to sustain the conditions under which her children can flourish.

Nel Noddings is a philosopher who has drawn from the maternal perspective to develop another influential account of caregiving, which highlights the caregiver's need for what she calls "engrossment" and "motivational displacement." We are "engrossed" in the "cared-for" to the extent we're able to occupy her perspective, which requires "stepping out of our own frame of reference and into the other's."[9] As the Na'vi would say, we must truly "see" the other, for recognizing her needs is an indispensible precondition of caring for her properly. Then we can give ourselves over to "motivational displacement," in which we are motivated by the needs of the other rather than merely by our own desires. Such empathetic engagement with other beings, including other species, seems to be the hallmark of the Na'vi way of being in the world. Consider a Na'vi who seeks to ride an ikran (mountain banshee): if she approaches the ikran simply as an object to bend to her will, she'll never be able to make the bond. When the ikran seeks to "kill" her, she will fail to recognize it as an act of "choosing," interpreting it instead as an aggressive provocation and an invitation to respond in kind. Making the bond with an ikran requires an intricate dance, in which one must accurately interpret the nature and the needs of the ikran in order for the partnership to be formed. Even before *tsaheylu* is consummated, the Na'vi must be able to occupy the perspective of the other.

And, just like the *tsaheylu*, the caring relationship between two human beings involves more than just an intellectual grasp of the other's situation. It requires emotional engagement. Philosopher Annette Baier (1929–2012) has pointed out one reason why care ethics puts such a premium on emotions:

> It might be important for a father figure to have total control of their violent urges to beat to death the children whose actions enrage them, but more than control of such nasty emotions seems needed in the mother or primary parent, or parent-substitute, by most psychological theories. They need to love their children, not just control their emotions.[10]

Love provides the motivation for caring. But emotions are also important to the care perspective because they sometimes allow us to grasp aspects of a situation that may not be available from a justice perspective.

Caring is complex and messy. There's no simple, one-size-fits-all formula that will tell us how to care, since genuine caring requires sensitivity to the needs of particular individuals as they arise in highly specific situations. This may be one of the reasons why philosophers have often preferred the clear-cut, impersonal rules of the justice perspective, where abstract, formal reasoning dictates what's right and wrong, without any messy complications or emotions. According to Noddings, "ethical argumentation has frequently proceeded as if it were governed by the logical necessity characteristic of geometry."[11] And many philosophers have argued that that's how it should be, since sentimental biases can so often cloud our ability to act rationally and to make truly responsible ethical decisions.

Consider the destruction of Hometree. Parker Selfridge did the math, concluded that his obligation to the stockholders was more important than the lodging preferences of "the blue monkeys," and made his decision, confident that he was doing the right thing. His inability to empathize with the Na'vi and to understand the world from their perspective ("We try to give them medicine, education, roads. But, no, no, no, they like mud!") leaves him unable to see their attachment to Hometree as anything other than irrational intransigence. According to his own "rational" calculations, taking the lives of a certain number of intransigent Na'vi is an acceptable price for getting the surviving Na'vi to move. Of course, later, as flames engulf Hometree, Selfridge looks on with an expression that suggests that even he is affected by the horror of what he had done. But we can imagine a truly hard case like Quaritch dismissing that emotional reaction as mere sentimentality that clouds one's judgment and softens the resolve to do what must be done.

In contrast, consider Neytiri, who feels the awful weight of her action when she's forced to kill the viperwolves who are attacking Jake, recognizing that what she must do is a serious harm to both herself and her world. That's because the maternal perspective of the Na'vi enables her to see much more than the "sky people" can. When she looks at Jake's fierce attackers, what she "sees" is not just the mortal threat they pose to Jake, but mothers, pups, and their own struggle for survival. When she slays them, she mourns for them and the families they leave behind. This "engrossment" and "motivational displacement" is bound up with a distinctive perspective, one that becomes more and more accessible to Jake as his own motivations and attitudes begin to mirror those of the Na'vi and as he comes to appreciate the perspective of the mother.

Mother Takes Sides

Emphasizing the maternal origins of care ethics doesn't mean that men aren't capable of caring. Neytiri's father, Eytukan, clearly cares deeply for his people, with an attentiveness and concern not unlike the feelings of a mother for her children. Nor should we suppose that care ethics has no room for justice. Most care ethicists recognize that both the father's voice and the mother's voice must be included in a full account of our moral responsibilities. As Baier observes, "there is little disagreement that justice is a social value of very great importance, and injustice an evil."[12] Moreover, most care ethicists acknowledge the inevitability of conflict in a world where the interests of everyone don't necessarily coincide. On a planet where "the strong prey on the weak," there will be a place for masculine warrior virtues of the sort Quaritch exemplifies – such as physical courage, strength, endurance, and pride – alongside the maternal caring ones. Caring might require mounting your ikran, grabbing your quiver of poisoned arrows, and going into battle to protect those you care about. For this reason, warriors like Jake and Tsu'tey have an honored place within Na'vi society. Neytiri is also an excellent warrior. And so, for that matter, is Eywa.

Before leading the battle against the "sky people," Jake pleads with Eywa: "See the world we come from. There's no green there. They killed their mother, and they're gonna do the same here. ... I will stand and fight. You know I will. But I need a little help here." It's at this point that Neytiri speaks the words that we quoted earlier, about how Eywa is a nurturer, not an adjudicator of conflicts: "Our Great Mother does not take sides, Jake. She protects only the balance of life." Yet Neytiri is not entirely right. Like any good mother, Eywa bestows her care on all her offspring equally, remaining impartial when disputes arise between them; but, when the very survival of that caring relationship is imperiled, she can't remain on the sidelines. As Noddings writes: "The one-caring has one great aim: to preserve and enhance caring in herself and in those with whom she comes in contact."[13] When the intricate web of relationships that comprises life on Pandora is under assault, protecting the balance of life means taking sides and joining the fight.

"All I ever wanted in my sorry-ass life was a single thing worth fighting for," reports Jake in his opening voiceover. In the end, he found what he was looking for in Eywa. Jake has learned that the masculine perspective of the warrior is incomplete, that it needs the feminine ethic of caring to give a worthy meaning and purpose to the fight. Without that care perspective, the world can easily devolve into a living hell.

Notes

1. For more on contract as a basis for ethics and on the communitarian alternative, see Chapter 14 by Dale Murray.
2. William Shakespeare, *As You Like It*, Act II, Scene VII, lines 44, 51–53, and 66.
3. Carol Gilligan, *In a Different Voice: Psychological Theory and Women's Development* (Cambridge: Harvard University Press, 1993), 171.

4. Ibid., 172.
5. Nel Noddings, *Caring: A Feminine Approach to Ethics and Moral Education*, 2nd ed. (Berkley: University of California Press, 2003), 1.
6. Sara Ruddick, *Maternal Thinking: Toward a Politics of Peace* (New York: Ballantine Books, 1989), 17.
7. Ibid., 77.
8. Ibid., 115.
9. Noddings, *Caring*, 24.
10. Annette Baier, "The Need for More Than Justice," in her *Moral Prejudices: Essays on Ethics* (Cambridge: Harvard University Press, 1995), 30–31.
11. Noddings, *Caring*, 1.
12. Baier, "Need for More Than Justice," 19.
13. Noddings, *Caring*, 172.

"Eywa Will Provide"
Pantheism, Christianity, and the Value of Nature

Jason T. Eberl

"Haven't got lost in the woods, have you?" With this layered question Colonel Miles Quaritch confronts Jake Sully on his return from an extended stay with the Na'vi. Quaritch senses that Jake is starting to see the world as the Na'vi do, which is a problem, since the Na'vi stand in the way of his employer's economic interests on Pandora. In a rare film review published by *L'Osservatore Romano*, the quasi-official newspaper of the Vatican, a representative of the Roman Catholic leadership also voices concern about the effects of spending too much time among the Na'vi and worries that the intoxicating visual beauty of James Cameron's cinematic masterpiece may lure unsuspecting viewers into the "woods" of Pandora and the Na'vi's eco-centric worldview.[1] This reaction may not be surprising to some. After all, a pro-imperialist and anti-environmentalist stance is consistent with the church's long history of making strategic alliances with and conferring spiritual blessings on *conquistadores* and others who raped the land and the indigenous populations of the "new world" to exploit its resources. This history of conquest may in turn seem to follow a tradition that ostensibly began in the Book of Genesis, when God said to the first human beings: "Be fruitful and multiply, and fill the earth and subdue it; and have dominion over the fish of the sea and over the birds of the air and over every living thing that moves upon the earth."[2]

Avatar and Philosophy: Learning to See, First Edition. Edited by George A. Dunn.
© 2014 John Wiley & Sons, Inc. Published 2014 by John Wiley & Sons, Inc.

Recent history, though, shows a different attitude emerging among Christians of all denominations. For instance, the Vatican, under the leadership of Pope Benedict XVI, spearheaded a number of pro-environmental initiatives, such that the retired pontiff has been nicknamed "the green pope" in some circles. One example is a list of "ten commandments for the environment," a statement of environmental principles released by the Vatican.[3] Another is the installation of solar panels on the roof of the stadium-size auditorium where papal events are held.[4] The Vatican is also on track to become the world's first "carbon-neutral" state by participating in a reforestation project in Hungary to offset its fossil fuel consumption.[5] Finally, Pope Emeritus Benedict has directly addressed environmental concerns:

> In nature, the believer recognizes the wonderful result of God's creative activity, which we may use responsibly to satisfy our legitimate needs, material or otherwise, while respecting the intrinsic balance of creation. If this vision is lost, we end up either considering nature an untouchable taboo or, on the contrary, abusing it. Neither attitude is consonant with the Christian vision of nature as the fruit of God's creation ... Nature is at our disposal not as "a heap of scattered refuse," but as a gift of the Creator who has given it an inbuilt order, enabling man to draw from it the principles needed in order "to till it and keep it" (Gen 2: 15) ... it is a wondrous work of the Creator containing a "grammar" which sets forth ends and criteria for its wise use, not its reckless exploitation....[6]

Such moral teaching and practical measures represent an alternative interpretation of God's initial command to humanity – an interpretation that recasts the command in terms of *stewardship* as opposed to *domination*.

If the Vatican has adopted a "pro-green" attitude, then why the negative reaction to *Avatar*? Is there anything about the Na'vi's relationship with their world and with other animals that goes against traditional Christian doctrine? Is there some common ground between the respective spiritualities of the Na'vi and Christianity? Let's explore these questions to see if there's a sound philosophical ethic within the Christian intellectual tradition that shares *Avatar*'s view of nature as valuable *in and of itself*, not just as a tool for humans to use for their own purposes.[7]

"They're Fly-Bitten Savages Who Live in a Tree"

As it turns out, the focus of the Vatican's critique isn't *Avatar*'s pro-environmental, pro-indigenous population and anti-imperialist message, but rather the theological cloak in which these messages are wrapped. Traditional Christian theism holds that God is both *transcendent* and *immanent*, meaning that God exists wholly outside of the created universe, outside of space and time, yet interacts with the created universe in myriad ways – most directly through incarnation in the person of Jesus of Nazareth. Compare this with Eywa, the Na'vi "All Mother." Eywa is also worshipped as a divine being; but, unlike the Christian God, she doesn't merely interact with the world of Pandora but *is* Pandora *itself*, manifested through the intricate neural network among the plant and animal species that inhabit it, the Na'vi among them. Divinizing the world in this way constitutes *pantheism* – the thesis that God is everywhere, in everything, and does not exist outside of the universe in any fashion. Thus *L'Osservatore Romano*'s central criticism of *Avatar* is that this film "shows a spiritualism linked to the worship of nature, a fashionable pantheism in which creator and creation are mixed up."[8] Vatican Radio asserts that *Avatar* "cleverly winks at all those pseudo-doctrines that turn ecology into the religion of the millennium. Nature is no longer a creation to defend, but a divinity to worship."[9]

Described in this way, the theology of *Avatar* is indeed inimical to traditional Christian theism's foundational belief in a transcendent creator. But this doesn't mean that the ecological attitudes linked to the Pandoran worldview are necessarily at odds with those linked to traditional theism. While the latter doesn't view God as existing solely *within* the world, it does understand God to be intimately united with the world as its creator and the constant sustainer of its existence. God didn't just get the ball rolling and then leave the universe to its own devices – a view known as *deism* – but is actively involved, even now, in maintaining creation in existence. Furthermore, according to various classical and contemporary Christian theologians, the world's *biodiversity* – the rich array of different created beings – is a direct and necessary result of God's creative action. God doesn't want a uniform and monotonous world but one that testifies to God's goodness by containing a diverse variety of beings. Thus respect for *all* life forms may be morally required of those who profess to serve God's will, regardless of whether they view God as immanent or transcendent.

Regrettably, Christians have not always recognized the moral value of nature and nonhuman animals but have all too often regarded them merely as "tools" to be used in any way human beings see fit. Lynn White, Jr. describes the traditional interpretation of the Book of Genesis, which, he contends, is one of the primary roots of the modern ecological crisis:

> Man named all the animals, thus establishing his dominance over them. God planned all this explicitly for man's benefit and rule: no item in the physical creation had any purpose save to serve man's purposes ... [Christianity] not only established a dualism of man and nature but also insisted that it is God's will that man exploit nature for his proper ends.[10]

White's point is effectively illustrated in this first-hand account of the traditional Christian view of humanity's relationship to the other animals and "things" that populate our environment:

> Brute beasts, not having understanding and therefore not being persons, cannot have any rights ... We have no duties to them ... Brutes are as *things* in our regard: so far as they are useful to us, they exist for us, not for themselves; and we do right in using them unsparingly for our need and convenience, though not for our wantonness.[11]

This disdain for the rights of nonhuman creatures is also on full display in Parker Selfridge's contemptuous dismissal of the Na'vi as "fly-bitten savages who live in a tree," whose interests are therefore owed no consideration when things of value to human beings are at stake. If this is his attitude toward nonhuman creatures whose appearance and capabilities so closely resemble our own, it should come as no surprise that he has even less concern for the interests of the other "brute beasts" of Pandora.

"You Are Not in Kansas Anymore. You Are on Pandora"

Despite the attitude that dominated Christian thinking for millennia and remains influential among many Christians to this day, there are other strands within the Christian tradition that are much more friendly to ecological concerns. Lynn White himself proposes Francis of Assisi (1182–1226) as "a patron saint for ecologists,"[12] on account of his love of nature and his belief in the equality of all creatures.

Let's consider another highly influential source for Christian thought: the medieval philosopher and theologian Thomas Aquinas (ca. 1225–1274). The life of Aquinas may not supply us with stirring anecdotes of biophilia in practice, as does the life of Francis, but in his writings we find solid philosophical and theological reasons to adopt a more ecologically friendly view of the relationship between God, human beings, and the rest of creation.

Aquinas understands the created universe to manifest God's *being*, *goodness*, and *beauty*. In God, these qualities are *infinite*, so they could not be replicated exactly by anything that is not God. Nevertheless, Aquinas writes:

> [God] brought things into being in order that His goodness might be communicated to creatures, and be represented by them; and because His goodness could not be adequately represented by one creature alone, He produced many and diverse creatures, that what was wanting to one in the representation of the divine goodness might be supplied by another. For goodness, which in God is simple and uniform, in creatures is manifold and divided and hence the whole universe together participates in the divine goodness more perfectly, and represents it better than any single creature whatever.[13]

God saw fit to create not just one form of finite goodness – human beings – but a plentitude consisting of innumerably different forms and degrees of created goodness. One could thus argue that the extinction of species has a direct and negative impact on the manifestation of the divine in nature.[14] Aquinas even asserts what may pass for a theological truism on Pandora: "God is in all things, and innermostly."[15] But, as Jill LeBlanc notes, "this view is not pantheism: God is not all things."[16] Rather God's essential nature is to be a transcendent creator, present to all beings as the source of their existence. But Aquinas believes that God is also "present" within created beings in another way: as the source of an internal motivation that inspires them to strive to be as much like their creator as they can within the limits of their own essential nature, calling forth whatever forms of being, goodness, and beauty are proper to the flourishing of each species. "Flourishing" refers to the actualization of a creature's essential capacities, to its living the sort of life for which it was meant.

On Pandora, for example, animals such as viperwolves flourish by doing what's necessary to stay alive – hunting, fighting off predators, reproducing – and by forming communities based on mutual aid and affection. The Na'vi flourish through similar activities, but also by using their intellects to perfect those pursuits and to seek greater knowledge and wisdom for their own sake. The divine is manifested through these activities when, in *harmonious* fashion, these activities produce higher degrees of being, goodness, and beauty, each individual being doing its naturally ordained part to contribute not only to its own flourishing, but also to the flourishing of other beings in its environment. For example, the Pandoran warbonnet fern produces nectar that attracts insects, which provide food for a certain species of bird that has developed a close relationship with the warbonnet. By feeding on these insects, the birds protect the warbonnets from them.

It's worth noting how different the flora and fauna on Pandora are from their earthly counterparts, which is exactly what one would expect were it God's will that life evolve on other planets in ever greater diversity. The evolution of life on this planet is just another aspect of creation growing ever nearer to what it can never perfectly reproduce: the infinite being, goodness, and beauty of its creator.

To manifest the qualities of God in nature, it's not enough for many different types of beings to exist. Each individual member of each species must seek to *perfect* itself – striving to "be all that it can be" (in the spirit of the US army slogan of the 1980s). Hence each warbonnet and each octoshroom strive to be the best plant they can be, by seeking nourishment and other necessities for its survival and reproduction. Each viperwolf and each thanator seek not only their own survival and reproduction, but also pleasure and the avoidance of pain, as part of their *sentient* animal nature. As one moves up the evolutionary chain, various capacities distinctive of each species emerge, which animals instinctively seek to exercise and perfect: sturmbeests protect their young, tetrapterons want to hunt, and social animals in general want to associate with other members of their species. These activities may serve ends like survival and reproduction, but they're also activities that animals may come to value for their own sake, as essential components of a good life for that species.

Finally, each Na'vi and each human being seek perfection as living, sentient, social, and *rational* animals. Thus everything in creation is seeking the divine in its own way. In the words of Aquinas, "all things, by desiring their own perfection, desire God."[17]

"We Will See If Your Insanity Can Be Cured"

The premise that everything in the universe has its own intrinsic purpose – its immanent striving toward both its own flourishing and the flourishing of other beings with which it shares its environment – provides an initial foundation for the idea that everything also possesses its own intrinsic *value*. Aquinas holds that any being's existence is good or valuable in itself, since he understands the properties of *being* and *goodness* to be *commensurate*.[18] This means that, the greater degree of existence a being enjoys, the greater its intrinsic value and the value of any act that supports its flourishing. It is good that this being continues to exist and flourish; the world is richer for it. A merely living organism is a lower grade of being than a sentient animal, which in turn is a lower grade of being than a rational animal – human, Na'vi, or otherwise. Hence the existence and flourishing of a rational animal are worth more than those of a nonrational animal, which in turn are worth more than the existence and flourishing of an organism that is neither rational nor sentient. But all creatures have some degree of goodness, so actions that support the life and health of any plant or animal will have a positive moral value, while actions that threaten life and health will have a negative moral value. Neytiri expresses her recognition of this fact when she says that it's "sad" that she killed the viperwolves. Something of value was preserved – the life of a rational creature – but it would have been better if the viperwolves didn't have to die. The "sky people," on the other hand, seem incapable of feeling sadness for the losses suffered by other living creatures, which makes them blind to the moral atrocity of their bulldozing the forest.

From a moral point of view, when we evaluate our treatment of sentient beings capable of feeling pleasure and pain – such as human beings, Na'vi, and other animal species – we need to take into account whether our actions cause them needless suffering or bring them greater joy. We observe the Na'vi's desire to minimize suffering when we see Neytiri teaching Jake how to make a "clean kill" when they hunt. In addition, social creatures – such as human beings, the Na'vi, and many other highly evolved species – seek harmonious coexistence, friendship, and love, making the promotion of satisfying relationships another fulcrum for moral evaluation. We learn that the Na'vi value such relationships when Neytiri shows Jake the litter of young viper-wolves playing together with their mother; his eyes grow wide with wonder at the tender love between these creatures, whom he had previously regarded only as vicious predators. It is unimaginable that the Na'vi would ever confine intelligent and social animals in cages, depriving them of the opportunity to form satisfying relationships with members of their own kind.

Finally, rational beings with an inherent desire to gain knowledge for its own sake – such as human beings and the Na'vi – benefit from acts that lead them toward truth and are harmed by acts that lead them away from it. Jake benefits from the education he receives from Neytiri – an education not only in techniques of surviving in the forest but, even more importantly, in learning to "see" the forest in all its alluring beauty. This natural beauty is worth knowing, Aquinas would say, because it affords us a glimpse of the eternal beauty of God. Jake's deception, on the other hand, harms the Na'vi – and not just because it makes them vulnerable to the rapacious schemes of the "sky people," but also because it thwarts their natural desire as rational beings to know the truth.

Being and goodness are also commensurate with *beauty*: the more a being flourishes, the greater its inherent, objective beauty.[19] A healthy plant or animal is more beautiful than a sickly specimen of the same species. Likewise, a healthy, flourishing environment is more beautiful than a landscape that has been ravaged by strip mining, clearcutting, or the sort of bulldozing the Resources Development Administration (RDA) Corporation inflicts on the Pandoran rainforest. The instinctive and inescapable *aesthetic* reaction we have to the natural world – an experience well captured with respect to Pandora, given the benefits of 3D IMAX projection technology – is also a recognition of the intrinsic value of those beautiful natural objects, living and nonliving alike, that compose the biosphere.

We have thus far defined three aspects of the Christian worldview: the variety of beings as a manifestation of God's nature in the created universe; the interrelated and interdependent nature of the elements and creatures that comprise the biosphere; and the inherent goodness of allowing beings of all types to flourish in their essential natures. Collectively they provide a foundation for the moral duties of human beings and Na'vi toward other animals and the rest of the biosphere that sustains our existence. Summing up these points, Thomistic philosopher Peter Cvek writes:

> From the divine perspective, all beings are good, and the life of every being has value. All beings, rational and non-rational, exist for the sake of the perfection of the universe. Moreover, since all beings contribute to the common good and perfection of the natural order as a whole, divine providence has ordained that, as much as possible, all beings should be preserved in existence.[20]

He concludes: "Accordingly, human beings have a duty to seek the preservation of the natural order, at least with respect to the preservation of each natural species."

"She's Always Going on About ... the Spirits of Animals"

Aquinas's view may be termed "non-egalitarian biocentrism,"[21] since he believes in a hierarchy with plants at its base, nonrational animals distributed along the middle rungs, and rational animals perched at its apex. We may not want to treat these as *sharp* categorical distinctions, however. Some nonrational animal species have the most rudimentary capacity for sensory awareness and locomotion, which makes them functionally only marginally better than higher levels of plant species. Others have a high degree of cognitive, affective, and volitional capacity, which puts them right on the dividing edge between "nonrational" and "rational."[22] Aquinas links gradations in *value* with an increasing capacity for volitional action, reserving for the ultimate moral category of "person" to signify "what is most perfect in all of nature": rational beings, who (he believes) are inherently endowed with "high dignity."[23] This category covers not only human beings but also nonhuman species like the Na'vi – since they, too, are clearly rational beings who freely direct their own behavior within a social moral framework.

Unfortunately, this hierarchical view leads Aquinas to reduce the value of all nonrational creatures to mere resources to be exploited by rational beings:

> We refute the error of those who claim that it is a sin for man to kill brute animals. For animals are ordered to man's use in the natural course of things, according to divine providence. Consequently, man uses them without any injustice, either by killing them or by employing them in any other way.[24]

Aquinas does concede that cruelty to the other animals is wrong, but not because of any duties we owe them. His sole concern is that cruelty to nonrational animals might instill habits in us that would make it easier to act cruelly to our fellow human beings. These oft-quoted assertions show that Aquinas may in some ways have been a typical representative of the Christian attitude that Lynn White criticizes as preparing the way for our contemporary environmental woes. On the other hand, they sit uncomfortably in the larger context of his ethical framework as well as with his understanding of the relationship between God and creation. Even great philosophers may lapse on occasion and miss the implications of some of their own insights.

Let's compare Aquinas's views on using nonrational animals with those of the Na'vi. The Omaticaya are willing to kill other animals for their own survival, but they would never allow another creature to suffer needlessly. Even when killing is unavoidable, they still perceive the death as a "sadness." The slain animal is honored as a "brother," who has sacrificed himself for those among his fellow animals who make up "the people." In addition to hunting for food, the Na'vi make other uses of their fellow animals, though typically in ways that seems more *cooperative* than exploitative. When the time comes for Jake to bond with an ikran, the winged creature must first "choose" Jake by trying to kill him, while the other ikran ignore him and fly away. Jake must then subdue his ikran, wrestling it to the ground and forcing the bond that will link the two together for life. Once the bond is formed, however, ikran and rider become one, in a way that no longer looks like a relationship of brutal domination and subjugation. On the contrary, their relationship now expresses a continuum of life shared between them. Similarly, when Neytiri teaches Jake to ride a direhorse, she instructs him to feel the animal's heartbeat, breathing, and strength as a necessary precondition for being able to *command* her. Would it be too much of an oxymoron to call this a relationship of "cooperative servitude"?

Even if rational animals sometimes need to use nonrational animals for the sake of their survival and flourishing, this doesn't mean that the nonrational have only an instrumental value – that their existence is only meaningful insofar as they may serve the purposes of persons. Rather it's evident that we nonsociopathic human beings recognize at some level the intrinsic value of other animals whenever we feel *pity* for their suffering. The capacity to feel pity is premised on an implicit recognition of a "kinship" between rational and nonrational animals – the fact that we have a shared capacity to suffer.[25] Many nonvegetarians prefer to live in blissful ignorance of the factory farming techniques and other forms of suffering that animals experience before arriving at their dinner table. It's not that they aren't aware that such suffering is occurring; they just don't want to confront those facts directly, because they know it will evoke a reaction of pity that may take the fun out of a family dinner at their favorite steakhouse. For the same reason, people who don't want to be motivated to give money to charities that provide food for starving children turn the TV channel or the magazine page when faced with a full-color image of a five-year-old orphan with a distended belly. This sort of deliberate ignorance doesn't excuse those who elect to eat meat or neglect their duty to support charitable causes, since their choice to avoid stimuli that would awaken appropriate moral emotions is itself a blameworthy decision.

According to Aquinas's hierarchy of being, human beings may justifiably use nonrational animals to support their own life. It would be permissible for a human being to kill an animal for food[26] or to save her own life from a predatory attack *if* there are no other viable options – just as Neytiri kills the viperwolves to save Jake in their first encounter, albeit with sadness and regret. But, as Christian philosopher Andrew Tardiff argues, it wouldn't be justified to kill an animal for food if vegetarian options were available, or to kill an animal in self-defense if nonlethal means were feasible.[27] Even when violence is justified to secure a higher good, only the least amount of violence necessary should be tolerated. Anything beyond that minimum – any *disproportionate* violence – is morally unjustifiable.[28] It goes without saying that any purely arbitrary – and certainly any outright *cruel* – treatment of animals is summarily ruled out.[29]

"The Most Hostile Environment Known to Man"

When human beings first arrive on Pandora, it's obvious that this world isn't meant to be a Garden of Eden for us. We even need oxygen masks just to walk around outside. Colonel Quaritch, proud of the scars he's earned on Pandora, doesn't hesitate to instill an adversarial attitude among the new arrivals:

> You are on Pandora, ladies and gentlemen. Respect that fact, every second of every day. If there is a hell, you might want to go there for some R & R after a tour on Pandora. Out there beyond that fence, every living thing that crawls, flies, or squats in the mud wants to kill you and eat your eyes for jujubes ... If you wish to survive you need to cultivate a strong mental attitude. You got to obey the rules. Pandora rules.

Later on he remarks to Jake while working out: "This low gravity will make you soft. You get soft, Pandora will shit you out dead with zero warning." Quaritch's descriptions leave us wondering how anyone, Na'vi included, could survive – let alone thrive – in such a world. Yet the problem isn't so much the environment as the confrontational stance that human beings have taken toward it, as opposed to the cooperative stance of the Na'vi.

Quaritch may regard Pandora as worse than "hell," but it's possible to give it just the opposite interpretation. Pandora is an "unfallen" world – a metaphorical Garden of Eden – characterized by a beautiful *harmony* among its inhabitants that's disrupted only when beings who aren't native to that world violently invade it. Probably the most symbolic of the names James Cameron chose for his characters is Grace Augustine. Augustine of Hippo (354–430) was a Christian philosopher and theologian who developed an astute and influential account of humanity's "fallen" nature in his theological reading of the story of Adam and Eve. Augustine shares the standard Christian belief that, prior to the fall, the first couple exercised complete "dominion" over the rest of creation, including the other animals. But he then describes the "wonderful way" they ruled over other animals in the prelapsarian (pre-fallen) world – "with the power of reason, not by brute force"[30] – which is also a strikingly apt description of how a Na'vi "rules" over the animal with whom she's made *tsaheylu* (the bond). Neither violence and cruelty nor the arbitrary use of other animals to cater to purposeless human whims were part of the pre-fallen world.

Nor did human beings exploit or abuse each other; the first biblical account of violence occurs in the Book of Genesis after human beings were banished from Eden.[31] Were it not for the fall, we would have resembled the Na'vi in our moral attitude not only toward other animals and our environment, but toward each other as well.

Filling in the details of Augustine's account, Aquinas describes how, before the fall, animals followed the commands of human beings "of their own accord" – as *subjects* following a leader, not as *slaves* obeying a master.[32] He further notes that in the prelapsarian world we didn't need to eat animals to survive.[33] In Genesis, immediately after setting human beings over the other animals, God announces that all plant life has been "given" to human beings and the other animals for food.[34] No mention is made of other animals also having been given to us for food. Genesis implies an initial state of *vegetarianism* that was rescinded later, after the fall, at the time of Noah – apparently as a concession to the violent tendencies of fallen human beings.[35]

Just as greedy and arrogant human beings disrupt the harmonious world of Pandora, the introduction of sin – stemming from human pride and greed – disrupted the prelapsarian harmony of our own world.[36] With their prideful arrogance, the "sky people" feel justified in putting their own needs ahead of those of all other creatures. Moreover, when they attempt to lure the Na'vi with consumer goodies – "lite beer" and "blue jeans" – they play the role of the tempting snake in the Garden. But then Pandora comes to light not only as an unfallen world, but as a world that resists the lures that caused us to fall. *Avatar* is a Garden of Eden story with a happy ending.

According to Augustine and Aquinas, through the grace bestowed by God by means of the redemptive sacrifice of Jesus Christ, a future restoration of prelapsarian harmony – the coming of the "Kingdom of God" – is now made possible, although it has yet to be realized.[37] Two important points are worth highlighting here.

First, the word *grace* means "gift" and is thus connected not only to the character of Grace Augustine, but also to Pandora itself, whose ancient Greek name means "all-gifts," and possibly "all-giver." Pandora – personified as Eywa – gives every living thing within its biosphere what it needs to flourish, until its ecological balance is disrupted by interlopers who didn't even have enough sense to protect their own world from ecological devastation. As Jake tells Eywa in his heartfelt prayer on the eve of battle, the Earth from which he came can no longer be an "all-giver" to human beings because of the harm they caused by upsetting the ecological balance. But this doesn't need to be our future. Pandora could be a "giver" to humanity by providing a model for how we can live in communion with our world. Jake receives the lesson, but unfortunately most of the other human beings on Pandora fail to listen and learn. Grace Augustine, of course, already knows this lesson. Her character thus signifies both the fall that is averted on Pandora and the knowledge that might be the instrument of humanity's potential renewal.

Second, the "Kingdom of God" needs us to help bring it about. We're not called to sit passively, waxing nostalgically for our prelapsarian past and hoping that God will grant us a better future. We're called to *cooperate* with God in making that hoped-for future a reality. Scriptural depictions of the Garden of Eden and of the post-apocalyptic kingdom are signs of what's possible, standards against which the present order of things must be judged, and reminders that the evils of this world are not part of God's original purpose. We realize the kingdom by acting now as if it had already come. That means putting our world back in harmony, a key feature of which is ecological balance among all living creatures and in the biosphere as a whole.

"I See You, Brother, and Thank You"

While *Avatar* and Christianity present distinct theological worldviews, similar moral lessons can be drawn concerning the intrinsic value of animals, other living beings, and the environment as a whole. Building on the moral worldview inherited from Aquinas and others in the Christian tradition, theologians and philosophers have begun to emphasize an ordering of living beings in the natural world that isn't premised on human beings possessing a "manifest destiny" to use and abuse other animals as they see fit. Rather, both rational moral reflection and our natural capacity for sympathy should lead each of us to recognize the intrinsic value not only of other animals, but of all living things and of the biosphere as a whole. All reflect, to varying degrees, the being, goodness, and beauty of God.

At the root of good and evil is our *moral attitude* toward the other beings affected by our actions and the *purpose* those actions serve. A Na'vi who kills a viperwolf in self-defense or hunts a hexapede as a source of food when no other options are available – and who recognizes that even an unavoidable killing is a "sadness" – has a completely different moral attitude from a human being on Pandora who bulldozes a forest full of animals for economic gain or, for that matter, from a human being on Earth who hunts for sport or subjects animals to cruel "factory farming" conditions for the sake of efficiency and of reaping maximum profits. These actions don't befit the dignity of the so-called "persons" whom God placed in a position of stewardship over creation. It's scary to think what would happen if God, who has absolute dominion over human beings, were to treat us as we treat those who have been entrusted to our care.

Notes

1. See Alassandra Rizzo, "Vatican Slams *Avatar*," *The World Post*, January 12, 2010, at http://www.huffingtonpost.com/2010/01/12/vatican-slams-avatar-prom_n_419949.html (accessed April 3, 2014).
2. Genesis 1: 28. All translations are from the New Revised Standard Version.
3. At http://www.catholicnews.com/data/stories/cns/0803279.htm (accessed June 16, 2010). See also Woodeene Koenig-Bricker, *Ten Commandments for the Environment: Pope Benedict XVI Speaks Out for Creation and Justice* (Notre Dame, IN: Ave Maria Press, 2009).
4. At http://www.catholicnews.com/data/stories/cns/0702971.htm (accessed June 16, 2010).
5. At http://www.catholicnews.com/data/stories/cns/0704015.htm (accessed June 16, 2010).
6. Pope Benedict XVI, *Caritas in veritate* (2009), §48, at http://www.vatican.va/holy_father/benedict_xvi/encyclicals/documents/hf_ben-xvi_enc_20090629_caritas-in-veritate_en.html (accessed June 16, 2010).
7. Of course, the views of the Vatican or Roman Catholicism in general do not necessarily reflect those of the wider Christian community, with its various denominations. The general trend, though, of moving toward a "green" theology is widespread among Christians. See, for example, Willis Jenkins, *Ecologies of Grace: Environmental Ethics and Christian Theology* (New York: Oxford University Press, 2008); or James Schaefer, *Theological Foundations for Environmental Ethics* (Washington, DC: Georgetown University Press, 2009).
8. Rizzo, "Vatican Slams *Avatar*."
9. Ibid.

10. Lynn White, Jr., "The Historical Roots of Our Ecologic Crisis," *Science* 155 (1967), 1205.

11. Joseph Rickaby, *Moral Philosophy, or Ethics and Natural Law* (1901), quoted in Peter P. Cvek, "Thomas Aquinas, Natural Law, and Environmental Ethics," *Vera Lex* 1 (2000), 7.

12. White, "Historical Roots," 1207.

13. Thomas Aquinas, *Summa theologica* (hereafter *ST*), trans. Dominican Fathers (New York: Benziger, 1948), I, Quaestio 47, art. 1.

14. See Jill LeBlanc, "Eco-Thomism," *Environmental Ethics* 21 (1999), 302.

15. *ST*, I, Quaest. 8, art. 1.

16. LeBlanc, "Eco-Thomism," 306.

17. *ST*, I, Quaest. 6, art. 1, *ad* 2.

18. See LeBlanc, "Eco-Thomism," 305. For further information on the commensurability of being and goodness, see Eleonore Stump and Norman Kretzmann, "Being and Good," in Scott MacDonald, ed., *Being and Goodness* (Ithaca, NY: Cornell University Press, 1991); Paul Vincent Spade, "Degrees of Being, Degrees of Goodness: Aquinas on Levels of Reality," in Scott MacDonald and Eleonore Stump, eds., *Aquinas's Moral Theory: Essays in Honor of Norman Kretzmann* (Ithaca, NY: Cornell University Press, 1999).

19. See Aquinas, *ST*, II.2, Quaest. 27, art. 1, *ad* 3; John Haldane, "Admiring the High Mountains: The Aesthetics of Environment," *Environmental Values* 3.2 (1994), 97–106; Montague Brown, "Natural Law and the Environment," *Proceedings of the American Catholic Philosophical Association* 63 (1989), 221–234.

20. Cvek, "Thomas Aquinas," 16–17. See Thomas Aquinas, *Summa contra Gentiles* (hereafter *SCG*), trans. Vernon J. Bourke (South Bend, IN: University of Notre Dame Press, 1991), III, 65.

21. See Cvek, "Thomas Aquinas," 18.

22. See Judy Barad, "Aquinas's Inconsistency on the Nature and the Treatment of Animals," *Between the Species* 4 (1988), 103.

23. *ST*, I, Quaest. 29, art. 3.

24. *SCG*, III, 112.

25. See LeBlanc, "Eco-Thomism," 300.

26. See *ST*, II.2, Quaest. 64, art. 1.

27. Andrew Tardiff, "A Catholic Case for Vegetarianism," *Faith and Philosophy* 15.2 (1998), 210–222.

28. See *ST*, II.2, Quaest. 64, art. 7.

29. See Peter Drum, "Aquinas and the Moral Status of Animals," *American Catholic Philosophical Quarterly* 66.4 (1992), 487.

30. Augustine, *The Literal Meaning of Genesis*, trans. Edmund Hill (Hyde Park, NY: New City Press, 2002), IX, 25.

31. See Genesis 4: 8.
32. See *ST*, I, Quaest. 91, art. 1, *ad* 4; LeBlanc, "Eco-Thomism," 298.
33. See *ST*, I, Quaest. 91, art. 1, *ad* 3.
34. See Genesis 1: 29–30.
35. See Genesis 9: 1–3.
36. Augustine and Aquinas would not limit the story of the fall and its effects to this physical planet, but would consider it part of the condition of the entire created universe; thus not even Pandora would be untouched by the effects of original sin.
37. Aquinas contends, however, that the establishment of the Kingdom of God will restore harmony only among all *rational* beings – God, angels, and human beings. Plants and animals will no longer exist, due to the fact that time would have ceased and there would be no further purpose to their existence; see *ST*, Supplement, Quaest. 91, art. 5.

The Tantra of *Avatar*

Asra Q. Nomani

When former Marine Jake Sully drapes his sinewy blue body around his Na'vi bride, Neytiri, his neural tendrils fuse with hers in one of the most unusual sex scenes ever produced on film. Critics and commentators have been dissecting the themes of the Hollywood mega-blockbuster, from its just war doctrine to its theories on environmental ethics. But there's a philosophical dimension that this otherworldly sex scene captures that most people have overlooked: the Tantra of *Avatar*. It's woven through the movie in its strong, sensual, feminist message, invoking the power of the feminine, the divinity of the goddess, and the virtue of spiritual liberation.

The characters Neytiri and Jake are the narrative vehicles for the telling of this romantic and seductive spiritual journey, which also conveys deeper lessons about how we can live with strength and moral clarity – and perhaps, if we're lucky, achieve a meaningful union with others and the world we share. In *Capturing* Avatar – a documentary about the movie's production included in the *Avatar* Extended Collector's Edition DVD – director James Cameron acknowledges that *Avatar* is "a love story." Moreover, it is the "sum total" of the "wonder" he has experienced in nature since his childhood days in rural Canada. The love story involves Jake first submitting to Neytiri as his teacher, then accepting her as his guide to becoming the man he needs to be before he can join her in their mind-blowing embrace. The wonder of nature is powerfully evoked in the Na'vi's relationship with another feminine wellspring of power and wisdom: Eywa, "their goddess, made up of all living things." Both are deeply tantric archetypes.

Avatar and Philosophy: Learning to See, First Edition. Edited by George A. Dunn.
© 2014 John Wiley & Sons, Inc. Published 2014 by John Wiley & Sons, Inc.

Weaving with Eywa

Archeologists and religious historians trace the roots of tantric philosophy to about 3000 BCE.[1] In the ruins of the ancient Indus Valley civilizations of Harappa and Mohenjodaro, in the region that was once India but is today Pakistan, archeologists have found ritual symbols representing yogic postures, mother goddesses, and fertility images conveying a powerful message of feminine divinity that would become Tantra. Before the philosophy we know today as Tantra emerged, though, the patriarchal tribes of the Aryans descended upon the Indus Valley civilization from the north, much like the "sky people" invaded Pandora. While the Na'vi people eventually repelled the "sky people," the Aryans came to stay, eroding much of the goddess culture of that ancient civilization. But the goddess worship that had been eclipsed by the Aryans would re-emerge in the tantric movement around the middle of the first millennium BCE. Religious historian Georg Feuerstein describes Tantra "as a full-fledged movement or cultural style extending over both Hinduism and Buddhism," the two dominant religious traditions in India at that time.[2] Within Hinduism and Buddhism, two major systems of Tantra have evolved into the twenty-first century. They assume somewhat different religious worldviews but nonetheless agree on many psychological and philosophical essentials that express themselves in *Avatar*.

The word *tantra* comes from two Sanskrit verbal roots, *tan* and *tra*. *Tan* means "to expand" or "to weave," which is just what Jake does in his avatar body when he weaves the tendrils of his neural queue with those of his teacher-lover Neytiri, the animals of Pandora, and the trees that connect him ultimately to Eywa, the source and personification of the living energy that runs through all things. *Tra* comes from a Sanskrit word *trayate*, which means "to liberate." It's by weaving himself into the world of Pandora, opening himself to its wonders, and adopting the ways of the Na'vi that Jake achieves the liberation he seeks. Of course, he must first come to understand himself and the true nature of his own needs and desire. Indeed, one of Tantra's deepest philosophical principles is inward self-discovery.

The powerful union of male and female energies in *Avatar* also reflects a core teaching of Tantra, which has been traditionally represented as the bond between the goddess Shakti and the god Shiva. Like the Na'vi with their worship of Eywa, Tantra acknowledges a primordial deity, Shakti, whose name comes from the Sanskrit word *shak*, which means "power." Her consort is the god Shiva. Eywa is never described in *Avatar* as having a male consort, but she clearly has ways of bonding with her worshippers that involve a profound opening of consciousness, of the sort that Tantra represents as the union of Shakti and Shiva. Tantra is about weaving male and female energies in a way that ultimately transcends gender. "Most of us are limited when it comes to recognizing both the male and [the] female aspects of our being," writes Tantric scholar Lama Yeshe. By uniting these two aspects, tantric meditation reveals "the magnificent blissful unified energy within us," showing us "what it's like to be a complete person, an emanation of totality."[3]

"These Dreams of Flying"

When Jake's boss, Dr. Grace Augustine, disembarks from pilot Trudy Chacón's Samson 16 and leads her team off into the forest, she directs Trudy's door gunner, Corporal Lyle Wainflee, to stay with the ship. "You the man, doc," replies Lyle, obediently. This ironic turn of phrase, with its facetious reversal of ordinary gender roles, nicely encapsulates the tantric attitude about men and woman. In Tantra, the woman is typically the teacher, according to Swami Muktananda (1908–1982), spiritual leader of the tantric Bihar School of Yoga. "In the tantric tradition, the woman is considered to be higher than the man," he writes, "the role of the initiator" being "shifted from the male to the female."[4]

In *Avatar*, Jake's teacher is Neytiri. She's the one who initiates him into the ways of "the people" and unveils for him the mysteries of Eywa. Neytiri is the farthest thing imaginable from a stereotypically helpless woman who waits for Jake to ride up on his direhorse to save her. She's the stronger member of their team, the one who saves Jake and teaches him how to survive in the forest. Most crucially, she's a *tsahìk* in training, destined to take her place as the spiritual leader of her tribe, the vehicle through whom the wisdom of Eywa is communicated to others. But she's only one example of the powerful current of female spirituality that runs through *Avatar*, which is also represented by Mo'at, Neytiri's mother and the current *tsahìk*. Mo'at is the one who directs Neytiri to teach Jake, a directive that Neytiri initially receives with a fit of pique, but that turns out to be a gift to both her and Jake. Even Grace, whose scientific mindset makes her an unlikely candidate for spiritual guide, plays a vital role in Jake's spiritual transformation, as the one who continually encourages him to attend to what Neytiri is trying to teach him in order for him "to see the forest through her eyes." Without his own tireless efforts, Jake can make no progress. But it's Grace who provides Jake with what he needs – including the avatar program and all the technical support from her scientific team – to undertake those efforts in the first place. At every turn, Jake's efforts are buoyed by the wisdom, initiative, encouragement, and energy of the women around him. And, of course, the ultimate source of that nurturing feminine energy on Pandora is the goddess Eywa, who first sends the sign that marks him as one chosen to receive her favor – of wood sprites floating down on him like dandelion seeds – thereby inducing Neytiri to spare his life and take him back to the village of her clan, the Omaticaya.

While they are vehicles of spiritual energy in *Avatar*, women are considered deities in Tantra. A woman who masters Tantra becomes a *dakini*, a "sky dancer" – a tantric deity who flies free of everything that keeps her hostage to ego, fear, and boundaries. She's free to be adventurous, aggressive, and bold in her search for enlightenment. And, having awakened her inner fire, she's also free to help others light their own. Her flight takes her through a spiritual voyage of clarity, fearlessness, and ecstasy that liberates her from worldly existence.

Significantly, *Avatar* opens with a visual and verbal meditation on flight and freedom. As the camera treats us to an aerial sweep over the lush green of Pandora, Jake recalls his own airborne aspirations. "When I was lying there in the VA hospital, with a big hole blown through the middle of my life, I started having these dreams of flying," he says. "I was free." Flight, of course, is a compelling metaphor for freedom, not just for freedom from physical limitations but also for spiritual liberation. But then, as if not ready for takeoff, Jake checks himself: "Sooner or later, though, you always have to wake up." It will take Neytiri to teach him that waking up and flying free don't need to be two different things.

Divine, Mind-Blowing Bliss

In *The Tantric Way*, authors Ajit Mookerjee, a longtime scholar and practitioner of Tantra, and Madhu Khanna, a scholar of Eastern and Western philosophies, explain that, unlike many other spiritual paths, Tantra doesn't require us to turn our backs on the joy of living a fully embodied existence in the world, forbidding our senses to feast on its voluptuous banquet of delights. The goal of Tantra is to be in the world even more fully, partaking of its riches with even greater awareness.

> Tantra provides a synthesis between spirit and matter to enable man to achieve his fullest spiritual and material potential. Renunciation, detachment and asceticism – by which one may free oneself from the bondage of existence and thereby recall one's original identity with the source of the universe – are not the way of tantra. Indeed, tantra is the opposite: not a withdrawal from life, but the fullest possible acceptance of our desires, feelings and situations as human beings.[5]

Part of that process of "acceptance" occurs through opening what Tantric practitioners call *chakras*. There are seven *chakras*, located at the tailbone, the genital area, the solar plexus, the heart, the throat, the middle of the forehead, and the crown of the head. These are "psychic centers in the body that are active at all times, whether we are conscious of them or not," according to tantric scholar Harish Johari.[6] One of the goals of tantric practice is to move energy through the *chakras* so as to produce progressively higher conscious states; this culminates with the opening of the crown *chakra* at the top of the head, whereupon one attains the highest and most surpassingly blissful state of consciousness. In *Avatar* Jake embarks on a journey of self-discovery and self-realization, advancing along a path that we can map out with the aid of these seven main energy centers or *chakras*.

Tantra weaves sexual energy into its unique brand of spirituality and religious devotion because one of the *chakras* is located at the sexual organs. Most of the attention that Tantra gets in the West focuses on how opening the *chakras* leads to "divine sex," a significant step up from the merely "great sex" to which readers of magazines like *Cosmopolitan* aspire. Indeed, as one tantric scholar writes: "A colloquial translation of Tantra would be 'mind-blowing.'"[7] And, true to form, when Jake mates with Neytiri, their neural queues weave together – literally – in "mind-blowing" tantric bliss.

Before that can happen, though, Tantra teaches that there's a certain amount of spiritual foreplay we must engage in – alone. Tantric teachers say that we can't achieve liberation in mystical union with another person until we begin to deconstruct our ordinary selves, liberating ourselves from the doubts, fears, duplicities, and confusions that make up our unenlightened egos. Georg Feuerstein writes that,

> in addition to strong faith in the teacher, in the process, and in them-selves, disciples also must embrace self-transformation through diligent discipline. The guru can lead his or her disciple to the eternal fountain, but cannot make them drink the elixir. Both grace and self-effort are needed to attain liberation.[8]

In *Avatar*, Jake goes on that journey. And we go along for the ride.

"Maybe You Should Teach Me"

The first *chakra*, called the *muladhara*, is located at the tailbone and concerns issues of basic survival. Surviving the attack of the viper-wolves is one of the first challenges Jake faces with Neytiri's help. After saving Jake, however, Neytiri inadvertently initiates this former marine into another tradition of Tantra. Grabbing his torch, she tosses it into the stream, against Jake's protests, leaving him momen-tarily in darkness. But, as he looks around, he sees the darkness recede as the forest turns on its own natural lights, leaving him surrounded – and, indeed, mesmerized – by the shimmering glow of bioluminescence. Ironically, it's only in the darkness that Jake can see the luminous beauty of the forest around him. What he sees is similar to what tantric practitioners visualize in their meditations. One of the aims of Tantra is to recognize the divine perfection of the world by seeing it as a *mandala* (Sanskrit for "circle") that represents "a celestial mansion." As *A Handbook of Tibetan Culture* explains, visualizing the *mandala* "plays a crucial role in tantric meditations."[9] In *Avatar* Jake suddenly finds himself encircled by a magnificent living *mandala*, a "celestial mansion" whose beauty eluded him while he was preoccupied with fear for his survival.

The second *chakra*, *swadhisthana*, at the genitals and the navel area, is the one most closely associated with tantric sex. But the biggest trip before divine copulation, tantric teachings say, is the celibate path, which involves finding union with our purer selves and overcoming bad habits and egocentric ideas. Renowned twentieth-century tantric Tibetan Buddhist master Lama Yeshe taught that "purification" from "the ignorant, negative mind" is a critical step toward "enlightenment."[10] That's certainly a step that Jake is encouraged to take when Neytiri points the tip of her bow at his throat and scolds him for stomping through the forest in a way that invited an attack by viperwolves and made it necessary for her to kill them. "You are like a baby," she admonishes. "Making noise, don't know what to do."

The third *chakra*, *manipura*, at the solar plexus, is about overcoming fear and attaining a sense of belonging. That's what happens to Jake as he presses Neytiri to accept him. "Why save me?" he asks. "You have a strong heart. No fear," she replies, leaning forward and regarding him for a moment with tenderness. "But stupid! Ignorant like a child." Leaping through the forest to follow Neytiri as she hurries away, Jake calls after her: "Well, if I'm like a child, then, look, maybe you should teach me." A critical threshold has been passed, as this fearless but spiritually stunted former marine opens himself to becoming Neytiri's student. Running through the jungle with Jake in close pursuit, she answers back: "No one can teach you to see. ... You're like a baby."

That may be true, but under Neytiri's tutelage Jakes progresses quickly toward maturity as he continues his journey through the *chakras*.

Tasting the Nectar

The Pandoran direhorse has a long tongue, which it uses to feed on the nectar of pitcher plants – its favorite food. As creatures of need, we human beings also have our favorite sources of pleasure and nourishment. In *Guide to Dakini Land*, meditation master Geshe Kelsang Gyatso describes the tantric principle of "experiencing nectar":

> Because we are beings of the desire realm we always take delight in seeing attractive forms, listening to beautiful sounds, smelling fragrant scents, tasting delicious food, and touching smooth and sensuous objects.

But he laments that most of the "delight" is "with a mind of attachment," clinging to sources of pleasure that are, as the Na'vi would say, "only borrowed," just like our little share of that "network of energy that flows through all living things." His guidance is to "taste the nectar" without attachment.[11] We should embrace the beauty of the present moment without judgment, expectation, acceptance, or rejection. When we can do that, we have reached a state of liberation – or *moksha*, in Sanskrit.

"Experiencing the nectar" is also part of Jake's education, which requires him to give his full attention to his present environment at every moment. He learns to recognize "the tiniest scents and sounds" of the forest, so that his own actions can always be a graceful response to whatever it has to offer him in that moment. As he gets to know the trails, the animals, the plants, and the landscape of the forest, as well the capabilities of his own body, his world grows steadily richer, more delightful, more like a partner in a joyful dance. It's a dance that begins with awkward, faltering steps but matures into a nimble ballet, a living expression of the Na'vi philosophy of interconnectedness.

In Tantra, as in *Avatar*, spiritual union isn't something attained only between a man and a woman. The Na'vi make *tsaheylu* with other animals too. Neytiri teaches Jake that, to become a warrior, he must do as the Na'vi do, taming and riding wild creatures by fusing his neural queue with theirs. She guides him through the exercise of making *tsaheylu* for the first time with a direhorse, instructing him: "Feel her. Feel her heartbeat. Her breath. Feel her strong legs." Jake commands the direhorse to go – and is promptly thrown off. But neither the resulting tumble in the mud nor the derisive laughter of Tsu'tey, the finest warrior on Pandora, is enough to dampen Jake's desire to learn, as he continues to throw himself into life on Pandora, racing across tree branches, taking even more tumbles in the process but grinning throughout. When he faces his ultimate challenge – riding the four-winged ikran – Neytiri guides him again: "Make the bond!" she cries, as Jake wrestles with the creature.

And then he's flying. It's not a dream this time.

Alien Sex and Sandstone Temples

"Come. Come," says Neytiri girlishly to Jake, after his initiation into the Omaticaya people. Luminescent fan lizards swirl in the air, as she guides him to the Tree of Voices, giggling.

"This is a place for prayers to be heard," she says, seductively caressing its luminescent, tendril-like branches against her cheek. "And sometimes answered."

Moments later, the answer arrives with a gentle kiss on the lips, the music serenading them as their kiss deepens and their passions rise. In the extended love scene included in the summer 2010 re-release, Neytiri pulls Jake down, bringing her braid to him. As he pulls his braid to hers, their neural queues intertwine. Gasping together, they seem slain. They kiss even more passionately, their wide eyes soaking each other up. Jake lifts her onto him as their bodies lock onto each other, surrounded by a curtain of luminescent branches. They wake up the next morning, spooning.

The image of Jake enlaced with Neytiri took me back to the erotic tantric sandstone temples I visited almost a decade earlier, in the northern Indian village of Khajuraho. Built by Hindu kings of the Chandel Empire from the tenth to the twelfth centuries, the most famous of the temples have images of divine, carnal acts carved around the highest points of their exterior walls. For tantric scholars and historians, this iconography celebrates the highest possibility of sexual union, captured in the mating ritual in *Avatar*. In *Khajuraho: The First Thousand Years*, Shobita Punja, a scholar of art history in New Delhi, writes:

> The temples of Khajuraho celebrate the union of opposites, the marriage of sky and earth, the play of light and darkness, the lively conservation of matter and space, of horizontal and vertical lines. The key to understanding Khajuraho lies in this central theme – the divine ecstasy of Shiva and Parvati [a Hindu goddess, considered to be a representation of Shakti], with all its philosophical implications: the unending dialogue between the form and the formless.[12]

But since, in addition to being a divine allegory, Jake and Neytiri's love story is also a human drama, their path to bliss is not without difficulties. When she discovers that he's been deceiving her about his collusion with Colonel Quaritch, she turns from him in anger. What will Jake do, now that his teacher has rejected him? Will he continue on the path of "purification"? Or will he return to being the broken man he had been before?

The fourth *chakra*, *anahata*, is the heart *chakra*, located at the center of the chest; it's what Neytiri touches in Jake to help him grow. Tantra is about us freeing ourselves from suffering by freeing ourselves from *maya* – illusion – and by opening our hearts to other possibilities. But, before Jake can be free, he must first decide which of his realities is "the true world" and which is "the dream." In other words, which is *maya* – his life as a human being or his life as a Na'vi? Casting his lot with the Colonel could make it possible for him to have the surgery that would restore the use of his human legs. Casting his lot with the Na'vi would forever foreclose that prospect, but it could also open him to new possibilities, which may not yet be within the reach of his imagination. He decides that his life with the "sky people" is the illusion. His heart is with the Na'vi.

The fifth *chakra*, located at the throat, is called *vishuddha*, which means "purity." It concerns the task of living truthfully; it reflects Jake's journey toward understanding his inner truth and expressing it honestly. First he was duplicitous with the Na'vi people, and then with Colonel Quaritch. Now, having discovered where his heart really lies, Jake must take his stand and fearlessly embrace his truth. And he does. He returns to Neytiri standing atop the fiercest creature on Pandora, the great toruk or leonopteryx – the "last shadow."

Dismounting the toruk, Jake walks directly through a throng of Na'vi to stand face to face with Neytiri, his teacher, whose eyes are wide with wonder. All pretense now set aside, they stand before each other, emotionally uncovered, their hearts speaking to each other in the words of the sacramental Na'vi greeting, "I see you." This moment resembles what in Tantra is called the "child pose." Two people hold their palms together at their heart in a traditional Hindu greeting, saluting each other with the word *namaste*, which means "I bow to the divine in you." They then gaze at each other as they strive to develop mutual empathy and to see each other's inner divinity.

The sixth *chakra*, *ajna*, is commonly thought of as "the third eye" because it's located between the eyebrows, on the forehead. It's about insight. One of the key ingredients of Tantra is the discovery of *atman* or true self. Jake must decide where his true self lies. Tantra teaches that with our true self we can experience *raga* (passion) and *kama* (sexual pleasure) together with someone else on the path to enlightenment.

"I Don't Want to Be Late for My Own Party"

Avatar concludes with a scene in which Jake dares to attempt to enter his avatar body permanently, passing through the eye of Eywa in a ritual that entails the death of his human form. Dying to one life, he is reborn to another. Earlier, Grace had died during an unsuccessful attempt to pass her spirit through the eye of Eywa. As Grace takes her last breath, we see her travel through what looks like a tunnel of pulsating light and energy, until everything dissolves into pure white radiance.

This scene is reminiscent of the tantric vision of death, which emerges in a verse from the *Tibetan Book of the Dead* that describes the *bardo* (transitional state) of dying:

> Now when the *bardo* of dying dawns upon me,
> I will abandon all grasping, yearning, and attachment,
> Enter undistracted into clear awareness of the teaching,
> And eject my consciousness into the space of unborn Rigpa;
> As I leave this compound body of flesh and blood
> I will know it to be a transitory illusion.[13]

Clarifying this verse, Sogyal Rinpoche writes: "The principle is that at the moment of death, the practitioner ejects his or her consciousness and merges it with the wisdom of the Buddha," which the *Tibetan Book of the Dead* calls "the space of unborn Rigpa."[14] In Tantric Tibetan Buddhism "the central presence" at death is the "radiant presence" of Buddha Amitabha, "the Buddha of Limitless Light," who represents "the limitless, luminous nature of our mind."[15]

In Tantra, the seventh *chakra* is the crown *chakra*, *sahasrara*, located at the top of the head. It's the channel connecting us to our spiritual nature, the doorway through which the life force of the universe enters us to flow through the six lower *chakras*. The ultimate expression of the tantric journey occurs when goddess energy – in this case, represented by Neytiri – guides the energy called kundalini to rise, through the other *chakras*, into the crown *chakra* at the top of the head; this rising results in an experience of union with the divine. This happens when Jake, in order to move from his human body to his avatar body, must pass his spirit through the eye of Eywa, achieving union with the goddess before being "breathed back" into another physical form.

Undulating bodies greet Jake as he arrives for the ceremony that will be both his funeral and his birthday party. Neytiri kisses both his eyes. She puts her hand on his right cheek. There's a suspenseful silence, until, on cue, Jake's avatar eyes open. He has survived the transformation.

In the tantric model it's Shakti, the goddess, who brings healing and enlightenment to the god Shiva. Jake and Neytiri are the Shiva and Shakti of *Avatar*. The word "avatar" comes from the Sanskrit noun *avatāra*, derived from a verbal root that means "to cross over." Jake's avatar is what enables him to "cross over" from the mortal world to the sublime universe of Pandora. In Sanskrit, however, *avatāra* refers to the descent of a god into human form, such as the blue-skinned Krishna of Hindu mythology, the most famous and beloved *avatāra* of the god Vishnu. But the movement in *Avatar* is in the opposite direction: not descent to lower regions but ascent to a higher form of existence. Jake is a broken mortal who "crosses over" into the body of what is, in many important respects, a higher being: he becomes one of the Na'vi, a race whose blue, Krishna-like skin and towering height makes them seem semi-divine. Most often, in tantric philosophy there is a goddess who guides the journey to higher realms. In *Avatar* that guide – that goddess – is Neytiri.

Tantric priestesses would welcome broken and wounded men returning from war, helping them to heal, just as Neytiri does for the broken warrior Jake. Some critics have said that *Avatar* follows a typical colonialist plot where a white man saves a native people. But Tantric philosophy helps us to discern the outlines of a different plot, with a different savior. Jake opens himself to Neytiri; so, according to the tantric model, it's actually Neytiri who heals and saves Jake, each one seeing the divine in the other and inspiring us to see the divine in ourselves and in others.

Namaste.

Acknowledgments

The author would like to thank George Dunn and Bill Irwin for their graceful, wise, and intelligent leadership in bringing this chapter to publication. She would also like to acknowledge Walter Robinson, a scholar of philosophy whose insights made this chapter more meaningful and thoughtful and whose generosity of spirit is the kind that makes collaboration a delight. Finally, she would like to thank Samir Nomani, her nephew, the founding president of the Milford High School Philosophy Club in Milford, MA and a young student of philosophy whose passion for the field is contagious and inspiring.

Notes

1. Katherine Anne Harper and Robert L. Brow, *The Roots of Tantra* (Albany, NY: SUNY Press, 2002), 40.
2. George Feuerstein, *Tantra: The Path of Ecstasy* (Boston, MA: Shambhala Publications, 1998), x.
3. Lama Yeshe, *The Tantric Path of Purification* (Boston, MA: Wisdom Publications, 1995), 150.
4. Swami Muktananda, *Nawa Yogini Tantra* (Bihar, India: Bihar School of Yoga, 1977), 4–5.
5. Ajit Mookerjee and Madhu Khanna, *The Tantric Way* (London: Thames & Hudson, 1977), 9.
6. Harish Johari, *Chakras: Energy Centers of Transformation* (Rochester, VT: Inner Traditions India, 1987), 1.
7. Jonn Mumford, *Ecstasy Through Tantra* (St. Paul, MN: Llewellyn Publications, 1994), 40.
8. Feuerstein, *Tantra*, 93.
9. Graham Coleman, ed., *A Handbook of Tibetan Culture* (New Delhi, India: Rupa & Co., 1993), 342.
10. Yeshe, *The Tantric Path*, 5.
11. Geshe Kelsang Gyatso, *Guide to Dakini Land* (New Delhi, India: Motilal Banarsidass Publishers, 1991), 36.
12. Shobita Punja, *Khajuraho: The First Thousand Years* (New Delhi, India: Viking, 1999), 179.
13. Sogyal Rinpoche, *The Tibetan Book of Living and Dying* (San Francisco, CA: HarperOne, 2002), 227.
14. Rinpoche, *Tibetan Book of Living and Dying*, 236.
15. Ibid., 236–237.

Part II

SEEING THE NA'VI
"YOU WILL TEACH HIM OUR WAYS"

Learning to *See* the Na'vi

Stephanie Adair

"You're like a baby. Making noise, don't know what to do,"
Neytiri scowls at Jake.
"Well, if I'm like a child, then, look, maybe you should teach
me," he protests.
"Sky People cannot learn," she replies, "You do not see.*"*

Scientists like Grace Augustine and Norm Spellman understand that that *seeing* is important to the Na'vi. They even understand that the significance of the expression *I see you* reaches far beyond a mere acknowledgment of someone having entered your visual field. But, despite all that, they haven't yet learned to *see* in the Na'vi way.

Grace is a scientist and ethnographer who has written *the* book on Na'vi culture, having learned their language and lived among them. Jake Sully, on the other hand, is a former marine who comes to the project not only ignorant of the Na'vi but without any scientific training whatsoever. Ironically, though, it's this uneducated warrior who in the end is really able to understand the Na'vi and to assimilate into their society. Grace may have dedicated her life to studying this culture, but there remains an invisible barrier that prevents her from really *seeing* the Na'vi.

Avatar clearly raises the question of how anyone can really come to know something new. Normally, we would expect an academic like Grace to be in the best position to acquire knowledge; but, when it comes to *seeing*, the unschooled Jarhead has the advantage. So what is it that occludes the vision of the "sky people"?

Avatar and Philosophy: Learning to See, First Edition. Edited by George A. Dunn.
© 2014 John Wiley & Sons, Inc. Published 2014 by John Wiley & Sons, Inc.

The Company Man, the Colonel, and the Grunts

Consider Parker Selfridge and Colonel Miles Quaritch. When they look on the elegant nymph-like Na'vi, the desire for possession and control blazes in their eyes, blinding them to what a travesty destroying the Na'vi's unique way of life would be. All that Selfridge and Quaritch care about is getting the Na'vi to leave Hometree. Any attempt to learn about their culture simply serves this goal. They give Jake the mission of figuring out what matters to the Na'vi, not because they're curious about their culture, but only so that they can control the "blue monkeys" by finding out what the Na'vi want and then leveraging it – either by promising them more of it ("lite beer" and "blue jeans," anyone?) or by holding it hostage until they agree to relocate ("This tree of souls place – yeah, I got them by the balls with that"). Learning how the Na'vi live, how their society is organized, and what rituals they observe – that may be useful to know too, the better to destroy them in battle.

Selfridge and Quaritch lack any recognition of others as valuable in themselves. Selfridge respects only the bottom line; making money for the company is his only goal. Access to the mineral deposit under Hometree will allow his company to defeat the competition, dominate the unobtanium market, and become an unstoppable capitalist force. Nothing else – not the lives of the Na'vi and mercenaries, not the destruction of the planet's ecosystem – even approaches the value of "all that cheddar." All that Selfridge sees when he looks at the Na'vi is an obstacle that stands in the way of a good "quarterly statement."

For Quaritch, on the other hand, violence seems almost like an end in itself. Thriving on violent conflict, Quaritch seems to value most his ability to overpower others. Most of the people with whom he has dealings are either his own soldiers, over whom he exercises power, or the hostile forces "beyond that fence" where "every living thing that crawls, flies, or squats in the mud wants to kill you and eat your eyes for jujubes." To Quaritch, even Pandora itself seems to be in on the fight, trying to lure him to his death with her insidiously low gravity. Pumping iron, he instructs Jake: "This low gravity'll make you soft. You get *soft*, and Pandora will shit you out dead with zero warning." Climbing into his amplified mobility platform (AMP) suit, Quaritch can hardly disguise the thrill he gets from the way this machine amplifies his power and transforms him into a ferocious giant. Since he places the highest value on power over others, the world appears to him as a throng of hostile forces that supply him with endless rows of enemies to dominate.

As leaders of the mission, Selfridge and Quaritch see Pandora only through the lens of their own preoccupations, especially their urgent desire to relocate the Na'vi. But there's a notable difference between Quaritch and his "grunts." The underlings are in a very different position from that of their commanding officer. It's not their job to criticize the goal of their mission, nor is it incumbent upon them to strategize about the most effective means of accomplishing it. Whatever their individual motives are for coming on the mission to Pandora – money, curiosity, bloodlust – their role as army grunts demands that they cultivate a strong sense of duty. Time and again, we see their sense of duty take hold. On Jake's first trip into the forest of Pandora, Grace orders the security operations (SecOps) mercenary to stay with the helicopter. "One idiot with a gun is enough," she sneers. Despite the insult and the palpable tensions between the SecOps and the scientists in the Avatar program (whom Quaritch derides as a "bunch of limp-dick science majors"), the soldier responds to Grace's command with respectful obedience: "You the man, Doc!" It's his duty to obey, even if she shows him no respect in return.

Not much later, SecOps pilot Trudy Chacón shows us that she recognizes a duty to obey her superiors, regardless of the consequences. As night falls, she tells Grace that they must discontinue until morning their search for Jake, who became separated from the others in the forest. "We're not allowed to run night ops," she announces. "Colonel's orders." Grace believes that Jake won't survive until morning, but Trudy feels bound by her duty to obey the orders of her commanding officer.[1]

Whatever else we think of this conscientious devotion to duty, it at least indicates that these SecOps grunts have learned to respect someone or something beyond their almighty egos and their private whims. Respect is the attitude we take toward persons and things we value as having some sort of intrinsic worth, and those values influence how we see the world. Selfridge and Quaritch, unlike their underlings, demonstrate no respect for others. For Selfridge and Quaritch, other human beings, the Na'vi, and even the Pandoran eco-system have worth only as means to monetary or military goals. That Jake, "a warrior of the Jarhead clan," comes from a group that cultivates respect may, ironically, have something to do with why he is able to learn to *see*.

Good Observation Isn't *Seeing*

The Greek philosopher Heraclitus (c. 535–475 BCE) said: "Much learning does not teach understanding."[2] Or, as Mo'at tells Jake: "It is hard to fill a cup which is already full." Far from enabling Grace to better understand the Na'vi, as one might expect, her extensive learning, dazzling credentials, and vast scientific expertise actually prevent her from *seeing* them truly. She looks at them with the eyes of a well-trained scientist, superimposing her ready-made framework on them – quantifying, analyzing, and categorizing them in an effort to render them scientifically "knowable."

Like the SecOps grunts, the scientists recognize a duty to follow a set of rules they didn't make. Their protocols prescribe everything, from how to use a tool or collect samples without contamination to the proper framework for interpreting data. These rules regulate scientific research, making it possible to produce results that can be reproduced by others. An unwarranted break with established protocols could cost the project its stamp of scientific validity.

In her experiments the scientist acts upon the object of her research not just physically, but cognitively, by interpreting the experimental results and deciding what they mean. Her manner of interpreting the raw data – the interpretative framework she employs to make sense of the world – plays a major role in determining her conclusions. For example, when Grace "wrote the book on Pandoran botany," her attention was most likely focused on the molecular, genetic, and biochemical properties of the local plant life. But, when she turns her trained eye on the forest to identify, label, and categorize each plant, her scientific and methodical approach might be the very thing that prevents her from *seeing* the forest as the Na'vi do. Likewise, if the scientists can't *see* the Na'vi, it may be because their interpretative framework isn't suited to the task of *seeing* the Na'vi as they see themselves.

Of course, scientists aren't the only ones who interpret their experiences in a way that runs the risk of falsifying them. The German philosopher Friedrich Nietzsche (1844–1900) described how any new experience "finds our senses ... hostile and reluctant," so that we unconsciously reinterpret every novel item into something more familiar and easier to understand. "Even in the midst of the strangest experience," he wrote, "we still do the same: we make up the major part of the experience and can scarcely be forced *not* to contemplate some event as its 'inventors.'"[3] *Avatar*'s scientists thus reinvent the strange landscape of Pandora as a world of curious scientific phenomena, something they have the tools to understand. And yet it could be argued that even the Na'vi don't see things as they *are*. No one escapes one's own subjective limitations so as to see the world objectively, as it *is* in itself. What we "see" is always guided by some set of concerns and interests. But the Na'vi way of *seeing* grows organically out of their active engagement with the world in which they live and that they deeply love. We might think that having an emotional connection to what you seek to know would be an advantage, but in the view of many scientists just the opposite is the case.

One thing that characterizes the scientific way of seeing is the high value it places on *detached* observation. Contemporary philosopher Alison Jaggar calls this the "myth of disinterested inquiry": the belief that emotions are a contaminant to be avoided in the search for knowledge.[4] Just as Grace cautions Norm against letting his saliva accidentally contaminate the samples he takes in the forest, so many scientists believe that interjecting yourself into your study contaminates good work. Of course, as Dr. Max Patel explains to Jake while he video-logs, "good science is good observation," and that's going to require some sort of interaction with whatever it is you're observing. But interaction in the service of scientific observation must still remain emotionally detached. That's a far cry from falling "in love with the forest and with the Omaticaya people," as Jake did in the course of learning to *see*.

The detachment that characterizes the scientists' way of seeing also comes out in how they relate to the avatars. They don't think of them as bodies, but rather as pieces of equipment. Norm Spellman communicates this sentiment when he introduces himself to his new colleagues as "Norm, avatar driver." "You guys can take them out tomorrow," a lab tech tells them, as if the avatars were a set of shiny new jet skis. The avatars enable a video game-like experience for the scientists, allowing them to steal a peak at life on Pandora and to grab a sample for later analysis in sterilized labs. Inasmuch as the scientists regard the avatars as mere vehicles, the "good observation" they're after cannot be a genuinely embodied experience of *really being with* the object of their study.

Norm's impersonal relationship with his avatar and his scientific adherence to rules quickly surface when he establishes his initial link. Preoccupied with working out any mechanical kinks, he runs through a careful round of tests ("touch your thumb to your fingers"). Compare that with Jake, who immediately feels this alien body to be *his own* and wants all the toe-wiggling, tail-flapping, leaping-and-jumping action he can get. Jake makes himself at home in his new body, whereas Norm inspects his avatar like an expensive new piece of lab equipment. We can almost hear him thinking: "I better learn to use this high-tech investment properly!"

"I Need to Take Some Samples"

The scientists see avatars as sweet new rides rather than actual bodies. But Grace's relationship to her Na'vi body brings out an additional element of the scientists' relationship to the Na'vi, one for which Western ethnographers studying indigenous cultures have also come under criticism. However much she may attempt to look and talk like a Na'vi, she still regards them as alien entities to be studied, curiosities to be put under the microscope. Faced with a radically different culture, Grace struggles to maintain an appropriate distance and detachment. This even plays out in her choice of dress. At the school, living among the Na'vi, she still wears human apparel rather than traditional Na'vi attire. The Na'vi women's breasts are exposed, being only partially covered by their necklaces. Despite Grace's desire to know and be accepted by the Na'vi, her own breasts remain covered.

For all her many disagreements with Selfridge and Quaritch, Grace shares their desire for mastery; she simply seeks mastery through knowledge rather than through physical domination. Positioning herself as the authoritative "knower," Grace approaches the radical otherness of the Na'vi as something to be assimilated into her scientific framework and mastered in the way a schoolchild masters her lessons.

That may be the right approach for measuring the speed of signal transduction between the roots of the forest or for isolating the primary compounds responsible for the bioluminescence of Pandora's flora and fauna. But it's not especially conducive to a genuine encounter with the Na'vi. Nor even perhaps to a genuine encounter with Eywa. As Jake carries the dying Grace to the Tree of Souls, she whispers dreamily: "I need to take some samples." She recognizes the tree as something extraordinary, but her fantasy remains thoroughly scientific. Not content just to *be* there with Eywa, she dreams of taking something from the place so she can analyze it, know it, and decide what it is.

While Grace lies dying on the roots of the Tree of Souls, her limitations crystallize. She is ultimately unable to enter her avatar as her real and permanent body, as her injuries have left her too weak to pass through the eye of Eywa. We could take her final inability to transcend her human limitations as a metaphor for how her detached scientific approach has failed to draw her into the wisdom of the Na'vi and their way of *seeing*. Observe as she may, as long as she is unwilling to commit her whole self and to risk being transformed by her encounter with the Na'vi, she will never learn to *see*. Her fatal wound symbolizes how deeply ingrained her commitment to one-sided, disinterested inquiry is: like the hole in her abdomen, it has left her hopelessly incapacitated. She is too weak to make the leap and too dedicated to knowledge as mastery to be altered at her core by an encounter with something radically new; her last words nonetheless betray the first glimpses of transformative sight: "I'm with her, Jake. She's real!"

Jake, Empty Cup of the Jarhead Clan

We wouldn't expect to learn how to swim without the muscular structure of our bodies changing in the process. How, then, could Grace imagine that she could truly come to know the Na'vi without being changed in the process?

Having no illusions about his own lack of education, Jake informs Mo'at that he has come to learn from the Na'vi. "We have tried to teach other Sky People," the *tsahìk* scowls. "It is hard to fill a cup that is already full." With self-deprecating humor, Jake replies: "Well, my cup is empty, trust me. Just ask Dr. Augustine. I'm no scientist." Accepting his status as a *skxawng* – a moron, in the eyes of both the

Na'vi and his human colleagues – he readily recognizes that he has many things to learn *from* Pandora, which is something quite different from Grace's and Norm's belief that there's much to learn *about* Pandora, that is, about the many unusual phenomena that cry out for scientific analysis and classification. But, as Grace's example shows us, genuine understanding is more than just obtaining a store of knowledge. Genuine understanding requires being open to transformation. Intertwining the processes of learning and becoming, *seeing* may be possible only for someone who starts out as an admitted *skxawng*.

Jake's empty cup and his lack of intellectual pretensions may be precisely why Eywa, whose seeds flow around him in a glowing anointment, recognizes him as having the potential to *see*. Unlike Grace and Norm, he hasn't made a vocation of collecting knowledge. But as a soldier he's accustomed to receiving instruction, and he's brimming with natural curiosity. Both his humility and his eagerness make him a suitable candidate for learning the ways of the Na'vi. Moreover, unlike his scientific colleagues, Jake is accustomed to living in the *here* and *now*. Indeed the abstract and reflective approach of the scientists actually takes them away from the *here* and *now*. Jake, on the other hand, embraces each moment on Pandora with full-hearted abandon. Why does Pandora strike Jake so forcefully? Without any scientific framework between himself and his experience ("I dissected a frog once"), Jakes encounters Pandora's marvels in a powerfully immediate way. Grace and Norm, on the other hand, are in direct contact with their scientific schema and only indirectly with the forest itself.

Jake embodies the joyful approach to knowledge that Nietzsche found lacking among many so-called knowers, whom he accused of approaching knowledge with an attitude of "gruesome seriousness" and "clumsy obtrusiveness."[5] Instead, Nietzsche proposed what he called *eine fröhliche Wissenschaft*, "a joyful science" that engages the object of knowledge in something like a seductive dance rather than solemnly squinting at it from an aloof distance. Jake has much in common with Nietzsche's jubilant investigator. Bubbling with the spirit of play, he gleefully embraces every experience and lives it with full emotional depth. When Grace advises him to "stand his ground" against the rhinoceros-like hammerhead titanothere, he fully commits himself to the moment, not only standing strong but charging forward a few paces and letting out his own territorial roar.

Loving and Learning

"Hey, it's not something you can teach," chortles Jake as Grace recounts the tale of his escape from the stampeding hammerhead titanothere. Jake isn't indifferent to learning, but he also seems to think that the kind of knowledge really worth having isn't directly teachable. How, then, does Jake learn to *see* if not through Neytiri's teaching him?

To answer this question, let's look at one of the most important things Jake learns: the integral and sacred role of the forest. Jake does not originally see the forest as the Na'vi do; he complains in his video log: "I really hope this tree-hugger crap isn't on the final." Overhearing him, Grace interjects: "This isn't just about eye–hand coordination out there, you know. You need to listen to what she says. Try to see the forest through her eyes." While Grace may *seem* to be proposing a type of learning similar to Na'vi *seeing*, that impression is misleading. Observation is crucial to Grace's research, but observation differs from *seeing* in that it allows the observer to remain the same. Grace apparently believes that, when Jake acquires the ability to see the forest through Neytiri's eyes, it will be like a pair of glasses he can put on when he needs to understand the Na'vi and take off when he is at home. But the Na'vi way of *seeing* is not like switching between lenses. It's more like transforming the eye itself.

Jake expresses his confusion as this disorienting and reorienting process of transformation takes hold. "Everything is backwards now," he reports, "like out there is the true world and in here is the dream." In time, his logs take a quite different tone from his earlier cynicism about "tree-hugger crap." With a tinge of wonder in his voice, he narrates: "I'm trying to understand this deep connection the people have to the forest. She talks about a network of energy that flows through all living things." In the end, after being accepted as one of "the people" – a full-fledged member of the Omaticaya clan – Jake comes face to face with his former cynical self in the guise of Parker Selfridge. Mocking Grace's scientific explanation of the sacred nature of the forest, the Resources Development Administration (RDA) officer howls: "What the hell have you people been smoking out there? They're just goddamn trees!"

What has happened to Jake to move him so far from Selfridge? Jake's new way of *seeing* the forest has not been brought about by anything specific that Neytiri told him, but by his time spent with her and the other Na'vi. The key may lie in what he confesses to Neytiri, in an effort to regain her trust after the attack on Hometree: "I fell in love with the forest and with the Omaticaya people. And with you." If that's right, then the attempt to teach *seeing* would be like trying to teach someone to fall in love – it just doesn't work that way. But love does happen, at least to those who allow it to happen to them. And when it does, we often come to see the world in a new light.

Some things are best known in a scientific, disinterested manner. But certain prominent aspects of Na'vi culture suggest that this sterile approach may actually be an impediment to understanding these people. Not only do visceral emotions play a crucial role in Na'vi culture – as we see when Neytiri stands protectively hissing and snarling over Jake's body, or when the aerial hunters sound their gleeful whoops and hollers – but central to the Na'vi way of life is the experience of *tsaheylu*, the bond. Since so many of the Na'vi's activities are dependent upon linking consciousness, it's doubtful that the sort of knowledge that scrutinizes its object from a safe distance will allow one to *see* the Na'vi. Recall Jake's first experience of *tsaheylu*. When Jake links with the direhorse, we see their eyes grow wide from the forceful intensity of shared consciousness. Neytiri coaches him: "Feel her. Feel her heartbeat. Her breath. Feel her strong legs. You may tell her what to do. Inside." Unable to handle the experience, Jake finds himself tossed into the mud. Tsu'tey stops by to laugh. "A rock *sees* more!" he scoffs, a verdict that confirms the close relationship between *tsaheylu* and *seeing*.

To truly *see* something in the Na'vi way, one must regard it lovingly, as valuable and worthy of respect, quite the opposite of how Selfridge and Quaritch see the world. Like *tsaheylu*, this way of seeing requires opening oneself up to an intimate connection with a creature that may be frighteningly different, while all the while one embraces this difference through a unifying love. The scientific ideal of disinterested objectivity is entirely at odds with this intertwining of knower and known. Moreover, the scientists make on their own the choice to study the Na'vi, not realizing that the Na'vi, like the ikrans they ride, must choose the scientists as well.

Seeing transforms because it depends on linking one's heart and mind with the object of knowledge. It emerges only through robust experiences with full-blooded emotional depth. Neytiri is right about those "sky people" who are only interested in taking samples and rushing home to analyze them: they will never learn to see.

Notes

1. As Trudy's character develops, her allegiance to military duty comes into conflict with her notion of what is right. Faced with the order to fire on Hometree, she realizes that this act cannot be justified by the duty to obey her commanding officer, so she swerves her helicopter around and heads back to the base.
2. *The Art and Thought of Heraclitus*, ed. Charles H. Kahn (Cambridge: Cambridge University Press, 1979), 37 (tr. 18).
3. Friedrich Nietzsche, *Beyond Good and Evil*, trans. Walter Kaufman (New York: Vintage Books, 1989), §192, 105.
4. Alison M. Jaggar, "Love and Knowledge: Emotion in Feminist Epistemology," in Alison Bailey and Chris Cuomo, eds., *The Feminist Philosophy Reader* (New York: McGraw-Hill 2008), 687–688.
5. Nietzsche, *Beyond Good and Evil*, Preface, 1.

It Doesn't Take an Avatar
How to Empathize with a Blue-Skinned Alien

Andrew Terjesen

Jake Sully went from being a self-centered individual, only concerned with regaining the use of his legs, to being the defender of an entire world. How did that happen? We might be tempted to give most of the credit to empathy, supposing that Jake's avatar allowed him to *empathize* with the Na'vi and concluding that his *empathy* forged a connection that enabled him to see beyond his own selfish desires.

In fact the idea that empathy is the root of morality is an old one. But was it really empathy that triggered Jake's moral transformation? And was his empathy really awakened by his experiences with his avatar?[1]

"A Demon in a False Body"

We might say that we *empathize* with others when we have an understanding of what they're thinking or feeling. This form of empathy, which psychologists call "cognitive empathy," doesn't require us actually to *feel* what they're feeling, only to *understand* what they're going through, even if only on a purely intellectual level. This cognitive empathy might help us make moral judgments by affording insight into the perspectives of everyone involved. Armed with such an understanding, we can then choose the action that does the best job of balancing everyone's legitimate interests. But could an avatar enable a human being to achieve cognitive empathy with the Na'vi way of thinking?

Avatar and Philosophy: Learning to See, First Edition. Edited by George A. Dunn.
© 2014 John Wiley & Sons, Inc. Published 2014 by John Wiley & Sons, Inc.

Among the purposes of the avatars is to allow human beings to function more effectively on Pandora. The larger, more durable bodies of the Na'vi – with their tough "bones reinforced in naturally occurring carbon fiber" – are better equipped for surviving the hazards of life on Pandora. Presumably the avatars share the Na'vi's enhanced skeletal structure, which gives their human drivers a similar boost in strength and resistance to injury. The avatars also allow their drivers to function without the gas masks that human beings usually have to wear outside. Of course, these physical advantages aren't the main reason for the Avatar program, at least not according to Selfridge. "Your little puppet show," he reminds Grace, exists to facilitate human interaction with the Na'vi. More specifically, it's about "winning the hearts and minds of the natives." Avatars overcome at least one possible impediment to human–Na'vi interaction: the difference in size and durability of their respective bodies.

While to us the avatars may look indistinguishable from the Na'vi, the Na'vi know when they're dealing with an avatar and not one of their own. They refer to Jake as a "dreamwalker" (*uniltìrantokx* in the Na'vi language) and, even more pejoratively, as a "demon in a false body." Among other differences, the avatars have five fingers instead of four, their neural queues (*tswin* in Na'vi) start at the top of the skull instead of its base, and they apparently smell bad (at least to Eytukan, who complains that Jake's "alien smell fills my nose") – all products of the hybrid nature of avatars that have been created from a mixture of human and Na'vi DNA. And, even if one doesn't have time to count fingers and isn't in the mood to take a deep whiff, the avatars also betray themselves by their awkward behavior in the forests of Pandora. Neytiri likens Jake's behavior to that of an ignorant and clumsy "baby" tramping through the forest, "making noise, don't know what to do."

Since avatars aren't biologically identical to the Na'vi, how can we be sure that "Jakesully" will see the forest in the same way as "the people"? These hybrid avatars might not replicate the sensory experiences of the Na'vi perfectly. And, even if they did, the avatar drivers can still never experience Pandora exactly as the Na'vi do. Though it may seem like a minor difference, the number of fingers you have affects how you manipulate objects and experience the world around you. In addition, the avatar drivers' understanding of the world is still shaped by their human memories and, of course, they can disconnect from their avatars at any time. The idea that Jake could understand the Na'vi by driving his avatar for a few months is as absurd as thinking that Bill Gates could understand what it means to be poor if he chose to live below the poverty line for a few months.

All these factors raise doubts as to whether avatars can really contribute much to cognitive empathy. But we're at an even greater disadvantage without them. For example, the Na'vi possess neural queues, an organ for which there is nothing comparable in our experiences. Without that organ for communing with Eywa and with the other creatures of Pandora, we might not be able to understand the depth of the Na'vi's connection to nature.

Before we dismiss the possibility of experiencing empathy for the Na'vi, however, let's bear in mind that even two beings of the same species will never have exactly the same physiological makeup and knowledge. Guests on *The Jerry Springer Show* sometimes try to deflect criticism of their unconventional life choices by bellowing back at their detractors: "You don't know me, you don't know my family!" But do you really need to experience an incestuous three-way with your father and daughter in order to pass judgment? The philosopher Edith Stein (1891–1942) didn't think so. Her doctoral dissertation, *On the Problem of Empathy*, explains how we can understand these Springer guests without – thank you very much! – having to experience the world exactly as they do. According to Stein, empathizing with someone is not the same thing as having his or her experience. Claiming that we can't empathize with others unless we experience the world exactly as they do puts too much of a burden on cognitive empathy.

Stein notes that empathy can be mistaken. For example, when Jake was first introduced to Grace, he might have mistaken her brusque demeanor for a sign that she lacks compassion, an initial impression that her later decisions refute. But we can also be mistaken about our *own* mental states. At one point, Jake admits that he's having difficulty with his dual existence. As he says in one of his logs: "Everything is backwards now. Like out there is the true world and in here is the dream." If he can be confused or mistaken about his own experiences (and even confused about what he wants), then it should be no surprise that he could be mistaken about other people. Even if the avatar bodies are not perfect reproductions of the Na'vi and the avatar drivers are not thoroughly shaped by Na'vi customs, the avatars can still provide some insight into the experiences of "the people." Particular beliefs about what it means to be Na'vi might be mistaken, but a lack of 100 percent accuracy doesn't mean that empathy is completely unreliable. If it did, we couldn't rely on other fallible faculties like vision or introspection.

So, even if avatar bodies differ from Na'vi bodies, their physiologies at least have many similarities. And even if the culture of the Na'vi is foreign to the avatar drivers in many ways, it's not entirely strange, since it bears a strong resemblance to the lifestyle of hunter-gatherer tribes on Earth. So it seems reasonable to believe that operating an avatar could be an aid to cognitive empathy, and that avatar drivers could make fairly reliable – albeit fallible – judgments about the Na'vi mindset. But are avatars the only way to achieve this sort of empathetic understanding of "the people"?

"I'd Say We Understand Them Just Fine"

The way Parker Selfridge talks about the Na'vi might give the impression that he doesn't really understand the inhabitants of Pandora. When Selfridge decides to send the SecOps to destroy Hometree, Grace shoves her way past security to rebuke him for putting "people" at risk. But before she can even finish her sentence, Selfridge bursts into an angry tirade: "No. No, no, no, no. They're fly-bitten savages that live in a tree! All right? Look around! I don't know about you, but I see a lot of trees. They can move!" These words put Selfridge's appalling ignorance about the Na'vi culture on stark display.[2] But is he really ignorant of the Na'vi? Or does he "understand them just fine," as Colonel Quaritch claimed only a short while before?

Don't get me wrong. I'm not trying to justify the behavior of the Resources Development Administration (RDA). My only point is that Selfridge's words reveal that he does understand the Na'vi, at least in some important respects. "Fly-bitten savages" are words of abuse that highlight certain qualities of the Na'vi that Selfridge doesn't like, chiefly because they make his job harder. But these are also qualities that he *understands*, in that he recognizes that the Na'vi have no interest in technology, modern luxury goods, or anything else he might offer in exchange for the right to mine for unobtanium at Hometree. In short, he has enough cognitive empathy for "the people" to recognize that any further attempts to negotiate are futile and that a superior show of force is much more likely to get them to relocate. And, harsh as it sounds, Selfridge is correct – the Omaticaya *can* find a new home, although it might never have the same significance for them as Hometree.

Selfridge and Quaritch show us that it's possible to achieve cognitive empathy for the Na'vi without being an avatar driver. Their judgments about what the Na'vi are thinking don't differ much from those of Grace and Jake. There's one crucial difference, however. Selfridge and Quaritch just don't care a lot about the effects of the RDA's actions on the Na'vi. It turns out that cognitive empathy – simply *understanding* what someone else is thinking or feeling – isn't enough to guarantee that we'll *care* about their feelings or act morally toward them. Cognitive empathy may influence our actions to some degree. It may be part of the reason why Selfridge initially favors a less aggressive approach to relocating the Na'vi. But in the end no amount of cognitive empathy can dislodge his belief that he's doing the right thing. In his mind, a handful of dead Na'vi are just unfortunate collateral damage.

Quaritch has even less compassion. His understanding of the Na'vi only fuels his belief that they must be subjugated or destroyed. He even uses his understanding of Na'vi religion to plot a psychologically devastating attack on Hometree. "Now, the hostiles believe this mountain stronghold of theirs is protected by their deity," he tells his forces. "And when we destroy it, we will blast a crater in their racial memory so deep that they won't come within 1,000 clicks of it ever again. And that, too, is a fact." Without the benefit of cognitive empathy, he would never have been able to recognize that "fact" or to formulate such a heinous plan.

But perhaps the problem with people like Selfridge and Quaritch is that their cognitive empathy never goes beyond the "facts." Their distant and "objective" perspective means that they never really experience the Na'vi point of view. That's why many people prefer to define empathy as the ability to put oneself in another person's shoes, vicariously experiencing the world from his or her subjective perspective.[3] Let's call this ability "reenactive empathy," since it involves not just understanding, but actually re-experiencing another's feeling and emotions. But will driving an avatar make it easier to achieve this kind of empathy? And will reenactive empathy necessarily affect our moral judgments any more than cognitive empathy does?[4]

"No One Can Teach You to See"

When Jake first meets Neytiri, he asks her to teach him how to "see." "No one can teach you to see," she scoffs. Neytiri is referring to "seeing" in the sense that Norm describes, which means "I see into you. I understand you." "Seeing" seems to be a case of reenactive empathy, but it's also described as a kind of perception – and, of course, we all understand that no one can teach you how to perceive. If you're walking through the forest and come upon a cluster of bright orange helicoradian – those striking plants with spiral leaves that coil up when touched – you just *see* the orange of the leaves immediately. No one can teach you to see it. Is reenactive empathy like that? Is it just another form of perception?

The philosopher Adam Smith (1723–1790) argued that what we call here reenactive empathy (or what he called "sympathy") isn't as simple and straightforward as ordinary perception. After all, just seeing a Na'vi writhing in pain doesn't necessarily cause the onlooker to suffer, at least not if the onlooker is as heartless as Quaritch. So what is it that someone like Quaritch is missing? Smith believed that reenactive empathy depends on an exercise of imagination. In his *Theory of Moral Sentiments* he writes:

> As we have no immediate experience of what other men feel, we can form no idea of the manner in which they are affected, but by conceiving what we ourselves should feel in the like situation... By the imagination we place ourselves in his situation, we conceive ourselves enduring all the same torments, we enter as it were into his body, and become in some measure the same person with him, and thence form some idea of his sensations, and even feel something which, though weaker in degree, is not altogether unlike them. His agonies, when they are thus brought home to ourselves, when we have thus adopted and made them our own, begin at last to affect us, and we then tremble and shudder at the thought of what he feels.[5]

Even if we can't be taught to perceive, imagination might be something that can be cultivated to some extent. Smith doesn't directly address this question, but his writings suggest that we can develop our empathetic imagination through practice and learning. For example, after learning more about Na'vi beliefs and attitudes toward nature, Jake is in a better position to imagine what Neytiri felt when she saved him from the viperwolves and to appreciate why she scorned his expression of gratitude. Better able to empathize, he can now see that, if anything, he should have apologized for making it necessary for her to kill his attackers.

In the twentieth century some philosophers, called theory theorists, argued that we could understand others by simply applying our theoretical knowledge of how behavior is linked to mental states. So, for instance, when Jake dismounts the toruk that he flew into the Na'vi gathering at the Tree of Souls, Neytiri's eyes grow wide and her breathing becomes slow and deep, which we somehow understand as a sign of amazement on her part. Theory theorists would argue that we're just making inferences about her mental state on the basis of our theory about how people – who in this case include the Na'vi – typically behave when they're amazed: they open their eyes wide and stare in the direction of the amazing spectacle. But other philosophers, called simulation theorists, hold a different view. They argue that we understand others by simulating their experiences or by putting ourselves in their situation, bypassing any need for logical inferences. We don't really need a theory to understand Neytiri's amazement, since we all know how amazed we would feel if someone flew a great leonopteryx into our prayer meeting. The simulation theorists seem to have an upper hand in the debate right now, as they're receiving strong support from recent neurological research that demonstrates a close relationship between understanding and simulation.[6] But does this mean that driving an avatar is necessary for understanding the Na'vi?

When Mo'at conscripts Neytiri to teach Jake Sully how to "speak and walk" as the Na'vi do, she seems to be suggesting that one can't understand the Na'vi without a physical reenactment of their way of life. Neytiri doesn't welcome her assignment, though, as we can tell from the huffy groan of protest she heaves in her mother's general direction. Even for those of us who are neither Na'vi nor avatar drivers, Neytiri's meaning is unmistakable. Clearly, then, even without the benefit of avatars, we can achieve a degree of reenactive empathy with the Na'vi, despite our biological and cultural differences. This situation is really no different from how we are able to empathize with nonhuman species here on Earth. For instance, the nurturing behavior of other primates is similar to that of human mothers, and this makes it easy for us to empathize with maternal monkeys and apes. In more difficult cases we can rely on veterinarians and "animal whisperers" to give us a good understanding of what goes through the heads of other species. Of course, animal behaviorists do seem to get their best insights into the minds of other species when they live among their subjects.[7] In a similar fashion, avatars could be an aid to empathy by making it easier for a human being to simulate being a Na'vi. Avatar drivers could then explain to their fellow human beings what it's like to be Na'vi.

So it seems that, while avatars are not required to experience reen-active empathy, they might still enhance the accuracy and depth of our empathetic understanding. Maybe the reason why most human beings on Pandora aren't greatly moved by the plight of the Na'vi is that they never had the benefit of an avatar experience. Consequently their ability to "simulate" the Na'vi point of view is underdeveloped.

"My Cup Is Empty"

Jake is clearly special. He's able to understand the Omaticaya much better than either Grace or Norm. As Mo'at notes in what may be a reference to Grace: "We have tried to teach other Sky People. It is hard to fill a cup which is already full." The implication is that the human beings who have previously interacted with the Na'vi are so filled with preconceptions about "the people" and Pandora that they cannot "see" things as the Na'vi do. We can safely assume that Grace had formed many beliefs about the Na'vi before she ever met them. Norm too comes filled with textbook information about "the people." Jake, on the other hand, doesn't know much of anything about the Omaticaya, and so it's with good reason that he can say "my cup is empty."

But perhaps we shouldn't take Jake at his word when he calls himself an empty vessel. His life as a marine is very much a part of him, as we see when he readily identifies himself to the Omaticaya as a member of the Jarhead clan, despite having been discharged because of his injuries. A better explanation of Jake's success in understanding "the people" may be that the contents of his "cup" already have something in common with Omaticaya ways. As Etukyan says, "this is the first warrior dreamwalker we have seen." Jake starts on the road to under-standing already steeped in many of the values that "the people" hold as a society of hunters, warriors, and shamans. Grace and Norm can't truly understand the culture of the Na'vi because they don't accept the underlying martial values. We hear Grace's dismissive attitude toward the warrior frame of mind in her characterization of the SecOps soldier assigned to protect her – she calls him an "idiot with a gun."

Of course, Jake's success with reenactive empathy doesn't always translate into moral action. That's not too surprising. Even though it's a different process from cognitive empathy, reenactive empathy is still just a way of understanding others. When people talk about empathy in relation to ethics, they often assume that empathetically experiencing someone's suffering will automatically move us to do something to alleviate that suffering. But that's not how it usually works. When we encounter suffering, we frequently experience "empathic distress" – a distress that stems from the recognition that another individual is in pain. But we can often make those unpleasant feelings go away simply by changing the channel or by finding some other way to ignore the problem. The fact that we can choose whether we engage in reenactive empathy – that we can turn it on and shut it off – means that we can't always rely on it to produce moral action. But is there a form of empathy that generates a concern for the suffering of others that can't be shut off?

"I Fell in Love"

Even as Jake is developing a deeper understanding of the Omaticaya, he still makes reports to Quaritch that are used to plan an assault on "the people." Meanwhile, he does nothing to help the Omaticaya, for instance by telling them why he was really sent, or what the "sky people" have in mind – until they're pretty much on Hometree's doorstep. His actions during this time may betray some ambivalence, but he doesn't seem to have been completely swayed to the side of the Na'vi. For all we know, he's still half-heartedly entertaining plans to get his legs fixed and to return to his human life on Earth. When he finally takes a stand and alerts the Na'vi to the danger they face, his duplicity is exposed. What he tells Neytiri at this point to repair his broken relationship with her and "the people" says a lot about what really led him to embrace the cause of the Omaticaya. "Look," he says, "at first it was just orders, and then everything changed. Okay? I fell in love. I fell in love with the forest and with the Omaticaya people. And with you." What spurs Jake to action is not simply his *understanding* of the Na'vi, but also – and primarily – his personal *relationship* with them. His reenactive empathy opens him to this relationship, but it's the loyalty and friendship he experiences as one of "the people" that generates his "empathic concern," his motivation to help them in their "time of great sorrow."

Jake's first act of defiance against the RDA corporation – his attack on the bulldozers that were clearing a path to Hometree – occurred the morning after he was mated with Neytiri. The timing might be a coincidence. Maybe he would have reacted in the same way if they had plowed through the forest a day earlier. But it does look as if the danger they posed to Neytiri stoked his rage against the machines. He had also been initiated into the tribe as one of "the people" the night before, so it is equally possible that it was his newfound connection to the Omaticaya spurred him on. The bulldozers were not just threatening the Na'vi anymore – they were threatening *his* people.

It seems safe to say that Jake lists the things he has come to love in ascending order of importance: the forest, the Omaticaya, and Neytiri. His love for the forest is not as strong as his love for the Omaticaya. Even as he prepares for his initiation, he doesn't seem to appreciate fully the Pandoran ecosystem, although he certainly tries. When killing an animal, he performs the proper rituals to show gratitude and respect, but performing religious rituals is not the same as understanding them. Almost until the end of the film, he doesn't quite get the deep connection that the Na'vi have to the forest. The notion of a "network of energy that flows through all living things" and the idea that "all energy is only borrowed" seem pretty mysterious to him. Even his prayer to Eywa at the Tree of Souls suggests that he's still wrestling with these ideas. Jake is much more concerned about the destruction of "the people" than he is about the destruction of the ecosystem.

And even his concern for "the people" seems to fall short of his concern for one Na'vi in particular, Neytiri. Jake is enamored of the beautiful future *tsahìk* from their very first meeting. His interest in her fuels his interest in learning about the Omaticaya, especially when she's assigned the task of teaching him. And it's in the process of learning about the ways of the Na'vi that he learns to appreciate the forest.

There's a tendency to think that empathetic understanding will automatically yield empathic concern. But some psychological studies suggest that empathic concern is generated not so much by empathetic understanding as by a feeling of connection or "oneness" with the other.[8] Jake's experience illustrates this idea as well. It's only when he sees his own well-being bound up with the well-being of "the people" that he's moved to decisive action.

"I Didn't Sign Up for This Shit"

If we're looking for another reason why we shouldn't place too much emphasis on empathetic understanding, let's consider the one character in *Avatar* who displays empathic concern for the Na'vi without any real understanding of them. Trudy Chacón is a former military, like Jake. Consequently she and Jake are on the same wavelength almost from their first meeting. Without an avatar or any special training in Na'vi culture, Trudy is motivated to help Grace and Jake in their efforts to protect "the people." In all likelihood, she's as puzzled by the Omaticaya beliefs as Jake was throughout most of his training. Nonetheless, she's the only pilot who refuses to fire on Hometree; she declares that she "didn't sign up for this shit" as she turns her Samson 16 back to Hell's Gate. And she breaks Grace, Norm, and Jake out of the brig, taking them to a remote location so that they can reconnect with their avatars and help the Omaticaya. Finally, she joins the battle on behalf of the Na'vi and ultimately sacrifices her life protecting the Tree of Souls.

Trudy has no great familiarity with Na'vi culture or their way of life, nor does she seem to share Jake's and the other avatar drivers' affection for the Na'vi. Yet she puts her life on the line to do right by Pandora and its inhabitants. She knows that the RDA's actions are morally indefensible and is undoubtedly aware that Quaritch is taking sadistic delight in this one-sided confrontation, for which he's been pushing all along. Trudy is thus our strongest evidence that empathic concern for the Na'vi doesn't require some special understanding of "the people" that only an avatar can provide. The recognition of suffering on which empathic concern is based can be achieved through a simple act of cognitive empathy – and the anguish of the Na'vi during the assault on Hometree is etched plainly on their faces, obvious even to someone who knows nothing about "the people."

Recognizing a connection with others appears to be the key to empathic concern; but we never learn exactly why Trudy responds to Omaticaya. Somehow she saw a connection between herself and the

Na'vi and became willing to die for them. Maybe the plight of the Na'vi reminded her of the experiences of her ancestors, who may also have suffered oppression and forced relocation. Or maybe she saw a connection between the person she wanted to be and how she treated "the people." Whatever the reason, Trudy is a unique individual. Most people find it too difficult to get beyond narrow self-interest (like Selfridge) or a narcissistic personality (like Quaritch) and make a connection with someone with a radically different way of life. An avatar might be a big help to such blinkered people, a way to get them outside their limited point of view and open themselves up to others. It certainly worked for Jake – though I think nothing short of a personality transplant will help Miles Quaritch.

Notes

1. For a discussion of how empathy actually works, see Chapter 6 by Massimiliano Cappuccio.
2. Selfridge's words also show a tendency to dehumanize the other.
3. In Chapter 6, Cappuccio uses a definition of "empathy" similar to the one presented here. However, he defines it a little more narrowly, as an embodied process. The definition presented here does not presume any particular mechanism for putting oneself in the shoes of another. For a more thorough discussion of what processes might be at work, see Chapter 6.
4. The phrase "reenactive empathy" is taken from Karsten Stueber and his book *Rediscovering Empathy: Agency, Psychology, and the Human Sciences* (Cambridge, MA: MIT Press, 2006). This form of empathy is called "reenactive" because it involves recreating the experiences of someone else by acting them out in our own mind (somehow).
5. Adam Smith, *The Theory of Moral Sentiments* (Indianapolis, IN: Liberty Fund, 2009), 9.
6. One of the most promising areas of research concerns mirror neurons. For more information, see Chapter 6.
7. For more on understanding the minds of nonhuman animals, see Chapter 18 by Wayne Yuen.
8. Robert B. Cialdini, Stephanie L. Brown, Brian P. Lewis, Carol Luce, and Steven L. Neuberg, "Reinterpreting the Empathy–Altruism Relationship: When One into One Equals Oneness," *Journal of Personality and Social Psychology* 73.3 (1997), 481–494.

6

"I See You" through a Glass Darkly

Avatar and the Limits of Empathy

Massimiliano Cappuccio

Avatar, a passionate movie about empathy, features characters who, in various ways, are able to experience the world through the eyes of another or, as the saying goes, to "put themselves into another's shoes." But, concealed beneath a surface of ecological pantheism, a contradiction lies at the heart of the movie's portrayal of empathy.

On the one hand, in ordinary empathy access to another person's mind is *mediated* by our perception of her unique embodied identity. In other words, we perceive what's going on "in there" – what she's experiencing, feeling, or intending – by paying attention to her body, including her gestures and facial expressions. Of course, it may be hard to "read" someone whose background, lifestyle, and experience of the world are radically different from our own. That's one reason why Jake Sully and other avatar drivers actually take on the form of the Na'vi when they want to get to know the blue-skinned humanoid inhabitants of Pandora. What better way to become familiar with the members of an alien species than to take on their appearance, along with some of the unique capabilities of their bodies, in order to live among them?

On the other hand, *Avatar* introduces us to a seemingly more direct way to connect with the minds of others: *tsaheylu* – "the bond." *Tsaheylu* is depicted as a computer-like exchange of information that's indifferent to how the bodies of the two individuals appear to each other. So is this really just a more direct form of empathy, bypassing the need for visible bodily clues and going straight to hidden recesses

Avatar and Philosophy: Learning to See, First Edition. Edited by George A. Dunn.
© 2014 John Wiley & Sons, Inc. Published 2014 by John Wiley & Sons, Inc.

of the mind? No, I don't think it's really empathy at all, but rather an entirely different way to understand others. As we'll see, appreciating how *tsaheylu* differs from true empathy can help to understand what empathy really is and why it's important.

Empathy in Blue

The word "sympathy," precursor to empathy, originally designated a polite sensitivity to social and cultural circumstances and the capacity to cope with them properly. The philosopher (and architect of modern economic theory) Adam Smith (1723–1790) was the first to characterize sympathy as an internal act that reproduces the experience of the other.[1] For example, when Jake pursues Neytiri across a thick tree branch, retaining his balance only with great difficulty, we in the audience live his tension in each of his smallest breaths. Our muscles contract along with his and we reproduce his efforts within our own bodies, thereby sharing his experience. By means of empathy, we inhabits Jake's body in a way analogous to how he inhabits his avatar.

The psychologist Theodor Lipps (1851–1914) compared this empathetic response to the sympathetic resonance of two musical strings: our bodies produce the same experience, just as the strings of different musical instruments vibrate at the same frequency when they're traversed by the same note.[2] When I empathize, my soul vibrates with that of another person, generating in my body an echo of her internal experience. The reason why we're able to feel the thrill and danger of Jake's acrobatic adventures in the forest is that to some extent they trigger corresponding automatic reactions in our bodies, such as tightened muscles and accelerated breathing and heartbeat. This "inner imitation" is, for Lipps, a form of union and hence of intimate understanding.

Thus empathy is not a matter of perceiving someone's behavior and then *reasoning* our way to conclusions about her inner life. It's not conceptual or abstract knowledge, but something we experience straightaway. We need only look at the person in front of us – her movements, her face, her hands – and we immediately recognize her as a living center of emotions, experiences, desires, and intentions, a being who is conscious, just like us, and completely different from any inanimate object. That's the power of empathy! For example, when Jake looks into the face of Eytukan, he doesn't see a neutral collection of facial features – nose, eyes, mouth, and forehead – from which he infers the pride of the Omaticaya clan leader. On the contrary, he sees Eytukan's pride directly, "in the flesh," embodied in his austere countenance.

The philosopher Edmund Husserl (1859–1938)[3] and his pupil Edith Stein (1891–1942)[4] developed Lipps' conception of empathy as an embodied process of *analogy*, that is, a process through which we experience the world *as if* we were in the other person's skin. For example, when we see poor Jake plummet out of the tree, crashing through the branches, and landing on his ass, we instinctively understand his pain *as if* we were in his place. Automatically, without even thinking about it, we associate Jake's pained expression with how we would form the muscles on our faces *if* we were suffering in the same way. When we wince, it means we're in pain. In the same way, we know that Jake is hurting. That's why we immediately see Jake's body as *injured* and *sore*. In short, when we empathize in this way, the other person becomes our "alter ego," an analogy, a way of vicariously experiencing our own possibilities.

Husserl and Stein stressed that our ability to establish such an analogy depends on how familiar we are with salient aspects of the other person's body, including its signals, gestures, and conduct. The more my bodily characteristics appear similar to yours, the more spontaneously you will empathize with me. That's why we empathize less easily with Pandoran hexapedes than with terrestrial dogs and cats. Mammals have bodies not too dissimilar from ours, so we find it easy to feel their pain. The pain inflicted on a beloved pet can even be intolerable to us. But we might not have as much sympathy for the six-legged herbivores hunted and killed by the Na'vi on account of their greater dissimilarity to us, even though we have no rational motives to doubt that their pain is just as real as that of a dog or cat. In addition, our level of sensitivity to the feelings of others is proportional to the degree of our empathic skills. Being masters of empathy, the Na'vi naturally feel close to every form of life, no matter how different it is from them.

Empathy Versus the Vulcan Mind Meld

Still, regardless of how fully a Na'vi can empathize with the physical pain of another, he will never feel any real pain in his own body as a consequence. By the same token, even when we empathize most strongly with a suffering loved one, what we feel is at most a global sense of discomfort rather than an exact reproduction of her physical sensations.[5] We certainly won't feel the *quality* of pain she's experiencing. Empathy can tell us a lot about her experience, but it doesn't reproduce that experience in us. That's a crucial point.

In short, empathy is not some magical telepathy providing direct access to the other's mind. It's always *mediated* by how the other's body looks and acts. Furthermore, it's *analogical*, based on our ability to recognize similarities between what's disclosed by the other's body and our own bodily experience. And, of course, our bodily experiences are never identical, however similar they may appear. Consequently empathy provides an access to the other's mind that's *relative* to our own perspective because it's drawn from our own experiences. It can only *simulate* what we would feel and how we would react if we were in the other's shoes. In short, my actions and emotional expressions appear meaningful to you only on the basis of particular possibilities available to your body. This makes absurd any ambitious dream of accessing another person's mind as such, of experiencing her thoughts and feelings directly, by means of some sort of "mental fusion" that bypasses the body, like Mr. Spock's Vulcan mind meld on *Star Trek*.

The Avatar program, therefore, seems to be based on the fundamentally correct intuition that, to understand the world of another, you need above all to experience her way of physically inhabiting that world. That means sharing her bodily skills, her way of riding, climbing, hunting, stalking, and shooting arrows. Of course, no one's mental life is entirely revealed by her body. But that's where our attempt to comprehend it needs to start. It's Jake's avatar body that allows him, by degrees, to understand Neytiri's worldview and motivations, as well as to imitate and acquire the panoply of physical skills through which she interacts with her world.

Of course, at the outset of Jake's adventures on Pandora, he was anxious and confused around the Omaticaya clan. Clearly, just having an avatar wasn't enough for him to understand Na'vi customs. On the other hand, without taking their appearance, he couldn't join their rituals, share their tribal customs, become a warrior of the clan, and finally come to their aid in their time of greatest peril. Jake's strength – as he will confess to the *tsahìk* Mo'at – is just that he arrived "empty" among Na'vi, without training or preparation, brimming only with impulsive and rough curiosity.[6] His new blue body and his lack of mental and cultural barriers make him capable of *filling* himself through his social interactions with the Na'vi, of becoming more and more similar to them – and eventually one of them. Needless to say, a proper *filling* requires an encounter capable of changing all the parties involved, which is what happens little by little between Jake and Neytiri as they learn from each other and mature in their relationship.

Empathy, *Tsaheylu*, and the iPod

Yet, even if being mediated through our ordinary perception of each other's bodies is a vital part of empathy on Earth, maybe things are different on Pandora. Consider how *tsaheylu* works. A Na'vi hunter can enter the mind of his steed through a direct neuronal connection, making a deep bond with the creature and taking control of its body. And *tsaheylu* doesn't work only with animals. Even the majestic trees of the forest, the roots of which preserve the memory of Pandora itself, are available for such a "bond." *Tsaheylu* involves some sort of brain linkage accomplished through an antenna-like appendage that, for the Na'vi, is hidden in a braid of hair. These antennas allow creatures to plug into each other's minds, like USB ports naturally evolved for networking functions and used to transfer data (memory), cognitive processes (motor control, perception), and even emotions and will. One creature's body becomes, in effect, a device to be activated and controlled by another, like a printer remotely operated from your PC.

Tsaheylu directly connects different minds, regardless of how their bodies function and appear. Once connected through *tsaheylu*, a direhorse sends and receives information as if she were directly reaching into her rider's consciousness, conveying thoughts and feelings that remain unchanged throughout all stages of the transmission. This is quite unlike ordinary empathy, in which it is impossible to tell if the experiences of the two parties are exactly the same. What's more, the Na'vi can even connect their pony-tailed neural queues to the Tree of Voices and download the memories and sentiments of their ancestors, much as you might download digital songs by connecting your iPod to the Internet. But notice this difference: iPods transmit and receive *unaltered* packages of information, which is why we can call them "transparent" media. Nothing is changed in the process of transmission except the location of the information. The very same data, encoded on some Internet site, are now (also) on my iPod. But, as we've seen, the content of an ordinary empathetic experience isn't like that at all. That's why we call empathy an "opaque" process, for it's not a simple transmission of unaltered information.

We should take seriously the difference between the Na'vi's direct mental linkage and human empathy mediated by bodily gestures and expressions. *Tsaheylu* looks similar to empathy because it allows the Na'vi to understand what others feel. If, however, the mind linkage accomplished through *tsaheylu* is the *transparent* process it appears to be, then it's dramatically different from the sort of empathy we're familiar with. Empathy isn't about transferring bits of information from one mind to another. It's about resonating with someone else's experience and giving it a meaning on the basis of our analogous experiences. Even if we could directly access a simple package of data stored in another person's brain, it would still need to be filtered through our respective cultures and personal histories and would assume different meanings for each of us.

In any case, human beings don't have neural queues equipped for *tsaheylu*, so the sort of mind linkage the Na'vi practice appears to be out of the question for us. However, contemporary researchers in neuroscience have discovered that our brains are in fact designed for a different sort of remote link with other minds, which makes use of brains cells called "mirror neurons." But what we know about these remarkable cells makes it even more certain that ordinary human empathy isn't just a weak, error-prone version of *tsaheylu*. It's something different entirely.

"Get Out of My Head!" *Tsaheylu* and Mirror Neurons

Mirror neurons are one of the most significant scientific discoveries of the last fifteen years. Originally discovered in macaque monkeys by the neurophysiologist Giacomo Rizzolatti and his team of researchers in Parma, Italy, mirror neurons are major candidates for explaining how empathy works at the level of brain functioning.[7] They're found in the premotor cortex – the area of the brain responsible for planning and executing actions – and have two very interesting properties.[8]

First, specialized mirror neurons fire whenever we perform actions
of a certain type, such as grasping, holding, moving away, ripping, or
bringing something to our mouths. Significantly, these mirror neurons
are able to distinguish between actions on the basis of their intentions
or purposes, regardless of the particular movements or tools they
happen to use. So, for example, a certain class of mirror neurons will
fire in Jake's brain whenever he grasps a piece of food with the intention of bringing it to his mouth, but not when he grasps an instrument
in the lab with the intention to move it from one place to another. But
the second property of these neurons is even more interesting, for
the mirror neurons associated with a certain type of action are active
both when we perform that action *and* when we attend to someone
else's performing it. In other words, neurons fire when Jake lowers
himself into his avatar link unit, and the same neurons fire when Jake
observes Grace or Norm executing the same set of movements, thus
allowing him to understand better.

Interestingly, the more familiar someone is with how to perform a
certain type of action, the more his mirror neurons will fire when he
sees that action performed.[9] Jake's mirror neurons undoubtedly fire
in an especially robust manner when he watches Neytiri battle
the viperwolves that attacked him, since he's also a warrior, a marine
trained in hand-to-hand combat. He may not be as proficient as
Neytiri at fending off six-legged reptilian canines, but at least
some of her fighting moves are probably already in his own combat
repertoire, so he understands their patterns and the intentions
behind them.

This dual function of mirror neurons – their role in both executing
and recognizing actions – makes it reasonable to assume that the
scaffolding for understanding the meaning of other people's actions
consists of our experiences performing those same actions firsthand.[10]
This neuroscientific model, therefore, seems perfectly in tune with
the philosophical model of empathy developed by Lipps, Husserl, and
Stein, except that neuroscience now locates embodied simulation
within invisible cognitive operations processed by the brain, instead
of the automatic reflexes of muscles and arms. But, if it's true that
mirror neurons are the neural basis of empathy, this is because they
engage our personal abilities and practical attitudes, not because they
provide an abstract depiction of an action. Mirror neurons testify that
empathy, as usually experienced by terrestrial creatures like us, is
nothing like a direct mental access.

But what if our mirror neurons could connect directly with the corresponding mirror neurons in another person's brain, let's say through a cable linking our skulls, *tsaheylu* style? Could a simple discharge of someone's "grasping" mirror neurons, communicated along that neural cable, inform us that she intends to grasp an object? In other words, could something like *tsaheylu* permit us to dispense with our own embodied knowledge of how to perform that action? No. It's likely that, even with a direct neuronal link to her mirror neurons, we wouldn't be able to understand that she was going to grasp unless we were already capable of grasping with *our own* bodies. If our mirror neurons are able to interact effectively with hers through a neural cable, this can only be because we've had *analogous* grasping experiences, *not* because the neuronal link enables some direct and smooth transfer of the *same* objective representation of the grasping action, like digitized information being downloaded from one PC to another.

That's why there must be an element of opacity (non-transparency) even in *tsaheylu*, as long as the latter is a vehicle of some sort of empathy. Even if Jake can plug right into his steed's brain, he can't *directly* access the very thoughts and purposes that the direhorse conceives in its mind, since Jake's experience of running, for example, is only remotely analogous to that of his six-legged mount. He would still need to see the direhorse's actions with his own eyes and to relate them to capacities of his own body. Opacity is a necessary condition for empathy in any possible world, even in worlds where brains can be directly linked. And this means that, even when we say "I see you," we still only see through a glass darkly.

How the Video Log Helps Us Think:
The Extended Mind Hypothesis

Opacity is a necessary condition for empathy, but empathy is not the only form of interpersonal communication. Human beings have other ways to get in tune that seem to be transparent, since the details of our bodies don't affect the information we want to share. To explain this point, we need to introduce the extended mind hypothesis, which challenges the traditional philosophical view that cognitive processes take place only within the boundaries of the skull.[11] We don't think with our heads alone. Some cognitive processes occur out in the world, involving non-neuronal parts of the body and devices situated beyond the skin, such as pen and paper, images, maps, and laptops.

Consider pen and paper. They're not just instruments for expressing thoughts previously conceived in the head. They can actually contribute to discovering new ideas on the fly. For example, when we're solving an equation or demonstrating a geometrical theorem, pen and paper are functionally encompassed in our mental activity and temporarily become structural components of it. In other words, we think *with* them, making them *parts* of our extended mind for as long as we use them as instruments for that purpose. Or consider the video log that Jake updates daily. If he wanted, he could use it to remember the events that occur each day on Pandora or to remind himself of his appointments the following day. The video log supplements his natural memory and in this sense it's an active element of his cognitive activity. That doesn't mean that pen, paper, and video logs "think," only that in some circumstances we can think better with them than we could without them.[12]

Not every augmentation of human powers is a case of extended mind. Consider the amplified mobility platforms (AMP) suits controlled by the SecOps troopers in *Avatar*. Colonel Quaritch's cybernetic armor enhances his speed and strength in his showdown with Jake, but it doesn't provide him with any extra insight, knowledge, intuition, or intelligence. *Tsaheylu*, on the other hand, may look like an excellent case of extended cognition. The Na'vi connect to the Tree of Voices to download the memory of the tribe and to learn from the past experiences of their ancestors in more or less the same way as Jake recalls his own past experiences with the aid of his video log. And, when Neytiri connects to her ikran, she can also access its emotions and feelings, as well as sending it mental commands that direct it to fly. The data received from her ikran are active elements of the mental activity that goes into riding. Even though the animal's body and senses are located outside her own brain, she can still use them to extend her usual cognitive functions. These seem like good cases of extended mind; but there's something quite puzzling about them.

Norm Spellman's Homework: The Socially Extended Mind

Now that we understand the extended mind hypothesis, let's focus on something called "the *socially* extended mind," in which cognitive processes don't simply make use of external objects, but also of other people and *their* minds. Imagine the following scenario: Norm Spellman needs to write a scientific report on the varieties of edible plants growing near the human land base on Pandora. As a student, he memorized the complete list of these plants, including their botanical names and taxonomical groups; but now he can't remember it very well. He can use several different strategies to bring it to mind, though. He could try to recall the information from his previous exploration of Pandora, he could look it up in his exobiology textbook, or if he's *really* desperate – he could ask his advisor Dr. Grace Augustine, hoping he's not bothering her too much. As far as the information is concerned, it makes no difference where he gets it. The information in the book and the information he would get from Grace is basically the same as the information stored somewhere in his head – after all, Grace is the author of the book he studied to become an exobiologist!

Of course, there's a huge difference between recalling the list by calling to mind past explorations – with all the associated tastes, smells, and colors – and reading this information from an impersonal academic book.[13] Asking Grace – that is, using her as part of his *socially* extended mind – is different in other ways, requiring some mutual linguistic understanding as well as a certain code of politeness. But, as long as Norm's primary concern is to get the data about the plants, it really doesn't matter how the information is packaged, implemented, stored, or obtained. He can empathize deeply with Grace or be indifferent to her – that might affect their relationship, but it won't change the list of plants. Regardless of how he recalls the list or how he interacts with others in the process, the information itself remains the same. In philosophy of mind, this principle is called "multiple realizability."[14]

But now notice how different the cognitive process is in empathy and in the socially extended mind. Let's imagine that Norm decides to ask Grace to help him with the information he needs for his report. When she comes into the lab, he carefully scrutinizes her face and her body language. He tries to discern whether she's busy, whether she's in a good mood, and basically whether it's a good time to bother her, all the while using his empathetic skills to try to understand her mental state. Whether he succeeds will depend on how well he can read her face and body to determine how it feels to be in her current situation. In this case, Grace's face and body aren't just the package around the information, as they are with the list of plants; here they're what constitutes the information. Consider how different it is to *read* the emotions *on* someone's face and to *read about* the same emotions *in* a book!

The principle of multiple realizability doesn't apply to empathy because the information that empathy conveys – for example, an understanding of Grace's current mood and intentions – can't be separated from its package. Empathy allows only an opaque (not a transparent) access to other minds, an access mediated by the body and dependent on our sensitivity to the other person's situation. The socially extended mind, on the other hand, grants a channel for sharing information that's indifferent to context – for example, a list that remains the same no matter how Norm obtains it. The difference between these two ways of relating to other minds comes down to this: Empathy deals with firsthand lived *experiences* such as feelings, emotions, and embodied intentions, while the socially extended mind is a way of storing and sharing *symbolic data* represented as words, numbers, or images. Both are necessary, but they are hardly the same.

Nature, Culture, and USB Portals

Avatar's fictional depiction of *tsaheylu* is fascinating, but also unrealistic, because it suggests a mix of empathy and the socially extended mind that blurs the boundaries between firsthand lived experiences and symbolic data. The puzzling thing is that the Na'vi minds can connect like nodes of a network of digital computers, yet they do it as a sort of empathic experience. But then, is this networking capability similar to empathy or to a socially extended mind? On the one hand, it seems that the *tsaheylu* offers an embodied understanding of private and subjective experiences – say, feelings of a pain, or the intention to sprint. On the other hand, when Grace describes the roots of the Pandoran trees as a brain-like network that can be accessed "to upload and download data," she suggests that experiences shared through *tsaheylu* are objectively encoded as symbolic data, not unlike songs stored in an iPod.

Now the problem is that, if *tsaheylu* were possible even in principle, then one of two things would have to be the case. First, empathy *could* be a transparent vehicle for transferring symbolic data; but then we would miss the important difference between seeing someone in pain and being informed by a newspaper that she is in pain.

Alternatively, the socially extended mind *could* grant access to private experiences; but that would probably put an end to sharing the sort of objective information that we convey with the aid of words and other symbols. In either case, we would be at a loss to understand how one and the same form of interpersonal communication could convey something that's at once as subjective as Grace's mood and as objective as a list of plants. And yet that seems to be what *tsaheylu* does. *Avatar* doesn't provide a clear explanation of how this could be possible, but maybe the sequels will offer more details.

In the meantime, what we know for sure is that on planet Earth nature provided human beings and some other animals with a capacity for empathy, while our culture has equipped us to share objective information through language and symbols. These two abilities are intertwined and never entirely independent, but we shouldn't lose sight of their difference.[15] The inherent limitations of empathy – its unsuitability for sharing objective knowledge – may be part of the reason why we had to become cultural beings and develop language and other symbol systems. Could we have evolved neural queues instead? Indeed, it seems doubtful that living beings could ever evolve a biological contraption to connect their brains directly, or that such a capacity could ever be useful in a purely natural or precultural context. From the standpoint of Darwinian evolutionary fitness, there are probably some very good reasons why natural selection didn't provide us with comfortable USB ports situated on the back of our necks!

Notes

1. Adam Smith, *The Theory of Moral Sentiments* (New York: Barnes & Noble, 2004 [1759]).
2. Theodor Lipps, *Ästhetik: Psychologie des Schönen und der Kunst*, 2 vols. (Hamburg and Leipzig: Leopold Voss, 1903–1906).
3. Edmund Husserl, *Cartesian Meditations*, trans. Dorion Cairns (The Hague: Martinus Nijhoff, 1973 [1931]).
4. Edith Stein, *On the Problem of Empathy* [1917], 3rd rev. ed. (Washington, DC: ICS Publications, 1989).
5. For more on the "simulation theory" of empathy, see Chapter 5 by Andrew Terjesen.
6. On the other hand, see Chapter 5 by Terjesen for an argument that Jake may not be as "empty" as he claims.

7. Giacomo Rizzolatti and Laila Craighero, "Mirror Neuron: A Neuro-logical Approach to Empathy," *Neurobiology of Human Values* (Berlin and Heidelberg: Springer-Verlag, 2005), 107. For a popular account of the discovery of mirror neurons, see Marco Iacoboni, *Mirroring People: The Science of Empathy and How We Connect with Others* (New York: Picador, 2009).

8. Giacomo Rizzolatti, Luciano Fadiga, Vittorio Gallese, and Leonardo Fogassi, "Premotor Cortex and the Recognition of Motor Actions," *Cognitive Brain Research* 3 (1996), 131.

9. Beatriz Calvo-Merino, Daniel E. Glaser, Julie Grezes, Richard E. Passingham, and Paul Haggard, "Action, Observation and Acquired Motor Skills: An fMRI Study with Expert Dancers," *Cortex* 15.8 (2005), 1243.

10. Vittorio Gallese, "Embodied Simulation: From Neurons to Phenomenal Experience," *Phenomenology and the Cognitive Sciences* 4 (2005), 23.

11. Andy Clark and David Chalmers, "The Extended Mind," *Analysis* 58.1 (1998), 7.

12. For a discussion of how extended mind theory can shed light on Jake's relationship with his avatar, see Chapter 11 by Ryan Smock.

13. Richard Menary, *Cognitive Integration: Mind and Cognition Unbounded* (New York: Palgrave Macmillan, 2007).

14. Michael Wheeler, "In Defense of Extended Functionalism," in Richard Menary, ed., *The Extended Mind*, (Boston, MA: MIT Press, 2010), 245–270.

15. John Sutton, "Exograms and Interdisciplinarity: History, the Extended Mind and the Civilizing Process," in Richard Menary, ed., *The Extended Mind* (Boston MA: MIT Press, 2010), 33–81.

Part III

SEEING NATURE
"TRY TO SEE THE FOREST THROUGH HER EYES"

Seeing the Na'vi Way
Respecting Life and Mind in All Organisms

Kyle Burchett

Jake Sully arrives on Pandora already disenchanted with the human race. His identical twin Tommy was murdered by a fellow human being for nothing more than "the paper in his wallet." Now, as Jake disembarks from the Valkyrie shuttlecraft, he enters a world where the same thing is happening on a grand scale, where human predators are ready to sacrifice the lives of countless living beings in pursuit of monetary gain. This disrespect for life is symptomatic of what the Na'vi see as the calling card of the "sky people," an insanity for which they have concluded there is no cure.

The Na'vi's intimate connection to all life on Pandora makes humanity's vicious attitude toward the natural world unfathomable to them. The Na'vi *see* the intrinsic value of *all* life. In their eyes, there can be no justification for the wanton destruction of life on Pandora. All of the unobtanium in the world can't buy back the lives destroyed in its acquisition. To disrespect life in others – whether plants, animals, or persons – is ultimately to disrespect oneself. The "sky people" act as if they were *apart* from nature rather than *a part* of it. Failing to *see* the intricate connections among all living things, they have no understanding of the moral significance of their actions – on Pandora or on Earth. The Na'vi, on the other hand, attempt to *see* through the eye of Eywa and to evaluate the moral significance of their actions by whether they uphold the balance of life.[1]

The "sky people" appraise life on Pandora in monetary terms. Parker Selfridge, the face of the Resources Development Administration

Avatar and Philosophy: Learning to See, First Edition. Edited by George A. Dunn.

(RDA) corporation, and his hired gun Colonel Miles Quaritch exemplify the worst qualities of blind human ignorance and arrogance. Like Tommy's murderer, they don't hesitate to take life for the sake of maximizing profits, without a thought for who or what gets crushed beneath their boot heels. Selfridge explains his corporation's position with the spine-numbing coldness of a genuine psychopath: "Killing the indigenous looks bad. But there's one thing the shareholders hate more than bad press, and that's a bad quarterly statement." The ruthless tactics the "sky people" employ to extract unobtanium from Pandora have led them to the brink of war with the Na'vi, whose way of life and very existence is threatened by the clearcutting of forests and strip mining of the land. Unless a cure can be found for the insanity of the "sky people," unless they can learn to *see*, they will destroy Eywa the way they destroyed their own mother, Gaia. Jake carries the weight and the fate of an entire world on his shoulders.

"They Killed Their Mother": The High Price of Insanity

The "sky people" pride themselves on their cleverness. Ironically, however, the cleverness of *Homo sapiens* can get in the way of truly rational behavior. The "sky people" are so mesmerized by their technological prowess that they are blind to their true place within a biosphere composed of interconnected parts, each one of which makes an essential contribution to the whole. Consequently their behavior toward their natural environment is anything but rational – unless imperiling one's own survival by wrecking the biosphere counts as evidence of superior reason. When corporate executives like Selfridge demonstrate their willingness to condemn humanity to extinction for the sake of short-term profits, they evince a deeply twisted, even logically incoherent system of values. How could the Na'vi not perceive human beings as insane, when these beings fail to *see* what is so incredibly obvious?

No organism can live outside of a fairly well-defined set of environmental conditions, and all life forms are inextricably linked to the environment in which they have evolved and are situated. The Na'vi understand this quite well and are baffled that human beings can't *see* the importance of maintaining the balance of life. The environment and the organisms that are *in* and *of* it play a vital role in one another's maintenance and evolution. The biosphere makes the survival of individual organisms possible, as each plant and animal species helps to preserve the chemical and molecular makeup of the whole. Consequently, extreme alterations to the environment caused by strip mining and the clearcutting of forests can be devastating for an entire ecosystem. Prolonged environmental degradation on a global scale can lead to the extinction or massive die-off of countless species. As the removal of one species can alter the environment in a way that makes the latter less able to support other species, the result could be a chain reaction of mass extinction – precisely what seems to have occurred on the dying world of the "sky people." The "sky people" have no one to blame for this catastrophe but themselves, as we hear Jake acknowledge in his prayer to Eywa before the climactic battle scene: "See the world we come from. There's no green there. They killed their Mother. And they're gonna do the same here."

In his book *The Death of Our Planet's Species*, philosopher Martin Gorke warns that we are currently in the midst of a mass extinction event like the one just described. An analysis of the Earth's geologic record indicates that mass extinction events are common in our planet's history, although the current one is unique in not having a natural cause in some cosmic or geological incident, such as an asteroid collision or a cataclysmic volcanic eruption.[2] It is instead a direct result of the irrational behavior of *Homo sapiens*, the supposedly *rational* animal. A steady accretion of scientific data makes it increasingly obvious that our overexploitation of natural resources and burning of fossil fuels are the chief culprits. By even conservative estimates, if we continue reproducing and overexploiting the environment at the same alarming rate as today, at least 50 percent of all nonhuman species on the Earth will have become extinct within the next 100 years. Listen to Gorke's dire recital of where we are today:

> Species are dying worldwide at a rate of about three per hour, or more than seventy per day, and 27,000 per year, each a unique specimen of life that has gradually come to be over hundreds of thousands of years. Extrapolating from present trends, we can expect an even greater increase in the loss of species.[3]

Gorke reminds us that we of the current generation are not only front-row witnesses to the catastrophe, but also bearers of moral culpability. Humanity's culturally ingrained devaluation of nonhuman life prevents us from *seeing* the rationality of adopting a truly ethical stance toward other species. Our salvation, according to Gorke, depends on setting aside our anthropocentrism and adopting a holistic worldview that recognizes the intrinsic value of the biosphere as a whole and the rich pageant of species and habitats it comprises. As he explains: "In a comprehensive form of environmental ethics both human and nonhuman individuals as well as wholes must be given adequate moral consideration."[4]

When it comes to protecting the Earth's biosphere, perhaps a truly *rational* form of anthropocentrism would be enough. Even if we don't recognize the intrinsic value of *other* species, reason tells us that our *own* prospects for survival are dim unless we start protecting the balance of life on our planet. But this form of rational anthropocentrism gives us no reason to protect species alien to our planet. For the "sky people" to respect life on Pandora, they must overcome their anthropocentrism and learn to *see* in the Na'vi way. Just as Eywa's concern extends even to Jake and Grace despite their being alien to Pandora, so the "sky people" must learn to value all life, terrestrial or otherwise, for its own sake.

Philosophers, Dogs, and Viperwolves

The insanity of the "sky people" is exemplified by their irrational anthropocentricism, an attitude that has regrettably been prevalent in Western philosophy since the time of the ancient Greeks. The philosopher Aristotle (384–322 BCE) argued in the *De anima* (his treatise *On the Soul*) that every living thing – plant, animal, or human being[5] – possessed a soul; but he deemed the human soul alone to be capable of rational thought.[6] Plants were the lowest life form for Aristotle, because they were capable only of feeding, growing, and reproducing. Believing plants to be basically without movement (or motor function), Aristotle thought that they lacked the need – and therefore the ability – to perceive the world around them. He set animals on a higher rung due to their ability to move and perceive, but the pinnacle of mortal powers was the capacity for reason, which he believed belonged exclusively to human beings. Ultimately he used this hierarchical classification to justify human beings' exploitation of the nonhuman world. In his *Politics* Aristotle claimed that the natural order of things dictated that organisms lower in the hierarchy exist solely for the benefit of those above. No doubt something like this line of reasoning has significantly influenced the RDA's corporate philosophy concerning Pandora. It's simply taken for granted that human beings are naturally superior and therefore entitled to commoditize and exploit everything on Pandora, living or otherwise.

Like Aristotle, the philosopher René Descartes (1596–1650) placed human beings in a category apart from other living things. But, even more boldly, he insisted that human beings alone have minds, while nonhuman organisms are simply mindless automata or machines. He justified this belief by appealing to something that seemed as obvious to him as it does to many people today, namely that the supposed inability of the other animals to use language "attests not merely to the fact that the beasts have less reason than men but that they have none at all."[7] Another justification was the supposedly limited behavioral repertoire of the other animals by comparison to that of "rational" human beings.[8] To deny that a being has a mind is to grant oneself a moral license to commit acts against it that would otherwise be considered horrendous. One such act is vivisection – cutting open a living organism in order to view the workings of its internal organs – a practice that Descartes not only endorsed but also carried himself, without any qualms. Jonathan Balcombe, in his book *Pleasurable Kingdom*, offers a poignant description of how Descartes would conduct this cruel procedure:

> With his blessing, dogs were nailed to wooden boards by their four paws and flayed alive to see the circulation of their blood. The victims' cries, to Descartes and his disciples, were no more the basis for moral concern than the creaks and groans of crushed, rusty metal.[9]

Imagine the horror such a sight would have awakened in a Na'vi. With their ability to commune with individual life forms through the neural tendrils that extend from their braided queues, the Na'vi know with absolute certainty that other organisms on Pandora have a mental life. They can participate directly in the subjectivity of other beings, literally *seeing* through the eyes of the organisms with whom they are joined. When Neytiri chooses to save Jake's life from a pack of viperwolves, she recognizes the moral cost. The pain she feels at slaying these animals who "did not need to die" is palpable as she prays over their fallen bodies.

Seeing through the Eye of Eywa

It's apparent from their vicious treatment of life on Pandora that
Selfridge and Quaritch are – ethically speaking – staunch Cartesians
when it comes to nonhuman beings. The Na'vi, on the other hand,
take life only when this is necessary in order to preserve life, and each
life is taken with a respectful attitude and a prayer of thanks that
acknowledges the agency of the organism whose life is sacrificed.
Every interaction with another life form has moral import. To deny
one's ethical obligations to other life forms is to blind oneself to the
interconnectedness of all life within the biosphere. Since Eywa
embodies the collective consciousness of all life on Pandora, the
experience of each individual organism is ultimately *seen* through the
eye of Eywa. Consequently the Na'vi are aware that they must always
strive to uphold the balance of life. Not only will they be held
accountable by the organisms with whom they interact, but they will
also be judged by their own conscience – and ultimately by Eywa's
all-seeing eye. It is in *being seen* that one truly learns to appreciate the
depth of one's moral obligations. *Seeing* in this sense necessitates
respecting each part of the interconnected biosphere as an aspect of
Eywa to be valued for both its intrinsic worth and its contribution to
the global balance of life.

Neytiri is reminded of the ethical implications of her actions when
an atokirina alights on the tip of an arrow she had aimed at Jake with
the intention of taking his life. She realizes that this seed of the Sacred
Tree, a very pure spirit in tune with Eywa, *sees* her actions quite
clearly. As a future *tsahìk*, an interpreter of the will of Eywa, she
cannot afford to ignore such an obvious sign. At this point, however,
Jake does not *see*. When Neytiri saves him from the viperwolves, his
expression of gratitude may be well meant, but it's imbued with indif-
ference for the lives taken on his behalf. His indoctrination into
Aristotelian and Cartesian humanism is too deeply ingrained. "I just
wanted to say thanks for killing those things," he tell Neytiri, who
responds by striking him to the ground. Her reaction of utter scorn
and disgust indicates the regret she may be feeling at this moment for
not having killed Jake herself. How could it possibly be Eywa's will to
save the life of one who does not *see*, one who could actually be
thankful for a killing? "You do not thank for this," she rebukes
the ignorant dreamwalker. "This is sad. Very sad only." It takes the

intervention of more atokirina to remind Neytiri again that she is being *seen*. Eywa's decision to protect Jake Sully forces the Na'vi to reevaluate their own notion of what it means to *see*: *seeing* in the Na'vi way, *seeing* through the eye of Eywa, means recognizing the intrinsic value of *all life*, even if that life comes from an alien world.

Wild Justice for All

Human beings tend to believe they invented justice and morality, but many contemporary thinkers have challenged this anthropocentric notion. Some cognitive ethologists – biologists who study the minds of animals by observing their behavior – have concluded that a sense of justice is actually widespread in the animal kingdom. In *Wild Justice*, Marc Bekoff and Jessica Pierce propose that a sense of right and wrong is something that evolves naturally in many social species because of the advantages it confers.[10] Shared acts of kindness, known as reciprocal altruism, promote social harmony and contribute to the survival of the individuals and species involved. Bekoff and Pierce argue that the more socially complex a species' interactions, the more highly developed its inherent sense of right and wrong behavior is likely to be. On Pandora, where life forms are able to engage in the most intimate social interactions involving a genuine meeting of minds, we should expect a highly developed sense of justice to be widespread among life forms. It is doubtful that a Na'vi hunter could persuade his or her ikran to commit acts that are morally reprehensible to an ikran. Of course, such a scenario is unlikely in any case, due to the Na'vi's own sense of justice.

The Na'vi probably wouldn't be surprised to learn that, in experiments conducted on Earth, rats will adamantly refuse to push a lever for food if they know that it will also deliver an electric shock to another rat in a neighboring cage.[11] Bekoff and Pierce conclude that these rats sense that it is *wrong* to harm another member of their species with whom they are capable of interacting socially. While the decision to forego food rather than subject a fellow rat to torture may not promote the survival of a conscientious rodent in a laboratory setting, the moral sense shared between two rats would indeed prove advantageous to them in more natural situations. And we might add that these rats exhibit a deeper understanding of morality than

Descartes ever did in the laboratory. Despite the wealth of data supporting the theory that a sense of justice is not unique to human beings, many people still cling to the anthropocentric view. As Bekoff and Pierce explain: "A lot of people have caved in to this assumption [that human beings have morality and other animals don't] because it is easier to deny morality to animals than to deal with the complex reverberations and implications of the possibility that animals have moral behavior."[12]

The traditional view of a nature *red in tooth and claw* doesn't hold up under scrutiny, when observing the everyday lives of most non-human organisms. Even on Pandora, where Colonel Quaritch warns that "every living thing that flies, crawls, or squats in the mud wants to kill you and eat your eyes for jujubes," most animals pass the greater part of their lives nonviolently. It's the ignorance of the "sky people" that frequently elicits violent reactions from Pandora's animal life. Foolishly entering the territory of a hammerhead titanothere – and, even more foolishly, firing off a couple of rounds in the animal's direction – is bound to lead to an unpleasant confrontation. Since the "sky people" do not *see*, they have no understanding of the consequences of their behavior toward Pandoran life. "All this is your fault," Neytiri admonishes Jake, whose ignorant bumbling – "like a baby" – had provoked the viperwolves' attack that required her to kill them. At that time, Jake viewed them as nothing but walking, stalking nightmares. Later, however, Neytiri shows him a family of viperwolves enjoying an activity more common in their everyday lives – delighting in each other's company as a contented and highly social group. After witnessing the gentle playfulness and conviviality of the viperwolves, Jake no longer ignorantly demonizes them. As he learns to *see*, he begins to set aside the false belief that the law of the "jungle" is only competition and violence. The natural world is also a place of cooperation and tenderness.

Where There's Life, There's Mind

Grace Augustine is a scientist whose interest in the rational behavior of nonhuman beings represents a paradigm shift that challenges many of the reigning assumptions of her discipline. The contemporary philosophers of mind Alva Noë and Evan Thompson are providing a theoretical framework for this paradigm shift. Their theories shake the foundations of the Aristotelian and Cartesian belief that the rational mind is something apart from the rest of nature.[13] Instead they argue that where there is life there is mind, some degree of consciousness or sentience being present in every living being. While there might be significant differences between the consciousness of one organism (say, a bacterium) and another (say, a proud philosopher in his or her ivory tower), these are really just differences in degree rather than in kind.[14] Here we see a parallel to Bekoff and Pierce's argument on wild justice. Differences in the sense of justice between one organism and another might also be only differences in degree, ranging from the primitive sense of fairness exhibited by rats to the abstract principles of justice developed by human beings.

The conceptual framework provided by these theories is useful for describing the type of experience involved when various organisms on Pandora interact, whether those interactions occur within a single species or across species boundaries. The continuity of mind allows the Na'vi to connect with and understand the minds of other organisms, as the continuity of morality allows those interactions to be conducted in a manner that does not transgress the moral sense of the species involved. Without that continuity, harmonious interactions would be much more difficult, particularly when they involve a linkage of neural tendrils that permits the joined organisms to *see* as one.

Unlike Descartes, Noë and Thompson don't presume that human beings are the only organisms on Earth or elsewhere capable of rational behavior. The gradual and continuous nature of evolution makes the notion of our sudden preeminence as the sole possessors of mind not only utterly implausible but outright absurd. In the words of cognitive ethologist Donald Griffin: "Evolutionary biologists are rightly suspicious of claims that some trait suddenly appears *de novo*, without any precursors."[15] Of course, this statement equally applies to life on Pandora. Wherever it appears, life implies mind.

Consciousness is experienced by an organism as a whole; it is the result of body and sense organs interacting with a world of which the organism is an inextricable component. This entails the surprising corollary that an organism need not have a brain in order to have a mind. Plants on Pandora obviously have minds, as is evident from the behavior of those atokirina that remind Neytiri of her moral obligations.

"More Connections Than the Human Brain"

Soon after Jake is initiated into the Omaticaya clan, Neytiri leads him to a grove of trees that are sacred to the Na'vi. Connecting the end of his queue to the tendrils of one of the trees, he is amazed to hear the voices of several Na'vi. It is a Tree of Voices, through which the Na'vi have access to the minds of their ancestors, who live on within Eywa. The implications are astounding: the consciousness of each organism on Pandora does not cease at death but continues, embodied within a network of interconnected trees that are globally linked, through a complex root system that has "more connections than the human brain." The next morning, as one of the Omaticaya, Jake sees the RDA corporation's heavy machinery roll in to destroy what can never be replaced. Soon after, Tsu'tey rides up to survey the landscape ravaged by the "sky people" in their genocidal drive for profit. His look of helpless dread says it all: the "sky people" are utterly *insane*.

Sharing some of Tsu'tey's outrage, Grace attempts to enlighten Selfridge as to the significance of the trees that he so thoughtlessly destroyed. "What we think we know," she explains, "is that there is some kind of electrochemical communication between the roots of the trees, like the synapses between neurons." Her futile effort at explanation is met with befuddlement, as Selfridge bursts into sardonic laughter, snapping back: "What the hell have you people been smoking out there?" The notion that a network of trees can embody anything resembling consciousness simply makes no sense in his worldview. His cup, it seems, is already overflowing with assumptions that are beyond question. Deeply ingrained in Selfridge (and others) is the belief that plants are mindless automata, which exhibit as much behavioral versatility as an automatic door.

It may surprise some readers to learn that Grace's research on plant communication is not entirely science fiction. Due to the work of biologists such as Anthony Trewavas, the intelligence of plants is no longer the laughing matter that Selfridge makes it out to be. On the contrary, the unquestioned assumption that plants are mindless is being exposed as untenable by new research within the up-and-coming scientific field of plant neurobiology. In fact Grace's words to Selfridge sound a lot like those of real-world scientist Trewavas when he writes: "From the current rate of progress, it looks as though plant communication is likely to be as complex as that within a brain."[16]

The knee-jerk reaction of people like Selfridge may be to insist that plants are inflexible organisms unable to adapt to novel situations, but research by Trewavas and others clearly demonstrates that plants exhibit enormous adaptability to an incredible variety of environmental factors. Since plants are literally rooted in one location, they can't pull up and move to a different spot when environmental conditions drastically change. Consequently their survival depends on the ability to adapt to their surroundings by reacting intelligently to changing variables such as light, mineral composition, water, touch, temperature, space, neighboring plants, disease, insects, and many other factors. "Autonomic responses can be rejected," writes Trewavas, since "the number of different environments that any wild plant experiences must be almost infinite in number. Only complex computation can fashion the optimal fitness response."[17] Plants are not mindless automata; nor are they incapable of movement. Their appearance of immobility is due to our inability to *see* them in their own timescale. It takes sped-up video recordings or time-lapse photography for us to see how much movement is really going on. Plants interact with their environments, constantly performing meaningful actions in response to sensory stimuli.

Even regarding the Pandoran network of interconnected roots that Grace describes, truth may be stranger than fiction. Biologist Tom Wakeford refers to the root networks that connect large communities of plant species as the *wood wide web*. Botanists believe that most plant-to-plant interactions take place underground, in the hidden world of roots, where Grace noticed the chemical and electrical signaling that she compared to the many neuronal connections within the human brain.[18] The roots of plants on Earth may also have something in common with our esteemed brains. Flowing through plants are some of the same neurotransmitters found in the brains of human beings and other animals.[19] Exposure to environmental stress triggers a dramatic increase in the production of these plant neurotransmitters. On Pandora, where life forms developed the capacity for deep mental communion, plants may be among the most mindful organisms of all, due to their constant exchange of information through a globally linked root network. This would be especially true of the Sacred Tree – the Tree of Souls – whose animal-like seeds, the atokirina, are taken as signs of Eywa's will.

The idea of vast underground networks of interconnected roots that extend across Pandora may also be much closer to scientific fact than many people can fathom. Botanists now know that virtually all wild plants have fungal networks connected to their roots that can extend, in some cases, for several miles. Along the myriad pathways of this fungal root network, different species of plants and trees share resources with one another, in active displays of altruism. Discussing Suzanne Simard's research on such networks, Tom Wakeford writes:

> In their exploration of this wood wide web, Simard's teams have found what could be a new principle of dynamic underground interdependence. Shaded plants, many of which are young seedlings struggling for light, are subsidized by those already bathed in sunshine at the top of the forest canopy. There seems to be an equalization process going on underground. Supplies are shared both within and among species: to those without shall be given, and those with plenty shall have it taken away.[20]

These networks defy our long-held presupposition that nature is solely a domain of ruthless competition rather than cooperation. With an uneven distribution of resources both under- and above-ground, it's more rational for most plants to pool their assets and share. Underground root networks permit them to exchange both information and resources. On Pandora, this sharing is made possible by a linkage of roots that are as intimately intertwined as the joined queues of two Na'vi lovers, mated for life.

Last Shadow

When Jake learns to *see* the Na'vi way, he comes to understand what such *seeing* entails. As *seen* through the eye of Eywa, all life is intrinsically valuable. In order to fulfill his moral obligations in a world where he is now both *seer* and *seen*, he cannot sit back and allow the balance of life on Pandora to be destroyed by the "sky people" with their irrational ideologies.

In the final scene of *Avatar*, Jake attains the pinnacle of *seeing* by passing through the eye of Eywa and returning to the world of the Na'vi, a feat that perhaps no other living being on Pandora had ever accomplished. We can only imagine what a profoundly transformative experience it must be to achieve intimacy with the embodied consciousness of an entire world's biota. Jake's transformation bodes well for our own fate. For if – contrary to what the Na'vi believed before witnessing Jake's remarkable evolution from Jake of the Jarhead clan to one of "the people" – our insanity *can* be cured and we can learn to *see* the value of protecting the balance of life on Earth, there may still be hope that *Homo sapiens* can avoid its own extinction. Otherwise, Jake Sully may truly be our last shadow.

Notes

1. Since the appearance of life on Earth, life forms have adapted to countless biospheres. Due to cosmic and geologic events, a completely unaltered "balance of life" can't be maintained for a species like ours. The "balance" I refer to should be understood as the chemical and molecular composition of a planet's atmosphere, without which life would be impossible for many species. If, for example, carbon dioxide levels in the Earth's atmosphere increased too much, the balance of life would be greatly altered for many species, *Homo sapiens* included. Such a balance can be disturbed by human activities that radically alter plant or marine ecosystems.
2. Of course, since *Homo sapiens* is a part of nature, all actions undertaken by the species are ultimately natural. However, the natural events I refer to as cosmic or geological are essentially unavoidable. The human-induced mass extinction event, while probable, was not an absolute necessity according to the physical laws of nature responsible for Earth's other mass extinction events. Human beings are capable of choosing a path other than the one they currently stomp upon.
3. Martin Gorke, *The Death of Our Planet's Species: A Challenge to Ecology and Ethics* (Washington, DC: Island Press, 2003), 1.
4. Ibid., 209.
5. We should never forget that human beings are in fact animals. The culturally ingrained notion that we are distinct from the natural world is evident in how "human" and "animal" are generally understood to be mutually exclusive.
6. *The Complete Works of Aristotle*, ed. Jonathan Barnes (Princeton, NJ: Princeton University Press, 1984), Vol. 1, 659–660.
7. René Descartes, *Discourse on Method,* in *Philosophical Essays and Correspondence*, ed. Roger Ariew (Indianapolis, IN: Hackett, 2000), 72.

8. In making that argument, however, Descartes only betrayed his ignorance of what the other animals are actually capable of doing. For a fascinating overview of the incredible versatility of animal behavior, including their capacities for language and tool use, see Marc Bekoff, *Minding Animals: Awareness, Emotion, and Heart* (New York: Oxford University Press, 2002).

9. Jonathan Balcombe, *Pleasurable Kingdom: Animals and the Nature of Feeling Good* (New York: Macmillan, 2006), 26.

10. Marc Bekoff and Jessica Pierce, *Wild Justice: The Moral Lives of Animals* (Chicago, IL: University of Chicago Press, 2009).

11. This research was conducted in 1959 by Russell Church, although the findings haven't been fully comprehended or taken seriously until recently, due to anthropocentric notions that animals such as rats couldn't possibly be moral agents. Bekoff would never condone such cruel research, since he has a fundamental attitude of respect for all animals. He merely reports the findings in order to support his theory that animals are inherently moral beings.

12. Bekoff and Pierce, *Wild Justice*, 10.

13. See Alva Noë, *Out of Our Heads: Why You Are Not Your Brain, and Other Lessons from the Biology of Consciousness* (New York: Hill and Wang, 2009), especially chapter 2, "Conscious Life," and Evan Thompson, *Mind in Life: Biology, Phenomenology, and the Sciences of Mind* (Cambridge: Cambrige University Press, 2007).

14. For a brilliant discussion of the social lives and communication of bacteria, see Myra J. Hird, *The Origins of Sociable Life: Evolution after Science Studies* (New York: Palgrave Macmillan, 2009).

15. Donald R. Griffin, "Afterword: What Is It Like?" in Marc Bekoff, Colin Allen, and Gordon M. Burghardt, eds., *The Cognitive Animal: Empirical and Theoretical Perspectives on Animal Cognition* (Cambridge, MA: MIT Press, 2002), 472.

16. Anthony Trewavas, "Aspects of Plant Intelligence," in *Annals of Botany* 92 (2003), 1–20, at 6.

17. Anthony Trewavas, "The Green Plant as an Intelligent Organism," in František Baluška, Stefano Mancuso, Dieter Volkmann, eds., *Communication in Plants: Neuronal Aspects of Plant Life* (Berlin: Springer-Verlag, 2006), 3.

18. In addition, research is currently being conducted into volatiles released by plants above ground as a medium of plant-to-plant communication. See, for example, Velemir Ninkovic, Robert Glinwood, and Jan Pettersson, "Communication between Undamaged Plants by Volatiles: The Role of Allelobiosis," in František Baluška, Stefano Mancuso, and

Dieter Volkmann, eds., *Communication in Plants: Neuronal Aspects of Plant Life* (Berlin: Springer-Verlag, 2006).

19. For more details, see Aaron Fait, Ayelet Yellin, and Hillel Fromm, "GABA and GHB Neurotransmitters in Plants and Animals," in František Baluška, Stefano Mancuso, and Dieter Volkmann, eds., *Communication in Plants: Neuronal Aspects of Plant Life* (Berlin: Springer-Verlag, 2006).

20. Tom Wakeford, *Liaisons of Life: From Hornworts to Hippos: How the Unassuming Microbe Has Driven Evolution* (New York: Wiley, 2001), 49.

8

They're *Not* Just Goddamn Trees
Hegel's Philosophy of Nature and the Avatar of Spirit

James Lawler

The title of the film *Avatar* specifically refers to the extension of the consciousness or spirit of a human individual into the body of an artificially created human–Na'vi hybrid. But there's another way to understand the title, a way that's in keeping with the worldview of the Na'vi people. In their view, the whole of their planet – its precious mineral, its plants and animal life, as well as the Na'vi themselves – makes up the body or avatar of a higher consciousness, a divine spirit that presides over the entire planet and is known to the Na'vi as the goddess Eywa.

Undoubtedly the Na'vi worldview will strike some people as nothing more than "pagan voodoo." But if we're looking for philosophical grounds for the Na'vi's beliefs about Eywa, we need look no further than the nineteenth-century German philosopher Georg Wilhelm Friedrich Hegel (1770–1831). In his *Philosophy of Nature*, Hegel argues that Nature is the embodiment – or, as we might say, the "avatar" – of what he calls the Absolute Spirit or God. Contrary to the orthodox Christian belief that God is wholly distinct from the world, Hegel does not regard the natural world as separate from the Divine Spirit. He even argues that the findings of science, when properly interpreted, require this understanding of nature as the embodiment or avatar of Spirit. But, to reach this understanding, he believed it was first necessary to develop a critique of *empiricism*, the inadequate form of science that has become dominant in modern times.

Avatar and Philosophy: Learning to See, First Edition. Edited by George A. Dunn.
© 2014 John Wiley & Sons, Inc. Published 2014 by John Wiley & Sons, Inc.

Spirit-"Driven" Avatars

For empiricism, reality consists solely of measurable physical bodies, whose movements can be explained by the impact or influence of other such bodies. Nothing moves itself and nothing is real except for discrete physical entities and the motion they impart to each other. But Jake's experience of "driving" his avatar – not to mention our ordinary experience of moving our own bodies – belies this picture of reality, since it doesn't make a place for consciousness or will, powers that Hegel assigns to spirit (when talking about the individual) or Spirit (when talking about God or the Divine Spirit that animates nature as a whole). But Hegel doesn't believe that spirit is something separate from the bodies it inhabits and animates. The individual spirit requires a body to realize itself, just as it requires the natural world as a tangible arena in which to realize its goals. And that natural world, Nature with a capital N, is itself an extension of Spirit with a capital S.

In its most primitive state, Nature is Spirit in a state of unconsciousness, or perhaps we should say *latent* consciousness, much like the state we are in when asleep. Natural evolution can then be understood as a long and gradual process of awakening, in which consciousness and will make their appearance in progressively more robust forms. The culminating moment of the process is the emergence of self-conscious beings – like ourselves and the Na'vi – who can become aware of their identity with the Absolute Spirit or God, which has been the hidden "driver" of this whole evolutionary drama. We are able to come to this realization, however, only by recognizing our unity with one another. That's why Hegel defines the Divine Spirit as "'I' that is 'We,' and 'We' that is 'I.'"[1] The spirit or consciousness of the individual human being or of the Na'vi can fully realize itself only by overcoming her separation from Nature and other beings like herself – a separation that's enforced by empiricism through its denial of consciousness and will to the natural world.

The Hungry Na'vi

In his *Philosophy of Nature* Hegel contrasts two approaches to nature: the theoretical and the practical. While the practical approach sees the natural world as something *for us*, something to be used for our own purposes, the theoretical approach stands back and looks at nature as it is *in itself*. The Resources Development Administration (RDA) mining operation is a good example of the practical approach, since it's wholly motivated by a practical interest in gaining and exploiting Pandora's precious commodity, unobtanium – the "little gray rock" that, according to Parker Selfridge, "sells for 20 million a kilo."

The RDA is exceptionally rapacious, but a more benign form of the practical approach to nature was the primary standpoint of human beings in the earliest period of their history, when they lived as hunters and gatherers in tribal communities. This approach begins when an individual first senses her dependence on nature. She may experience this dependence first as hunger, a need for something that exists outside of her. Nature supplies what she needs and she reaches out to appropriate and consume it. But in time the human use of nature became more sophisticated, as we began to shape nature into tools for our own use. The Na'vi do this as well, turning a wide assortment of beings of the forest into means for achieving their own purposes. For a particularly spectacular example, consider how they tame and bond with the winged ikran as a means of aerial transportation. In this way they surmount their initial sense of dependence on nature. Hegel succinctly expresses the complex interrelationship of the individual with nature in the terms of his *dialectical logic*:

> The negation of myself which I suffer within me in hunger is at the same time present as an other than myself, as something to be consumed; my act is to annul this contradiction by making the other identical with myself, or by restoring my self-unity through sacrificing the thing.[2]

By "dialectic" Hegel means an interaction that begins in opposition or conflict but ends in the recognition of a higher unity, as when an initially hostile natural world is turned into an accomplice in the pursuit of our goals. What Hegel analyzes in abstract logical terms reflects the first-hand experience of Na'vi hunters. They first experience a negation, a lack of what they need in order to survive, and they recognize nature as supplying what they need. Nature is at first encountered as something other than themselves, as an animal or plant existing outside of them, an object of their desire or an obstacle to its satisfaction. Through their activity they negate their separation from these natural beings. They "sacrifice the thing" by appropriating it for themselves, putting it to use for them, or consuming it as food. Through "the other" – the rock they transform into a tool, the tree they use as a dwelling, the animal they consume for nourishment – they overcome the negation in themselves and are restored to "self-unity."

For the Na'vi, however, the "sacrifice of the thing" is not a simple destruction, but is done with the intention to preserve and respect the spiritual essence of the natural world, which they regard as a singular being, the goddess Eywa. The alien "sky people," on the other hand, destroy without renewing, out of an unquenchable thirst for money, oblivious to their own deep interrelationship with nature. They are unlike the Na'vi, who have an implicit understanding of the dialectic between self and other, "the people" and nature. Everything for them is connected in "a network of energy that flows through all living things." Nothing is fundamentally dead. Parker Selfridge, the head of the mining operation, has this holism in mind when he complains: "You throw a stick in the air around here, it's gonna land on some sacred fern, for Christ's sake!" Selfridge doesn't get it, but Hegel would understand.

"Just Goddamn Trees"

Early in the film, as Grace and Norm explore the jungle of Pandora with instruments designed to digitally probe the microstructure of the roots of the forest's trees, Jake wanders off to do some exploring of his own. Fascinated and delighted with the awesome beauty of the planet's life forms, he wanders through the forest absorbed by the breathtaking scenery, exploring the behavior of the local flora by playfully interacting with it. Contrasting Jake and the scientists shows us two different approaches to nature: one narrowly focused on the microstructure of "samples," from which it pieces together an under-standing of the whole; the other given over to direct sensuous experi-ence and astonishment. Jake later describes himself to Mo'at, the Na'vi *tsahìk*, as an empty cup, signifying in part that his outlook on the world isn't biased by scientific preconceptions.[3]

Both Jake and the scientists take up a theoretical stance toward the forest of Pandora, seeking not to transform nature into something *for us* but only to understand or contemplate it as it is *in itself*. When Jake is riveted with wonder at the beauty of the forest, he isn't thinking about how to put it to use for him. But the theoretical approach of empiricism is different. While the scientists attempt to build up a concept of the whole on the basis of the microstructure of the parts as revealed in the "samples" they take, Jake never loses sight of the surface phenomena of Pandora – the minerals, plants, and animals in their wholeness.

The theoretical stance of empirical science resists the lure of sheer admiration for the myriad individual beings of the natural world as they present themselves to ordinary sensuous experience. It attempts instead to penetrate to the intelligible and universal features underlying these appearances, the hidden laws of nature that cause these beings to appear and act as they do. In so doing, Hegel argues, empirical science isn't just contemplating nature as it appears *in itself*, but is actually transforming the natural world into something *for us*, something scaled down to human understanding. Empirical science substitutes its own inventions – such as images on a computer screen – for the things themselves, killing the living spirit of the natural world. Hegel puts it like this:

> The more thought enters into our representation of things, the less do they retain their naturalness, their singularity and immediacy. The wealth of natural forms, in all their infinitely manifold configuration, is impoverished by the all-pervading power of thought, their vernal life and glowing colors die and fade away. The rustle of Nature's life is silenced in the stillness of thought; her abundant life, wearing a thousand delightful shapes, shrivels into arid forms and shapeless generalities resembling a murky northern fog.[4]

While Jake is naively admiring the beauties of Pandora, Grace and Norm are sticking syringes into roots and studying images on a computer screen. Oblivious to the strangeness of their fascination with a computer screen in the midst of the radiant splendor of nature, they're convinced that they're grasping the very reality and secret core of the thing itself. It turns out that what they're measuring is the "signal transduction" between the roots of the trees, which Grace believes constitutes a biological mechanism that supplies scientific confirmation for the Na'vi belief in the interconnectedness of life on Pandora. She attempts to explain her discovery to an uncomprehending Selfridge:

GRACE: There is some kind of electrochemical communication between the roots of the trees, like the synapses between neurons. And each tree has ten-to-the-fourth connections to the trees around it. And there are ten-to-the-twelfth trees on Pandora.

SELFRIDGE: Which is a lot I'm guessing.

GRACE: It's more connections than the human brain. Get it? It's a network. It's a network. It's a global network, and the Na'vi can access it. ...

SELFRIDGE: What the hell have you people been smoking out there? They're just goddamn trees.

Selfridge sees only the trees, but as a scientist Grace also sees their recondite molecular structures and the electrical signals through which they communicate, believing these to be the true mechanism of reality. But, from Hegel's perspective, what is missing from Grace's analysis is the unifying principle that binds all these parts together, the Spirit that makes Nature more than just an assortment of separate elements that interact in interesting ways, namely a unified whole in which rocks, plants, and animals are all organically connected parts. Grace may have identified the mechanism that connects all life on Pandora, just as a neuroscientist can describe some of the mechanisms of our brains. But, as long as we attend only to "mechanisms," all we'll ever see in nature or in other people is a machine. We'll remain blind to the inner reality of Spirit.

Who, then, draws closer to Pandora as it is *in itself* – Jake with his admiration of the rich variety of its sensible forms, or Grace with her samples, digital reductions, and mathematical formulas? How can these abstracted elements plumb the natural world in itself? While real nature exists precisely in its irreducible sensuality and multiplicity, empirical science inevitably whittles this sprawling source of wonder down into abstract thoughts, intangible generalities, and simplifications, turning it into something it's not. Not unlike the exploiters who seek to turn the forests of Pandora into a mining operation, empiricism ends up transforming nature into something *for us*, even as it pretends to grasp nature as it is *in itself*.

The Romantic Alternative: "Feel Her"

Recognizing that scientific knowledge transforms the world as it is in itself into abstract concepts devised by the mind, Hegel's great predecessor Immanuel Kant (1724–1804) concluded that it's impossible to know things as they are in themselves. In his summary of the history of philosophy, Hegel argues that Kant correctly recognized that the empiricist approach to science leads to an impasse that renders it unable to grasp living reality as it exists outside our minds.[5] But Hegel argued that there are two possible ways to solve this problem.

One way is to adopt the standpoint of intuition and feeling, rejecting abstract thought as a kind of fall from grace or original sin. In this perspective, popular in the romantic movement of Hegel's time, human existence was once a paradise in which we were one with nature and with each other. Our separation and alienation from nature came later, along with the egotism that separates us from one another. Science is an expression of the loss of connection with nature that characterizes technological civilization, which regards nature not as a unified whole but as an assemblage of resources for human exploitation. Scientists, with their mechanistic models of nature, are essentially in league with the practical exploitation of the Earth. Their arid abstractions abet the arrogant approach of commercial interests, whose dismissive attitude toward nature is captured well in Selfridge's remark: "They're just goddamn trees."

As a way to return to nature as it really is *in itself*, the romantic movement urged people to stop taking empirical science as their guide and to adopt instead an approach based on pure feeling. This feeling approach to nature is also suggested in *Avatar*. Neytiri teaches Jake to bond with the direhorse by weaving the tendrils of his neural queue with those of the animal's neural whip. Something happens, a powerful connection between the man and the beast. "That is *tsaheylu*. The bond," Neytiri says. "Feel her. Feel her heartbeat. Her breath. Feel her strong legs."

Hegel acknowledges that there's something "lofty" in the romantic ideal, with its elevation of intuition and feeling over abstract knowledge. Of course, it's important to feel our bonds with nature, as Jake connects with the direhorse and the winged wonders of Pandora. But, as a general framework for understanding nature, this romantic ideal can lead to fanciful inventions of all sorts, including the belief that there are

> favoured ones, seers to whom God imparts true knowledge and wisdom in sleep, or that man, even without being so favoured, can, at least by faith in it [i.e., in our immediate oneness with Nature], transport himself into a state where the inner side of Nature is immediately revealed to him, and where he need only let fancies occur to him, i.e., give free play to his fancy, in order to declare prophetically what is true.[6]

In other words, the danger is that relying solely on feeling and intuition leaves us too credulous, too ready to believe any oracle that comes down the pike purporting to speak in the voice of nature. We need to make a place for reason as well.

The Dialectical Alternative: "All Energy Is Borrowed"

Luckily, there's another way to surmount the problems associated with empirical science – its reduction of concrete, sensuous reality to lifeless abstraction – a way that doesn't require us to abandon science altogether. According to Hegel, an authentic philosophy of nature will *begin* with the achievements of empirical science, but then will seek to transform them through a deeper form of comprehension, which Hegel calls *dialectical reason*.

As we've seen, empirical science thinks of the world as consisting of discrete objects or elements that can be observed, measured, and then represented through abstract ideas that scientists regard as approximations of reality. Scientists never question the assumption that reality can be broken down into its individual components, which can be adequately understood in isolation from each other. Science analyzes these objects of direct experience – Selfridge's "goddamn trees" – into their underlying parts, such as leaves, branches, and roots. These in turn are thought to be composed of even more fundamental parts, such as cells, molecules, atoms, and electrons. When asked how much lab training he's had, Jake replies: "I dissected a frog once." Even a layperson like Jake knows that empirical science is all about dissection – taking a knife to nature in order to isolate and study each of its individual parts, so that we may figure out how they work.

According to Hegel, at a certain stage in the evolution of science it was necessary to dissect, or even vivisect the frog – to break the living whole into its component parts and examine them one by one. The only problem is that vivisection kills the spirit that makes the frog a unified, living being. Our way of knowing the parts conceals what makes them parts of a *whole*. But, as our understanding of reality deepens, it is inevitable that scientists will become more and more aware of the interconnectedness of things. As long as they remain wed to their old assumptions, however, they're incapable of adequately comprehending this interconnected reality. To make the transition to a higher stage of scientific thought, it is necessary to adopt the *dialectical logic* proposed by Hegel, according to which things are what they are only through their relationships with other entities.

Grace attempts to defend what seems to her scientific mind like a novel idea, namely that the world of Pandora consists of an interconnected living network. But Hegel would argue that this idea is even more radical than Grace suspects, since thinking through its full implications would force her to face the inadequacy of her own empiricist method of thinking. The logical basis of empiricist thinking is the principle of identity, $A = A$: a thing is just what it is, and not something other than itself. Parker Selfridge understands this standard logic perfectly well: trees are just goddamn trees. And if Grace and her colleagues suggest something different – that these trees are somehow more than just trees, that they "communicate" with each other and form a "network" – well, they must be smoking too much of the local weed.

Hegel's philosophy suggest that, for Grace's argument to become convincing, we would need to abandon the empiricist logic that defines reality as a collection of separate identities, each of which is what it is and not something else. Reality just doesn't correspond to this logic. Nothing has a truly separate existence, since everything exists only in relation to other beings in the surrounding world. The Na'vi have a firm grasp of this principle, recognizing that they're nothing apart from their vital connection with the natural world. As Neytiri sums up the folk wisdom of the Na'vi: "All energy is borrowed."

According to Hegel, we can recognize the truth of the folk wisdom contained in the nature religion of early cultures without having to abandon science. But the philosophy of feeling and intuition promoted by nineteenth-century (and contemporary) romanticists only superficially resembles the nature religion of early cultures. The romantic turn to intuition or feeling is the perspective of alienated modern individuals who seek to recover the perspective of people bound together in a form of life that the modern world has irrevocably lost. But we can't return to the tightly knit, tradition-based kinship societies of the past. We can only move forward, relating to nature and to each other in new ways, which incorporate the findings of modern science in a *dialectical* understanding that recognizes the essential interconnectedness of all beings.

This new understanding is reflected in Grace's discovery, made only at the moment of her death, that there's something more to Pandora than what's "measurable in the biology of the forest." There's the reality of its overarching and unifying spirit, the Goddess Eywa. "I'm with her, Jake," she says as her own spirit leaves her body and is united with the spirit of Pandora. "She's real!"

"The Eye of Eywa"

Hegel interprets the scientific laws of his own time as implying that Spirit, the reality that animates the *macrocosm* or the universe as a whole, expresses itself in the form of matter. It's not unlike how our own minds or spirits express themselves through our bodies, except that Hegel believes that the material world "emanates" or flows from Spirit, on which it remains dependent for its existence. Matter, therefore, is Spirit in its external or outward manifestation. But the *microcosm* of the tiniest particle of matter remains connected to every other particle and to the universal whole. Matter is not simply passive and inert, moved only by external impact. Rather the elements of matter actively reach out to one another in a mutual attraction, which Hegel believes is the real force behind Newton's law of gravity. Each bit of matter "involves" others in itself, an "involution" that gives rise to evolution, as individuals link together to evolve into higher levels of complexity. As Hegel puts it: "Evolution is thus also an involution, in that matter interiorizes itself to become life."[7] The reaching out of one bit of matter to another is already an embryonic form of consciousness. Only in this way is the evolution of conscious beings out of unconscious nature conceivable.

Anticipating Charles Darwin's (1809–1882) theory of evolution, Hegel sees evolution – from inanimate to animate to human forms of existence – as arising from an inner tension within the natural world itself, a natural dialectic in which things overcome their relative isolation by binding together in ever larger wholes, achieving higher forms of consciousness or spirit until they reach the stage of self-conscious human existence. But, unlike Darwin, Hegel believes that each individual participates in its own evolution by actively linking with others. Evolution is not solely the product of selection by outside forces.

Human history continues this evolution of forms of consciousness in three stages. First, there's the stage of the earliest peoples living in unity with nature, a way of being represented movingly by the Na'vi of *Avatar*. Later comes the stage at which people separate themselves from nature and their fellow human beings, ruthlessly exploiting the world and each other, as graphically depicted by the invaders of Pandora and their savage violation of the planet and its people. Finally, when the highest stage is reached, there's a return to the original unity and a renewed respect for nature and for one another, but in a way that involves thought as well as feeling and that preserves the gains of science. That appears to be the ideal and the hope proposed by the ending of the film.

When Jake passes through "the eye of Eywa" at the conclusion of *Avatar*, leaving his former body and his former life behind and becoming fully embodied as part of "the people," he implicitly recognizes the truth of Hegel's definition of Spirit. He overcomes the separation from nature and other beings that's imposed by an egotistical technological civilization. He can now connect to the divine spirit of the planet and become part of a mutually supporting community, an "'I' that is 'We,' and [a] 'We' that is 'I.'"

Notes

1. Georg Wilhelm Friedrich Hegel, *The Phenomenology of Spirit*, trans. A. V. Miller (Oxford: Oxford University Press, 1977), 110.
2. Georg Wilhelm Friedrich Hegel, *The Philosophy of Nature*, Part II of his *Encyclopaedia of the Philosophical Sciences (1830)*, trans. A. V. Miller (Oxford: Oxford University Press, 2004), 5.
3. For more on the scientific approach to the study of nature, see Chapter 4 by Stephanie Adair.
4. Hegel, *Philosophy of Nature*, 7.
5. Hegel's discussion of the relation between empiricism and Kant's "critical philosophy" is presented in chapter 4 of his "little logic": see Georg Wilhelm Friedrich Hegel, *Logic*, trans. William Wallace (Oxford: Oxford University Press, 1975), 60–94. This disccussion is followed by a section on "Immediate or Intuitive Knowledge" (pp. 95–112), the criticism of which leads to Hegel's own defense of dialectical logic.
6. Hegel, *Philosophy of Nature*, trans. A. V. Miller (Oxford: Oxford University Press, 2004), 8.
7. Ibid., 26.

9

"Everything Is Backwards Now"

Avatar, Anthropocentrism, and Relational Reason

Jeremy David Bendik-Keymer

There's a moment about halfway through *Avatar* where Jake Sully wakes up disoriented from the link to his avatar. "Everything is backwards now," he says, "like out there is the true world and in here is the dream." I call this the inside-out moment. Jake's life in the Resources Development Administration (RDA) mining colony seems unreal, while his avatar life seems real.

The inside-out moment comes at the midpoint of the film, not long before the rite of passage in which Jake becomes a member of the Omaticaya clan. It feels pivotal to the plot of the film. Out of the 35 chapters of the DVD, the inside-out moment occurs in chapter 18, right in the middle.

"Conversion" comes from the Latin *conversio*, which designates a turning around, an about-face. *Avatar* depicts what is an about-face for the former marine Jake Sully, who ultimately will no longer be human while, ironically, becoming more *humane* than he ever was before. Jake begins the film part opportunist, part solid marine, but he ends up as a self-sacrificing Na'vi hero who puts the welfare of Ewya and life on Pandora ahead of his own self-interest. Along the way, we watch his capacity for empathy and wonder grow. Jake the Na'vi depicts a *humane* person with deep, life-encompassing

Avatar and Philosophy: Learning to See, First Edition. Edited by George A. Dunn.
© 2014 John Wiley & Sons, Inc. Published 2014 by John Wiley & Sons, Inc.

relationships that take on responsibility for the future. This, I believe, is the explicit message of the inside-out moment.

Deep Humanity in an Alien Avatar

A being has moral standing if, *morally*, it makes a difference how we treat that being. A standard question raised in environmental ethics is: *Who* counts? *Who* has "moral standing"? If you think only human beings count, you're an anthropocentrist, someone who puts human beings – *anthrōpoi* in ancient Greek – at the center. If you think that all living beings count somewhat, you're a biocentrist, someone who puts life – *bios* in ancient Greek – at the center. And if you think that whole ecosystems count, believing, for example, that to destroy a wetland is morally objectionable above and beyond the loss of individual lives and livelihood, then you're an ecocentrist, someone who puts the *oikos* – "house, home, dwelling-place" in ancient Greek – at the center.[1]

Of course, there are shortsighted and enlightened versions of anthropocentrism. The shortsighted version was epitomized in April 2010 by the ill-starred managers of then British Petroleum (BP), who chose short-term profit over long-term sustainability, discounting the interests of the sea life and birds of the Gulf of Mexico. A more enlightened anthropocentrism would have understood that taking care of the macro-ecosystem of the Gulf of Mexico is, in the long term, even in BP's interest. After all, like any other corporation, BP depends on maintaining a good image with its customers, who in turn depend on a healthy natural world. Enlightened anthropocentrism takes into account the long-term and large-scale factors that contribute to human prosperity, treating everything nonhuman mostly as a means or as an impediment to that goal. In *Avatar*, the RDA corporation offers another example of anthropocentric thinking, arguably just as shortsighted as that of BP.

Rather than frame the issue in terms of shortsighted versus enlightened anthropocentricism, however, it is more helpful to think about superficial versus deep humanity. *Avatar* suggests that a *superficial* sense of our humanity involves shortsighted anthropocentrism. But it also suggests that acting from what is most deeply human involves something more than simply enlightened anthropocentrism. *Deep* humanity, as I will call it, embraces ecocentrism. Deep humanity is the view that, because our own humanity matters, we ought to be considerate toward life and considerate with our home – our *oikos*. Deep humanity is not superficial anthropocentrism or human chauvinism. It does not only entail being human, but also acting in ways that are deeply *humane*. One reason why I find *Avatar* so interesting is that it pushes us to acknowledge a distinction that's still not common in Environmental Ethics, the distinction between superficial and deep humanity.

Using standard environmental ethics taxonomy, we might say that *Avatar* depicts a confrontation between people with a shortsighted anthropocentric worldview and an alien race with an ecocentric worldview. The shortsighted anthropocentrists are on the side of the RDA, engaged in an enterprise that treats the Na'vi as obstacles and Pandora as a giant resource. By contrast, the Na'vi think that the ecological order of their entire planet counts. Pandora, to them, is Ewya: a *personality*, not an object.

That signals something. The question of who counts can be spelled out in terms of the distinction between something we treat as a mere object, to be used for our purposes, and some being we recognize as a partner in our universe. If, for example, I regard some wetland down the road as merely a resource or a nuisance, I'm treating it as an object. As long as it concerns me only as a useful object or as an obstacle, it lies outside the reach of my moral consideration. But if I conceive of the wetland as a partner in my moral universe, I can't help but give it moral consideration. I must respect it and care about it for its own sake, not merely for mine. I may even treat it as if it had a personality, as the Na'vi do when they regard their world as the embodiment of Ewya.

People with the *virtue* of a deep sense of humanity – as opposed to superficial or inhumane people – commonly hold that life isn't something you may just abuse. Think of Mahatma Gandhi (1869–1948), who is often held to have a consummate sense of humanity. Or think of Rachel Carson (1907–1964), author of *Silent Spring*, the book that is often credited with launching the modern environmental movement. Such people have empathy for all sorts of living beings, and they quite often identify with the land – and sea – around them to the extent that their sense of their own dignity depends on their care and respect for that ecosystem. There are numerous examples of people with a deep sense of humanity, but my favorite is my uncle Bill, a retired farmer from Avon, Ohio.[2] When killdeer nests appeared in his field – killdeer are birds that nest in the dirt – uncle Bill would drive his tractor around them. He was very matter of fact about what he was doing. It was nothing ideological for him, just something decent people do because those birds are trying to live too. In this and similar ways, people centered on being humane are not anthropocentric in the sense commonly used in environmental ethics. They have aspects of bio- and ecocentrism in their characters, and this makes them more like the Na'vi than like the mining mercenaries and corporate functionaries.[3]

Accordingly, as Jake's world turns inside out, he illustrates a shift from anthropocentrism to ecocentrism, revealing to us a potential within our own sense of humanity. The film is thus an "avatar" for our untapped sense of ourselves. When we eagerly support Jake and the Na'vi, we are siding with a way *we* could be. The film cleverly seduces us into taking a different stance toward what is desirable for a human being by embodying our own potential in an alien.

"Out There Is the True World"

What more can we learn about deep humanity by examining Jake's gradual conversion? Jake's inside-out moment coincides with his waking up from his link. He feels his life has been turned inside out. He lives most of his life in his avatar. His human body isn't where he's acting, because he acts through the body of his avatar. The process of living as an avatar, just in and of itself, makes everything seem backwards.

But Jake has clocked a number of hours by the time he feels that things have turned inside out. We'd expect him to get more used to linking – not less. When he says that everything is backwards, he's not just talking about the disorientation one gets from switching in and out of avatar life. He explains how things are backwards by pointing to the "true world" out there with his avatar, as opposed to the "dream" world in here, where his human body eats and sleeps. How is the world in the jungle with the Omaticaya *true*, and how might the world inside the mining complex be false? And what can this idea of the "true" world teach us about our own humanity?

I take Jake to be saying that the world of the Na'vi is truer because it's more *authentic*, not simply more factual or more actual. After all, his world inside the mining colony is no less factual or actual than the world of the Na'vi – at least within the story the film tells. Moreover, for the world "in here" to be a dream, it must be devoid of some important aspects of reality. Yet the mining colony is as physical and tangible as the jungle is. It's not unreal in the sense of being immaterial; so its unreality must be located elsewhere, at the opposite pole from authenticity. The mining world is somehow inauthentic, *fake*.

The film tells us indirectly how the Na'vi world is more authentic. Not long after Jake's turnaround moment, he ends up pleading for Neytiri's understanding in front of the Omaticaya clan, after he has revealed his duplicity to them. "Look, at first it was just orders," he says, "and then everything changed … I fell in love with the forest and with the Omaticaya people. And with you." At first, Jake was bent on exploiting the trust of the Omaticaya on behalf of his employer. He was using them, treating them as objects to be manipulated for the sake of something his employers wanted. That smacks of the anthropocentric belief that nonhumans don't count.

Yet the film offers something subtler than just a critique of anthropocentrism. As it begins, we see Jake deciding to step into his dead brother's shoes. He's just identified Tommy's body, laid out in a cardboard coffin. And, while that body is being incinerated, before the cinders even fall, two corporate "suits" try to persuade Jake to take over his brother's contract, so they may recover the money they lost as a result of his death. They don't give Jake space to mourn but get right down to business, time being money. The pursuit of profit has outstripped their sense of humanity. When these corporate "suits" put money ahead of compassion, their hearts don't differ much from that of the murderer who killed Tommy for the money in his wallet. This sets up the real moral conflict of the film, in which the villain is not just anthropocentrism, but an exploitative attitude toward the world, including the world of other human beings.

Among the Na'vi, the entire world of life has a personality that bears the name Eywa. All life on Pandora is *kindred*, as in a big family. This feeling of kinship is evident in the Na'vi's attitude even toward the hostile elements of their planet. For example, after Neytiri wounds a viperwolf while defending Jake, she says a prayer over its dying body and then kills it as painlessly as possible. In rebuking Jake for being so stupid as to provoke an attack from animals who then had to be killed in his defense, Neytiri shows respect even for a predator. That's the opposite of exploitation. By some standards, it's surprisingly *humane*. Under Neytiri's guidance, Jake later manages to kill a hexapede without causing it needless pain – and with an attitude of respect. That's when she tells him: "You are ready."

In short, the Omaticaya have a relationship with the surrounding world of life that is like a partnership. In the terminology of environmental ethics, they are ecocentric. But they also show us a deep sense of humanity, the way *we* can be when we are most humane. In so doing, they reveal – as we'll see in the next section – what it is that makes their world "true" and what, by contrast, makes the military–corporate world of the mining compound more like a bad "dream."

"Lost in the Woods"

Not long after Jake's inside-out moment, he's approached by Colonel Miles Quaritch. "Haven't got lost in the woods, have you?" Quaritch is right: Jake's new home is the woods. He fell in love with it along with the Omaticaya and Neytiri. Just moments before, we heard Jake tell his video log, "I don't know who I am anymore."

My hypothesis is that Jake feels alienated during his inside-out moment because he is transitioning away from a world that denies the real relationships with others that we are capable of having, relationships that tap into the deepest parts of ourselves. An unreal world is one that's devoid of important relationships. The authenticity of a world depends, in turn, on the richness of the relationships it offers.

Perhaps the woods are more real to Jake than the "dream" because they teem with beings who call out to him as potential partners, offering him many possible relationships and a chance to enter into something larger than himself. By contrast, the environment of the mining colony – governed by an exploitative outlook that regards the planet as an object – has a shortage of genuine relationships. What relationships there are seem thin and functional, like the tense opposition between Grace and Selfridge, or the harsh camaraderie of Quaritch and his mercenaries. The soldiers insult each other and even make fun of Jake's disability.[4] Under Selfridge, they are driven by greed and, under Quaritch, they are spurred on by fear.

Avatar's conversion story traces relationships that grow between Jake and Ewya, Jake and the Omaticaya, and Jake and Neytiri. These circles of life are connected. They come together at the end, in the climactic moment after the final battle with Quaritch, when Jake – the disabled and wounded soldier – is "seen" and loved for who he truly is by Neytiri, a member of a totally different species. Their relationship transcends his disability, the species boundary, and his former mindset.[5]

This sort of connection makes the world of the Omaticaya and Ewya authentic to Jake, while also deepening his sense of humanity. His deepening relationship with the world of life is the source of Jake's deepening sense of humanity, the way he becomes more humane. Here's where I think *Avatar* really advances beyond standard discussions in environmental ethics. Not only does the movie work with the novel category of deep humanity, but it also depicts "relational reason," the logic that deepens our humanity.

Relational reason is an expression for the logic of relationships, for the conscious process of trying to connect with a "who" – or, as the philosopher Martin Buber (1878–1965) called it, a "you."[6] When I reason relationally, I figure out how to connect with another being whom I take to be a person or to have something like a personality. To me, that being is then a subject, not an object; a "who," not a "what"; a person (or a person-like being), not a thing. The distinction between a "who" and a "what" is so basic that we teach it to our children when, for instance, we tell them that it's one thing to kick a rock and quite another thing to kick a dog.

The important point to stress about relational reason is that it helps us understand concretely and precisely what the world of the mining colony lacks such that its absence makes the colony seem unreal once Jake becomes aware of it. Relational reason is a basic part of human consciousness that works by interacting with everything that can be a possible subject or a "who" for us, for instance other living beings and systems of life. We can find personality and potential connection in all manner of living things, no matter how strange. To deny that connection is to deny a part of ourselves. Some psychologists and biologists even have a name for the elemental wonder and joy we experience when connected to the world of living things. They call it *biophilia*.

The world of the mining colony may deny the connection to life "in the woods," but the Omaticaya don't. Using relational reason, they continually try to connect with each other, to "see" each other. They also see and connect with other living beings – the viperwolves, for instance – and even with their entire ecosystem. They feel their world to have a personality, which they call Eywa, just as a farmer who knows the seasons, peculiarities, and riches of her land might feel that it has personality as well. The Omaticaya and the Na'vi generally acknowledge their relational capacities in a way the mercenaries and corporate functionaries do not. And *that* is what makes the world "out there" authentically human, whereas the world "in here" is false, denying important human relationships.

Jake becomes aware that the teeming world of life around him presents the possibility of many vital relationships. Even early on, during his first trip into the forest, he finds it to be a source of wonder. Lost in childlike curiosity, he drifts away from Grace and Norm to look at the spiral plants called "helicoradians." His wonder only increases under Neytiri's tutelage, until he finally falls "in love with the forest." Love is the ultimate relationship. And the teeming possibilities for relationship come to make "the woods" seem truer to Jake than the military–corporate world. By contrast, when the denizens of Hell's Gate cordon off much of that world – both mentally and physically – and treat it only as a mere resource or obstacle, they deny the true potential for human relatedness present in themselves. They deny their potential for deep humanity. And to do that is to deny an important aspect of one's reality.

At the end of the film Jake becomes a Na'vi, no longer human. But, in becoming nonhuman, he has become more humane. Ironically, by becoming an alien, Jake has become more recognizable. We see him, because he has let himself see and be seen.

"Everything Is Backwards Now"

The explicit message of *Avatar* concerns the value of discovering our deep humanity. It can be a moving message for those of us who are aware of our potential for connecting with our *oikos*, our dwelling-place on the planet. Yet there is a further layer to the inside-out moment, one that makes that moment turn around and take in the world of film-making itself: Hollywood, the production and distribution industries of mass market filmmaking, and the way we escape from our humdrum reality by watching fantasy films.

With its luminescent fantasies that fulfill a variety of wishes, isn't cinema like a dream? And don't we know, at some level, that once we leave the cinema we come back to the true world? Our lives – where we work, suffer, love, feel angst, endure insomnia, make food, and scrub counters – are in the real world, whereas the world of magical warriors is a fantasy.

But the real world is also the corporate world of profit seeking and the vast military apparatus that protects it, a world that makes a place for *Avatar* in part because it is a staggeringly profitable film. It is a world where many of us, at least in the United States, enjoy going to movies on Friday night while our military maintains a constant presence around the world. This is not to say that the US military – or the armed forces of other nations – are simply profit-mongering mercenaries like the SecOps in *Avatar*. Nor is it to say that James Cameron's film was made only for the sake of profits, either. Rather it's to say that our fantasy space inside the cinema is supported by a vast corporate and military order that belongs to a larger society, which is unsustainable and tragically at odds with the Earth's cycles of life. The world outside the theater, the world that makes our experience inside the theater possible, has much in common with Jake's life inside the mining colony, which comes to feel like a dream to him. The true world is out there for us, but we have yet to find it.

To put it bluntly, our mainstream institutions right now are at odds with our potential for deep humanity. Most of us are complicit in institutions that have not yet worked out a deeply human relationship with Earth. Our world's consumption patterns are unsustainable, and many scientists believe that we are heading toward potentially catastrophic climate change. Moreover, we are in the middle of the sixth mass extinction since life on Earth began, a mass extinction *we* are causing and that threatens to eliminate half the life forms on Earth in this century alone.[7] Our institutions perpetuate this unsustainable situation in a wasteful lifestyle closed off to the needs of other forms of life on this planet. In fact it's possible that you saw *Avatar* in a concrete shopping mall built over what used to be a thriving wetland.

So the happy ending of *Avatar* is a dream, while *our* world is closer to a nightmare, ecologically speaking. But that nightmare could give way to a true world if only our mainstream institutions could be reformed to express deep, life-encompassing relationships that are mindful of the future of life.

Notes

1. Any good reader in environmental ethics can be consulted for more information on the various positions taken by environmental ethicists. One reader I particularly like is David Schmidtz and Elizabeth Willot, *Environmental Ethics: What Really Matters, What Really Works* (New York: Oxford University Press, 2002). See also Dale Jamieson, *Ethics and the Environment* (New York: Cambridge University Press, 2008). The classic representative of biocentrism is Albert Schweitzer, while the classic representative of ecocentrism is Aldo Leopold. Anthropocentrism is pegged on so many philosophers and religions that it is best simply to read through an environmental ethics reader to get a sense of the term.

2. See Bendik-Keymer, *The Ecological Life: Discovering Citizenship and a Sense of Humanity* (Lanham, MD: Rowman & Littlefield, 2006), chs. 4–6. I developed there the idea of deep humanity through reading the work of Cora Diamond; see in particular her *The Realistic Spirit: Wittgenstein, Philosophy and the Mind* (Cambridge, MA: MIT Press, 1995).

3. I think that we can begin to see what ideally ought to matter to us by focusing on people of excellent character. Of course, this method could be considered question-begging, since one person's good character may be another person's bad character. But I hold only that it's a good place to start. Seeing a whole human being at work in real life, with all her or his dispositions, is often a better way to glimpse what matters than focusing on an abstract or fragmentary action. See Jamieson, *Ethics and the Environment*, as well as Ronald Sandler, *Character and Environment: A Virtue-Oriented Approach to Environmental Ethics* (New York: Columbia University Press, 2007).

4. For more on how Jake and others relate to his disability, see Chapter 11 by Ryan Smock.

5. Martha Nussbaum calls transcendence like this "humane." See her *The Frontiers of Justice: Disability, Nationality, Species Membership* (Cambridge, MA: Harvard University Press, 2006).

6. Martin Buber, *I and Thou*, trans. Walter Kaufmann (New York: Touchstone/Simon & Schuster, 1996).

7. See Martin Gorke, *The Death of our Planet's Species* (Washington, DC: Island Press, 2003).

Part IV

SEEING OUR BODIES
"THEY'VE GOT GREAT MUSCLE TONE"

10

The Identity of Avatars and Na'vi Wisdom

Kevin S. Decker

What is the self? It's the thing closest to us and it makes each of us who we are – but, for all this, it's a pretty slippery concept. In *Avatar*, Jake Sully struggles with his sense of self at a variety of levels, including the *metaphysical*: who or what is this "Jake" who can move between a human and a Na'vi form with the aid of link unit technology? But Jake's not the first person to worry about the nature of personal identity. The writings of a couple of the most famous ancient Greek philosophers, Plato (c. 429–347 BCE) and his student Aristotle (384–322 BCE), are full of sophisticated metaphysical speculations about the nature of the self. And philosophers haven't stopped speculating to this day.

The Continuity of the Self: Your Future Is in His Hands[1]

Plato and Aristotle share a basic metaphysical assumption about personal identity that is held by many people even today. In their book *Philosophy in the Flesh*, George Lakoff and Mark Johnson call this shared conjecture the "folk theory of essences."[2] It goes somewhat like this: "Every entity has an 'essence' or 'nature,' that is, a collection of properties that make it the kind of thing it is and is the causal source of its natural behavior."[3] Consider the savage, panther-like thanator, one of the first Pandoran creatures that Jake meets up

Avatar and Philosophy: Learning to See, First Edition. Edited by George A. Dunn.
© 2014 John Wiley & Sons, Inc. Published 2014 by John Wiley & Sons, Inc.

close and personal. This creature seems to be genetically coded for predatory behavior. If we were to see one nuzzling up to Jake affectionately rather than trying to shred him with its teeth, we would probably say that it was "acting against its nature."

It turns out that the folk theory of essences has a lot to do with how we think about ourselves, whether we have avatars or not. Again, Lakoff and Johnson:

> We have in our conceptual systems a very general metaphor in which our Essence is part of our Subject – our subjective consciousness, our locus of thought, judgment, and will. Thus, who we essentially are is associated with how we think, what judgments we make, and how we choose to act. According to the folk theory, it is our Essence that, ideally, should determine our natural behavior.[4]

"However," as these authors continue, "our concept of who we essentially are is often incompatible with what we actually do." Examples of this abound in society. Think of the gay or lesbian person struggling with his or her identity from within a heterosexual marriage, or the smoker who takes up cigarettes again after convincing herself that she no longer needs to smoke. This incompatibility produces the notion that we each have an authentic, true, "essential" self, tucked away inside. We might even come to think of our body as a container that somehow masks our real self.

After all, the experiences we call "mental" are often quite different from those we call "bodily." For example, when Jake is tossed from the back of a direhorse, the resulting *physical* pain has certain specific locations in his body, such as his aching tailbone. But when he witnesses the destruction of Hometree, his soul is gripped by a profound *psychological* pain that is unlike anything physical, in that it's not located in any particular part of his body. Even if we describe the scene as *heart*-breaking, that doesn't mean that Jake's psychological anguish is really taking place in his chest. Considerations such as these have led many philosophers to conclude that the mind (or soul) is something immaterial and, as such, distinct from the body. It's not hard to see how this idea of a two-part self found a home in some of humanity's major religious traditions. On this view, a person "essentially" is a *soul* or *spirit* that has, or occupies, its body only temporarily. Many philosophers and religious thinkers went so far as to claim that our "inessential" mortal frame was actually an impediment to genuine knowledge and virtue, so that we should look forward to the day when we finally get to cast it aside. The soul, seat of faith and reason, is the place of our real identity; it's what we really are. Or so reasoned a long line of philosophers, stretching from Socrates (469–399 BCE) to René Descartes (1596–1650).

But everything changed with the ideas of John Locke (1632–1704), a prolific British thinker and physician, who, according to one of his admirers, "raised the problem of personal identity in the form in which [later] philosophers have gone on discussing it ... [and] also proposed a solution which still has a great deal of force."[5] Inspired by the success of the seventeenth-century scientific revolution, Locke wrote his monumental book *An Essay concerning Human Understanding*, which made a case for *empiricism*, the theory of knowledge that demands evidence from the *senses* to establish the truth of any proposition about existence.[6] Dr. Max Patel sounds very much like a disciple of Locke when he remarks to Jake: "Good science is good observation." But if we use Locke's empiricism to judge whether we have good grounds for believing in an essential self, we get some surprising results.[7]

Locke distrusted the old arguments on behalf of the folk theory of essences. He didn't necessarily discount the possibility that there are "essences," but he believed that, if essences do exist, human beings *are not wired to detect them*. This is because our ideas come from two sources, neither of which tells us what's *essential* about a thing. Locke writes:

> The understanding seems to me, not to have the least glimmering of any ideas, which it doth not receive from one of these two. *External objects furnish the mind with the ideas of sensible qualities*, which are all those different perceptions they produce in us; and the *mind furnishes the understanding with ideas of its own operations*.[8]

First, Locke claims, we rely on our senses to form our ideas of things. So all the thanators we've seen in the jungles of Pandora appear horribly vicious, but who's to say that being vicious belongs to their *essence*? Unlikely as it seems, another tribe of Pandoran natives may have tamed some! Closer to home, it was an Old World presumption that the essence of the common swan was to have white feathers, since every observed swan had this feature. This presumption was dramatically put to rest, however, when black swans were discovered in 1697 in Western Australia.

A similar argument can be deployed against the notion of an essential self. If there is an essential self, we certainly can't detect it with our senses, because everything that we can observe about someone, including her appearance and behavior, undergoes constant change over the course of her life. Sometimes these changes can be radical. The casual observer, for example, comparing the human Jake and the Na'vi Jake, wouldn't notice much in common except a slight facial resemblance. Closer inspection of Na'vi Jake's attitudes and behavior might reveal many continuities with his human counterpart, but similar continuities could also be observed between family members, twins, married couples, and close friends – and we don't typically say that this makes them the same individual! At a deeper level, although Dr. Augustine knows that Jake's Na'vi body has elements of Tom Sully's (and, by extension, Jake's) human genome, this only establishes a *biological* similarity between the two bodies. In short, there's nothing perceptible to an outside observer that would be sufficient to demonstrate that the human and the Na'vi Jakes possess the same essential self – or, as Locke put it, the same *personal identity*.

But perhaps there's another way to show that Jake retains his identity when he passes from his human body to his Na'vi avatar and back again. To pursue this, Locke turns inward, to subjective experiences, the *stream of consciousness* and *memory*:

> This being premised to find wherein *personal identity* consists, we must consider what *person* stands for; which, I think, is a thinking intelligent being, that has reason and reflection, and can consider itself as itself, the same thinking thing in different times and places; which it does only by that consciousness, which is inseparable from thinking, and as it seems to me essential to it.[9]

Locke would say that, if Na'vi Jake remembers his experiences in his human body, and vice versa, then Jake's personal identity extends across bodies. We might call the relationship between different "Jakes" at different times "psychological connectedness."[10]

This kind of connectedness manifests itself as a continuity of behaviors and beliefs that persist despite a complete change of body – as when Na'vi Jake carries out the mission assigned to human Jake, or when human Jake retains the love for Neytiri that he gained while in a different body in the jungles of Pandora. For Locke, shifting the ground to subjective experience had an important moral dimension. Suppose, for example, that the Na'vi decide that Jake must be punished for his deception on behalf of Colonel Quaritch and the Resources Development Administration (RDA) corporation. It certainly wouldn't satisfy their sense of justice to punish only the avatar body that Jake occupied while carrying out his ruse, unless, of course, Jake – the same Jake who perpetrated the wrong – was currently joined to that body in such a way that he actually experienced the hurt inflicted on it. As Locke argues, "in this *personal identity*" – based on continuity of consciousness and memory – "is founded all the right and justice of reward and punishment; happiness and misery being that for which everyone is concerned for *himself*, not mattering what becomes of any substance, not joined to, or affected with that consciousness."[11]

Locke seems confident that personal identity isn't dependent upon being "in" a particular body, or perhaps even on "having" a body at all. When he claims that "nothing but consciousness can unite remote existences into the same person, the identity of substance will not do it,"[12] he's saying that our essential self need not be lodged in any particular framework, physical or otherwise. The self he describes is roughly like a program that can be run on a PC, a Mac, or a UNIX system – any "platform" that can sustain your consciousness will ensure the continued existence of your personal identity. Locke's *Essay* features many *Avatar*-like body-switching scenarios, suggesting that it's possible for the same consciousness to be switched between "platforms" without any interruption of conscious awareness or personal identity.[13] But can that be right?

The Body and the Self: Nothing on Earth Could Come between Them

In *Avatar*, the presuppositions about personal identity that ground the linkage process between human beings and avatar bodies seems to follow Locke's insights quite faithfully. For one thing, when the Na'vi forms are about to be "decanted" from their amnio tanks, no one worries that an *existing person* will be "displaced" when Jake or Norm Spellman "move in." Everyone assumes that a body doesn't have to contain any particular mind – or, for that matter, any mind at all![14] Locke's view that moving from one body to another doesn't violate personal identity is reflected in the movie's depiction of human-to-avatar transfers.

But, even if we suppose swapping bodies in this way to be a real possibility, is it really true that it would leave psychological connectedness and personal identity pretty much as they were before the transfer?

Locke seems to be right about one thing: the key to our essential self lies in the stream of consciousness and in those memories of past conscious states that provide us with an inner sense of psychological continuity. But that can't be the whole story. We know from psychology, for example, that many of our established behaviors – which are surely among the things that make us who we are – depend not only on consciousness but also on *habits* and *motor reflexes* that are ingrained in our bodies. As Jake learns how to maneuver through the treacherous forest canopy on Pandora, he reports that, as a result of prolonged practice, "I can trust my body to know what to do." This sort of knowledge isn't a collection of facts that his conscious mind is able to recall, but a practical know-how lodged in his muscles and in his newly acquired reflexes. But some philosophers have taken this insight a step further, arguing that our personal identity is bound up with our experience of *the body as a whole* – that is, our experience not only of being embodied, but of having the *particular* body we do.

This way of talking about the essential self challenges the body-swapping scenarios of Locke and *Avatar*, urging us to attend not to far-fetched thought experiments but instead to our first-person experience of how mind and body actually interact, our ordinary sense of "what it's like" to be embodied. This approach, known as "existential phenomenology," offers an alternative to perspectives like Locke's – perspectives that, in the words of Robert Solomon, begin with the presupposition that there is "a rigid distinction between mind and body coupled with the presumption that we know the mind better than the body."[15]

The French philosopher Maurice Merleau-Ponty (1908–1961) is an authoritative voice for this alternative way of speaking about mind and body. He thought that traditional scientific and philosophical theories, while powerful, were unable to provide accurate and complete descriptions of our "phenomenal field," his phrase for the lived and immediate experience of thinking, moving, and occupying a world. The body is what makes this phenomenal field possible by situating us in the world, affording us a point of view, and opening up opportunities for action. Suspicious of approaches that divided the mind from the body, he warned that, if I ignore the fundamental grounding that my body provides for my sense of self, "I regard my body, which is my point of view upon the world, as *one of the objects of that world.*"[16] As Merleau-Ponty reminds us, *a point of view* is never just an object like any other – it's the very precondition for sensing any object whatsoever! Consequently, Jake Sully has this much in common with the rest of us: he has a much more intimate connection to his body than either Locke's thought experiments or Dr. Augustine's research presuppose.

In short, while Merleau-Ponty might agree with Locke that consciousness is essential to personal identity, he would add the crucial qualification that we fundamentally misunderstand the nature of our consciousness unless we recognize that it is *essentially* embodied. Like other thinkers in the tradition of existential phenomenology, he doesn't view consciousness as something that "drives" the body like the occupant of a vehicle – or of an amplified mobility platform (AMP) suit. To the contrary, he believes that consciousness and the body are so completely interdependent that any attempt to separate them in theory is bound to impoverish our understanding of both.

Na'vi Wisdom: An Extreme Taste of Reality

In fact, Merleau-Ponty's understanding of the essential self as the lived body seems to cut against the thinking behind *Avatar's* linkage process. Norm Spellman, despite 520 hours of field time using the link units, sees himself as merely his avatar body's "driver," perhaps because he's cultivated a scientist's objectivity about bodies in general. If so, this speaks to one of Merleau-Ponty's wider points: we run the risk of becoming so alienated to our bodies that we regard them as mere instruments when

> science understands everything, including living, feeling, and thinking bodies, as nothing more than a set of physical elements connected by causal relations. As a result, even the human body becomes pure exteriority, a mere collection of parts outside of parts, interacting with one another according to scientific laws.[17]

Jake's experience is more dramatic. When first linked to his Na'vi body, he has an *immediate* sense of how it works. He doesn't seem particularly affected by the fact that he's now nine-feet tall, breathes a different atmosphere, and has a different metabolism. He takes his body for an unauthorized spin, pumping his legs in a way denied him since his spinal injury, and demonstrates instant agility by leaping so as to avoid a soldier in an AMP suit.

Merleau-Ponty would regard this scene as simply incredible. After all, Jake's avatar, like any body, is not a *machine* to be operated by skillful technique – as is the aforementioned AMP suit – but a place from which his subjective consciousness must learn a very different way of directing itself in the world. Merleau-Ponty takes great pains to show how this kind of awareness can be achieved only through real-world practice and through the gradual development of what he calls a *body image*, "a total awareness of my posture in the intersensory world."[18] Swapping out a body, on this view, isn't something we could do as casually as moving from a wheelchair to a link bed. At best, it would produce severe disorientation, and perhaps even profound trauma.

But if certain aspects of the avatar program defy Merleau-Ponty's insights into the essentially embodied nature of consciousness, the ecologically inclusive "seeing" of the Na'vi seems much more congenial to his understanding of how inner and outer, mental and material, are deeply intertwined. Na'vi animism, modeled on Native American spirituality, implies a sense of identity in which the material and the spiritual are thoroughly integrated. When they're pulled apart, the result isn't just detachment, but "brokenness." Lenora Hatathlie Hill conveys a sense of this intertwinement in her description of a Navajo ceremony that marks the birth of a new child:

> When the child is born, the afterbirth is taken and offered to a young tree or to a greasewood bush. The child becomes rooted in the Earth, and when it is born the roots are like a little string. Our rootedness to the Earth is like tying a string to yourself and the other end to your mother. The string thickens with each Offering, with each ceremony, each member of the member, each generation.[19]

Here we find no essential difference between the spiritual and the material that could warrant treating consciousness alone as significant for personal identity.[20]

The ecology of Pandora lends support to these views. For example, Grace Augustine and Norm learn that the trees of the Pandoran rainforest have an interconnecting root structure[21] – a discovery that parallels the Omaticaya clan's reverence for the weaving loom, which they call *Eywa s'ilvi mas'kit nivi*: "Eywa's wisdom is revealed to all of us."[22] The Na'vi's relationship to certain animals also supports Merleau-Ponty's idea that "there is a logic of the world to which my body in its entirety conforms."[23] The Na'vi hair queue facilitates an immediate connection between the Na'vi and domesticable animals like the direhorses and the ikran that would make even the horse whisperer blush. When we think of how difficult it is for our scientists to prevent cross-species tissue transplants from being rejected, we can't help but marvel at the extraordinary degree of *biological* compatibility required for *tsaheylu*. But even more remarkable is the *psychological* fusion it establishes across species.[24] That, at least, seems to be what's implied when Neytiri says of the ikran: "Once *tsaheylu* is made, ikran will fly with only one hunter in the whole life." This indicates that the *tsaheylu* ("the bond") is no mere sharing of thoughts between a Na'vi and an ikran. Rather, the process of intertwining queues fundamentally changes the ikran.[25]

If we can't isolate the essential self, as Locke does, by focusing on consciousness to the exclusion of the body, other interesting consequences follow. The folk theory of essences says that a thing's natural behavior is determined by its essence and, in the case of persons, John Locke identified this essence as consciousness. But Merleau-Ponty's perspective on the deep interdependency of flesh and subjectivity implies that any attempt to separate someone's consciousness from her body would – assuming for the moment that such a thing is even possible – violently interfere with her body image and force her to develop a new one. So, to return to the insights of Lakoff and Johnson, any attempt to understand our essential self today would need to draw on what we know about how our bodies sense, think, and move. This knowledge would in turn need to take into account our best biological, psychological, and cultural theories, in addition to existential phenomenology's best descriptions of our embodied experience. It's hard to know where all these investigation might lead, but this much as least can be said: as more and more research in cognitive science begins to confirm and develop important phenomenological insights by Merleau-Ponty and others, the easy body swapping of *Avatar* seems more and more dubious, even in principle.[26]

The Identity of Avatars: It's Nothing Personal

In many ways, existential phenomenology coincides with Na'vi wisdom. Both view the body and consciousness as intimately related, and both recognize value in the effort to see things that appear separate as fundamentally intertwined. Being among the Na'vi produces a profound change in Jake's consciousness. Indeed, he comes to discover something about his essential self through intimate contact with these people who have no duplicity, who enjoy a simple and ecstatic rootedness in their world. So perhaps we can take the death of Jake's human body and the final transfer of his consciousness to his Na'vi form as an instructive metaphor, which shows us the impossibility of discovering our essential self while we contend with a divided nature. In the end our minds cannot be alienated from our bodies.

Notes

1. In the never-ending effort to find interesting section headings that may reward the reader for paying close attention, the headings in this chapter are all advertising tag lines taken from other famous James Cameron productions. I won't tell you which is which, but see if you can guess which section headings come from: *Titanic* (1997), *Strange Days* (1995), *Terminator 2: Judgment Day* (1991), and *The Terminator* (1984).
2. Lakoff and Johnson are philosophers and cognitive scientists who attempt in their work to redescribe traditional philosophical problems in terms friendly to modern science's study of the brain, the body, and the neural system. Cognitive scientists often talk about "folk theories" as popular explanatory models that are "intuitively clear" and "make up a culture's shared common sense." They often contrast folk theories with what the latest research tells us about how we work. See George Lakoff and Mark Johnson, *Philosophy in the Flesh* (New York: Basic Books, 1999), 352.
3. Ibid., 363.
4. Ibid., 282.
5. J. L. Mackie, *Problems from Locke* (Oxford: Clarendon Press, 1976), 177.
6. For more on empiricism – and on the critique of empiricism developed by the German philosopher Georg Wilhelm Friedrich Hegel (1770–1831) – see Chapter 8 by James Lawler.
7. Locke is also famous for his theories concerning the origins of government and of private property. See Chapter 16 by Dale Murray.

8. John Locke, *An Essay concerning Human Understanding*, ed. Roger Woolhouse (New York: Penguin, 1997), 110.

9. Locke, *Essay*, 302.

10. The phrase is Derek Parfit's, and it's taken from his book *Reasons and Persons* (Oxford: Clarendon Press, 1984), 215. Thank you to George Dunn for the examples of psychological connectedness.

11. Locke, *Essay*, 308.

12. Ibid., 310.

13. For one such scenario, consider the following: "For should the soul of a prince, carrying with it the consciousness of the prince's past life, enter and inform the body of a cobbler, as soon as deserted by his own soul, everyone sees he would be the same person as the prince, accountable for the prince's actions ..." (Locke, *Essay*, 306).

14. The film sends mixed messages about this. For example, Norm and Dr. Max Cullimore note that the avatar bodies have "great muscle tone" as a result of the success of "proprioceptive sim[ulation]s." These would presumably be "virtual exercises" in which spatial sense and movement are stimulated, but how could a creature devoid of a mind benefit from them?

15. Robert Solomon, "General Introduction," *Phenomenology and Existentialism* (Lanham, MD: Rowman & Littlefield, 2001 [1972]), 2.

16. Maurice Merleau-Ponty, *Basic Writings*, ed. Thomas Baldwin (New York: Routledge, 2004), 83 (italics added).

17. Gary Gutting, "Merleau-Ponty," in *French Philosophy in the Twentieth Century* (New York: Cambridge University Press, 2001), 188–189.

18. Merleau-Ponty, *Basic Writings*, 103.

19. Quoted in T. C. McLuhan, ed., *The Way of the Earth: Encounters with Nature in Ancient and Contemporary Thought* (New York: Touchstone, 1994), 400.

20. For more on Native American themes in *Avatar*, see Chapter 17 by Dennis Knepp.

21. For a discussion of the interconnected root structure of the Pandoran rainforest and how it is related it recent discoveries about the roots of terrestrial plants, see Chapter 7 by Kyle Burchett.

22. Maria Wilhelm and Dirk Mathison, *James Cameron's* Avatar: *A Confidential Report on the Biological and Social History of Pandora* (London: HarperCollins, 2009), 41.

23. Maurice Merleau-Ponty, *The Phenomenology of Perception*, in Donn Welton, ed., *The Body: Classic and Contemporary Readings* (Malden, MA: Blackwell, 1999), 174.

24. Take that, Thomas Nagel! See Nagel, "What Is It Like to Be a Bat?" *Philosophical Review* 83 (1974), 435–450. In this famous paper, which also addresses consciousness and identity, Nagel claims that there are

some kinds of experience – bat experiences, for example – that human beings could never have. His arguments for this claim are too complex and interesting to receive justice here.

25.   On the other hand, the Na'vi culture also supports beliefs that seem to affirm the distinctiveness of mind and body. For people with knowledge of the outsiders but no link transfer technology, they are remarkably accepting of Jake when he first arrives in his avatar body. They also believe, at the end of the film, that a total and complete transfer of Jake's self can be achieved if he can first pass through the Eye of Eywa.

26.   An excellent book on this subject is Evan Thompson's *Mind in Life: Biology, Phenomenology, and the Sciences of Life* (Cambridge, MA: Harvard University Press, 2007). For a first-rate discussion of the work of Thompson and others who are attempting to reintegrate mind into nature, see Chapter 7.

"I Got This"

Disability, Stigma, and Jake Sully's Rejected Body

Ryan Smock

The promise of adventure amid the vast ocean of space has always enticed me, so when I first heard about James Cameron's *Avatar*, I was hooked even before I stepped into the theater. Interplanetary travel, giant robotic bodysuits, and a marine joining and eventually saving an indigenous extraterrestrial race – this film had it all! But when I finally saw *Avatar*, I realized there was something going on that was more serious than whether Jake Sully would save the Na'vi or whether his relationship with Neytiri would work out. Lurking beneath all that nerdy sci-fi goodness were real issues of how the military community viewed and treated Jake as a disabled person and how Jake himself dealt with the stigma related to his condition.

These issues might not seem important at first glance, since most of the film concerns Jake's learning the ways of the Na'vi and the conflict between the Na'vi and the "sky people." In fact there's scarcely a reference to disability after the first 15 minutes of the film. Only occasionally do we see Jake in his wheelchair, and we never see any disabled Na'vi, despite all the hazards that they routinely face. (Evidently being virtually indestructible is one benefit of having bones reinforced with naturally occurring carbon.) After that first 15 minutes, there are only a couple of pieces of dialogue related to Jake's disability. Grace Augustine teases him – "I'd hate to have to force-feed a cripple" – as Jake tries to skip lunch to elope with Neytiri. And, of course, Colonel Miles Quaritch pledges to help Jake

Avatar and Philosophy: Learning to See, First Edition. Edited by George A. Dunn.
© 2014 John Wiley & Sons, Inc. Published 2014 by John Wiley & Sons, Inc.

regain the use of his legs in return for intelligence he gathers living as a mole among the Na'vi.

But Quaritch's offer reminds us that much of what Jake does in the film is propelled by a desire to get his legs – his *real* legs – back. When we recall how scornfully the former "army dogs" and marines among the SecOps treated Jake in the opening scenes, it's not hard to understand why Quaritch's offer would be such a powerful incentive for him. Jake's disability and his desire to overcome it are, in a sense, what sets the action of *Avatar* in motion and keeps it going for at least the first hour and a half, until a crucial turning point in the film when his desire to regain his human legs is superseded by his desire to protect the Na'vi.

"That Is Just Wrong"

The sky shatters as a Valkyrie shuttle enters the Pandoran atmosphere, flies past lush forests and a desolate mining site, and finally lands at a military outpost. As the shuttle's cargo ramp hisses open and thumps to the ground, the arriving personnel pour out, darting across the courtyard and into the nearby base – all except Jake, who's still setting up his wheelchair and struggling with his atrophied legs.

"Let's go, special case!" shouts the crew chief, glaring at Jake as he scoots himself onto the wheelchair. "Do not make me wait for you!" And as Jake rolls down the ramp and across the courtyard, other personnel take notice:

"Look out hotrod!" says someone as he whisks pass Jake in an amplified mobility platform (AMP) suit.

"Check this out, man," says another member of the SecOps to his partner, Corporal Lyle Wainfleet. "Meals on wheels."

"Oh man, that is just wrong," Wainfleet replies. But he's not admonishing his partner for his tasteless comment. He's commenting about Jake.

In *The Rejected Body: Feminist Philosophical Reflections on Disability*, philosopher Susan Wendell writes about how disabled persons are typically devalued as members of society. Seen as inferior to "normal" humans, they're often regarded with revulsion, and sometimes even with fear and anger.[1] They may be verbally or physically abused, neglected, harassed, forced to live in poverty, subjected to discrimination and segregation, and socially isolated. Jake experiences several of these forms of mistreatment within the first 15 minutes of the film, and we learn that he's suffered others in the past. In his voiceover monologue he tells us that, prior to coming to Pandora, he lived off the meager benefits paid to veterans and that proper restorative treatment was too expensive. We hear Wainfleet and the other SecOps verbally harass and demean Jake, despite his obvious physical courage and the wartime sacrifice that left him paralyzed from the waist down. In fact, throughout most of the film, Jake's interaction with military personnel seems pretty much limited to exchanges with SecOps pilot Trudy Chacón or with Colonel Quaritch. So why are disabled persons devalued, and why do they receive such poor treatment?

Wendell suggests that our society is structured in part by what she calls "disciplines of normality."[2] We have ideas about what it means to be biologically "normal," such as having all limbs and appendages, having a certain body shape, having full control over bodily functions like locomotion, the release of gases, and the ridding of waste, and having no deformities or blemishes. We also have ideas about what it means to maintain normal social activity. A normal person is expected to hold down a job, partner up with a boyfriend, girlfriend or spouse, frequent entertainment venues, and perhaps attend an occasional religious service. These disciplines are pervasive: we confront them everywhere and everyone internalizes them. People who are able to maintain these disciplines are considered "normal," while people who cannot are stigmatized as "deviant," "deficient," "inferior," or "disabled" – and this stigmatizing can be devastating.

At early ages, children who do not maintain normality – who can't, for example, control their bowel movements or their vocal pitch or volume, or who have difficulty learning or hearing – are bullied and subjected to "taunting, teasing, and the threat of social ostracism."[3] A child who pees her pants in elementary school, for example, might spend days, weeks, or even months being abused, harassed, or shunned – all for an incident that was completely out of her control. Taunting and teasing might abate as one gets older, but ostracism can continue into adult life, as one is forced to endure various forms of segregation. Adults who don't maintain the disciplines of normality are often barred from schools, entertainment venues, military service, hospitals, places of business, and even religious institutions.

This de facto shunning may in part be due to the fact that the disabled awaken in "normal" people fears that they might themselves slip outside the realm of normality. Wendell quotes author Susan Griffin's account of a revealing personal experience:

> Waiting in line to be served at a restaurant, I began to notice an older woman who was sitting at a table alone. She was not eating, and she seemed to be miserable. I assumed she was waiting to be met. Her expression, the paleness of her skin ... indicated to me that she might be ill, perhaps even seriously ill, perhaps dying. I imagined that she was nauseous. I was hungry. Yet as I looked at her I felt my appetite begin to ebb, a nausea seemed about to invade me by virtue of her presence. I was afraid that I might be seated next to her, so that I might become more nauseous ... I felt an anger toward her. Why was she sick in this restaurant? Why force people who are eating to participate in her misery? I wanted to shout at her that she should go home, but of course, I did not. I was deeply ashamed of my feelings. And because of this shame I hid them away.[4]

On seeing the ailing woman, Griffin became afraid that she might become nauseous and sick. Her first instinct was to get rid of the person who was causing her distress, and to do so through verbal abuse ("I wanted to shout at her") and through insistence on that person's ostracism ("she should go home"). Similarly, the hurtful remarks of Wainfleet and the other SecOps personnel toward Jake probably reflect their discomfort at being around someone who serves as a living reminder that suffering a debilitating injury is a very real possibility for combat-oriented soldiers. Jake's mere presence is likely to arouse in them a perhaps only semi-conscious fear of sharing his fate, a fear they try to stave off by making wisecracks and by keeping Jake, the source of their uneasiness, at a safe distance. They were obviously not ashamed of their feelings as Griffin was of hers.

Still, Griffin may not have been the only person in that restaurant plagued by shame – the sick woman may have been as well. Continual stigmatization of people as deficient, inferior, or disabled often forces them to assume those social roles, limiting their range of possible social activities.[5] The woman in the restaurant, for example, is type-cast as "sick." As such, she loses a measure of autonomy, may be excused from responsibilities like going to work and doing household chores, and is expected to keep herself away from most public events. Jake, in turn, is typecast as "crippled," which also regularly results in a loss of autonomy, responsibility, and opportunities for social activity. But, while the sick person is normally expected to recover and to reclaim her autonomy, responsibility, and public role in society, the cripple is usually thought to be unable to do so. He's considered terminally dependent, helpless, and pitiful, nothing but a "burden" on others.[6] These stigmas might bring about a sense of shame – shame for failing to live up not only to the disciplines of normality regarding the body, but also to disciplines of normality regarding social responsibilities and activity.[7]

"Maybe I Was Sick of Doctors Telling Me What I Couldn't Do"

Jake doesn't let himself succumb to the stigma of being crippled, though. He resists being typecast and therefore doesn't feel the associated shame – or, if he does, he never lets it show. Not once in the film does he refer to himself as handicapped or crippled. While setting up his wheelchair at the beginning of the film, he tells us in a voiceover that, even after his injuries barred him from active duty as a marine, he still retained the marine attitude. "I told myself I could pass any test a man can pass," he says, making it perfectly clear that he's not about to surrender his autonomy, responsibility, or social life. His disability may make it difficult for him to realize his goals, but it's an obstacle he believes he can overcome, a "test" this tough marine can pass. Most importantly, he doesn't let other people's opinions about what he can do affect his actions. He completely ignores Wainfleet and the others, continuing into the base according to his orders. And, when Grace attempts to help him into the psionic link unit, Jake refuses. "Don't," he says. "I got this."

But, inspirational as Jake's determination may be, the stigma persists, compounding his disability by adding social challenges to the physical obstacles he already faces. Jake's refusal to identify himself as disabled doesn't prevent others from doing so. And Jake's not feeling shame for not living up to the marines' standards of normality doesn't mean they don't try to force shame upon him. The intent to inflict shame on Jake by bullying him into internalizing a sense of inferiority is clearly what lies behind the words and actions of Wainfleet and others. Even Grace's attempt to help Jake into the link unit – as benevolent as her intentions may be – probably reflects a stigmatizing assumption that Jake is a helpless cripple who can't pull himself up. It seems that, no matter how hard Jake tries to live up to the standards of normality present in that society, the "normal" people never fail to notice his "deficiency."

Jake could relieve this social pressure in several different ways. He could convince his society to change its disciplines of normality to make them more accommodating. Or he could find a way around his "deficiency" in order to satisfy the established disciplines, perhaps through curative treatment or the use of prosthetics. Or he could join a different society, whose disciplines he could meet without the need for treatment or prosthesis. Many examples of these methods are already found in our world. The Americans with Disabilities Act of 1990 tries to re-write our disciplines of normality to include and accept people with disabilities into the larger society, punishing those who segregate or discriminate against others simply for having a medical issue. At the same time, research in plastics and robotics brings almost daily advancements in prosthetic technology: some devices enable paraplegics to run marathons, while others provide the blind with basic sight (mostly shapes and motion). And each year hundreds of thousands, perhaps millions, of people join or develop communities with more relaxed disciplines of normality. The deaf community is a very interesting example of such a community, as the categories of disabled and nondisabled seem to get reversed when one enters their social group. In "normal" society, the inability to hear is viewed as a deficiency. The deaf must learn a sign language and speak through interpreters in order to communicate with the rest of society, which puts them at a social disadvantage. In deaf societies, however, the "normal" person is the one with the disability; for sign language rather than speech is the norm for communication. Also, the "normal" person will often be unable to understand elements of deaf culture such as flashing lights or color themes.

Unfortunately for Jake, most of his human colleagues at Hell's Gate don't seem very inclined to change their disciplines of normality for his sake. So, to find relief from the stigmatization forced on him, Jake must either find a way around his disability or find a community with disciplines of normality he can meet. Here's where his avatar comes in. Through his avatar, all of the motor skills Jake previously lacked have been restored. He can walk, swim, jump, and do anything he could do before his injury – and perhaps even do it better than before, since avatar bodies seem to share the Na'vi's exceptional strength, resilience, and athleticism. On the other hand, his avatar can't breathe the oxygen-rich air that human beings require; and it's 10 feet tall, bright blue, and somewhat cat-like in appearance – qualities that make having such a body in a human establishment a handicap in itself, despite its outright coolness. Among the Na'vi, however, Jake finds a society whose disciplines are more amenable. Granted, he has to put in a lot of physical training and survive a dangerous rite of passage, as well as convince the Na'vi that he's not a *skxawng*.[8] For the most part, though, there aren't any disciplines he can't match. He can run and jump as well as the Na'vi; he dusts himself off and walks away from a 100-foot fall; and he even tames an ikran.

Is Jake Just a Gamer?

Waking up for the first time in his avatar, Jake assumes control of a body that's free from any disability. He can wiggle his toes – and, what's more, he can *feel* that he's wiggling his toes. Against the direction of the attending technicians, he stands and begins moving about the room. When the technicians urge him to return to the gurney, he brushes them aside with words that echo his previous comment to Grace: "It's okay. It's all good. I got this." Within seconds, he has pushed open a door and taken off running across a courtyard and through an obstacle course, nearly colliding with yet another soldier in an AMP suit. This time, however, Jake really *is* acting like a "hotrod." He finally skids to a halt in a patch of dirt at the forest edge, takes a deep breath, and scrunches his feet just to feel the dirt between those newly mobile and sensitive toes.

Of course, someone might object that those aren't really Jake's toes – they're the avatar's toes. Jake is inside the compound, lying in a psionic link unit that's relaying electrical signals between him and the avatar. He's not actually feeling dirt, only a virtual sensation of dirt that's being generated in his brain by the link. On this view, Jake's relationship with the avatar is like the relationship between the player of a video game and the character he's playing. In fact, the word "avatar," a term borrowed from the world of video games, suggests just such a relationship, in which Jake is "playing" his avatar from his link unit. Just as a video game player presses buttons to cause an onscreen character to act, Jake's rapid eye movements while in his link unit suggest that he's generating neural impulses that direct the avatar's actions. The only difference is that the gamer doesn't experience every sensation just as his onscreen character would experience it – for example, the gamer doesn't feel the weight of the sword in his character's hand – while Jake experiences all the sensations of his avatar *as if* they were his own.

As if, but some might say *not really*. On this view, if Jake experiences his avatar running and leaping *as if* they were actions of his own body, it's because he's literally living in a dream. He's like some gamer who becomes so enthralled in his virtual world that he can no longer distinguish it from the real one ("Everything is backwards now") and may even forget to stop and eat ("Don't make me force feed a cripple"). Given Jake's disability and the stigma attached to it, it's understandable how he might want to trade his reality for a dream and how he could become addicted to the virtual experience of running through the forest canopy and flying on the back of a giant airborne lizard, especially when these activities also involve the companionship of a beautiful blue alien. But, viewed in this way, Jake's not really overcoming his physical and social disabilities – not any more than the gamer is really transformed into a magic, sword-wielding dwarf.

That may not be the best way to think about Jake's relationship with his avatar, however, since his avatar doesn't simply transport him to a virtual world, but actually enables him to interact with the environment and creatures of Pandora. As Colonel Quaritch advises the new arrivals, Pandora is a rough place – and that's putting it mildly! The terrain can be treacherous (as we see when Jake and other Na'vi climb Mount Iknimaya), the creatures can be massive and deadly, and the atmospheric gases are poisonous for human beings. To do anything on Pandora beyond the fence that marks the boundaries of Hell's Gate, Jake needs his avatar. It can breathe the noxious air; and the naturally occurring carbon fibers in its bones and muscle tissue make it "very hard to kill," as well as allowing it to better cope with some of the unique environmental obstacles on Pandora. Jake's avatar is a prosthetic device that allows him to cope with an environment in which having a merely human body – even a so-called "normal" human body – constitutes a severe "disability."

In this respect, the avatar is actually similar to those AMP suits with which Jake keeps narrowly avoiding collisions. In the film's climactic showdown, Jake in his avatar faces off against Quaritch outfitted in his AMP. The AMP permits Quaritch to do many of the same things that Jake is able to do with the aid of his avatar: it augments his strength and mobility, it permits him to breathe while enveloped in a poisonous atmosphere, and, of course, it also makes him "very hard to kill." Quaritch in his AMP suit and Jake in his avatar are both operating prosthetic "devices" that technologically extend their powers and allow them to overcome the handicap of having a human body on Pandora. But Jake's avatar can do something that Quaritch's AMP can't. It not only artificially bumps up his motor skills but extends his perceptual abilities as well, allowing him to see, hear, and feel things that are occurring miles away. When operating his avatar, Jake isn't only lying snug in his link unit; he's also wherever his avatar is, doing whatever it's doing. That's because, when linked to the avatar, he really *is* his avatar – in a much more real sense than the gamer is the character he plays.

"Yeah, Baby, I Got This!"

To understand how Jake's avatar can really become a part of who he is, we need to consider an argument from two contemporary philosophers. Andy Clark and David Chalmers write that

> if … a part of the world functions as a process which, were it done in the head, we would have no hesitation in recognizing as part of the cognitive process, then that part of the world *is* part of the cognitive process.[9]

When a blind man uses a cane, he's using a tool. That at least is how we typically describe it, for the cane is something outside his body, "a part of the world" he uses to augment a particular ability, namely his ability to locate obstacles in his path. But when we think about what the man is *doing* with the cane – scanning the area around him for objects – it becomes apparent that the cane serves the same function as the eyes would under "normal" circumstances. In this way the cane ceases to be merely an external tool and becomes instead a part of the man's cognitive process. That's because the man's swinging of the cane is what we call an *epistemic action*, an action that interacts with the world in order to support cognition. By swinging his cane back and forth, the blind man determines whether the area around him is clear of objects and thereby whether he can walk unimpeded in a given direction. Since this action directly affects whether the man walks in that direction, Clark and Chalmers argue that the swinging of the cane is the same sort of process as the man's scanning the ground with his eyes.[10] If they're right and the cane does become part of the man's cognitive process, part of his extended mind, then we might even go so far as to say that the cane becomes an extension of his self, at least for as long as it's used to help him "see."[11]

Jake's avatar is a lot like the blind man's cane in that it enhances his ability to interact with the world. Through nerve impulses generated by the link unit, he's able to extend his sensory perception beyond the confines of his body and into the avatar, so that he experiences what the avatar experiences. This means that every action Jake directs the avatar to take is an epistemic action, since the information gathered affects how Jake further directs the avatar. When the avatar turns to face an ikran, Jake sees the ikran and uses his avatar to taunt it. And, when the ikran bucks the avatar and tosses it over the cliff, Jake directs the avatar to grab onto exposed roots to prevent a nasty fall. Jake's cognitive process thus comes to include the avatar, making the avatar an extension of his self. In light of this, it is not so much that Jake directs the avatar to act, as that the avatar's actions are his own. The avatar becomes as much a part of Jake as his human body.

Gaining control of his ikran, Jake steers it through the Hallelujah Mountains, crying: "Yeah, baby, I got this!" He thus celebrates his ultimate triumph over his disability, a triumph made possible by his avatar. Ironically, he uses the same words he had previously used to refuse well-intentioned, but in reality stigmatizing offers of help.

"One Life Ends, Another Begins"

Jake's connection to his avatar is as intimate as intimate can be: he experiences everything the avatar experiences because of his extended cognition, and every action performed by the avatar is *his* action. The avatar is literally an extension of Jake himself. In his video log, Jake reports: "My feet are getting tougher. I can run farther every day. I have to trust my body to know what to do." Of course, he's referring to the feet and the body of his avatar, not to his human body with its useless paralyzed feet, which apparently has spent most of its time entombed in the link unit for several months.[12] But Jake spends so much time linked to the avatar that his human body and the human society to which it belongs begin to seem like a "dream." The more time he spends in his nondisabled Na'vi body, the more he *rejects* his disabled human body. While we cheer for Jake at his having found a way to overcome his disability and escape social stigmatization, his newfound happiness of being inducted into Na'vi culture has come at a price.

Dividing his time between two different bodies – one disabled and one not – means that Jake must juggle two competing disciplines of normality. Being human, he's compelled to uphold the disciplines of human society. When unable to do so because of his disability, he's ostracized by his peers. While piloting his avatar, however, Jake is part of Na'vi society and obliged to uphold their disciplines. Indeed Jake goes above and beyond Na'vi disciplines of normality when he tames the toruk, earning a special place in the Omaticaya tribe. The contrast between his overwhelming success with his avatar body and his utter failure with his human body causes Jake to dissociate himself from the latter: he rejects his "inferior" disabled body in favor of adopting and maintaining his "superior" nondisabled one. Consequently, in the final scene, Jake discards his disabled human body in order to live permanently as the avatar.

Most of the discussion surrounding *Avatar* when it was released concerned its pro-green message, its uplifting theme of preserving nature instead of simply exploiting and abusing it. Oddly enough, it was never asked whether the film had anything to say about disability or the stigma that accompanies it. Clearly the film champions Jake's determined attitude, his refusal to be defined by his disability, and his belief that despite his physical challenges he can still "pass any test a man can pass." That certainly sends a positive, anti-stigmatizing message. Yet the fact that Jake never affects any change in his society's disciplines of normality tends to stifle any inspirational message that might be gleaned from his admirable determination. In the end, Jake overcomes stigmatization only by being given a "replacement" body and by becoming part of a different society. That he's required to abandon both his human body and human society in order to find peace paints a pretty bleak picture of the prospects for disabled people here in the real world.

And that is just wrong.

Notes

1. Susan Wendell, *The Rejected Body: Feminist Philosophical Reflections on Disabilities* (New York: Routledge, 1996), 31.
2. Ibid., 87–89.
3. Ibid., 88.
4. Ibid., 61.
5. Ibid., 58, quoting Erving Goffman's book *Stigma: Notes on the Management of Spoiled Identity*.
6. Wendell, *The Rejected Body*, 44.
7. Ibid., 85.
8. As we find out in the movie, this word means "moron."
9. Andy Clark and David Chalmers, "The Extended Mind," *Analysis* 58.1 (1998), 8.
10. Ibid.
11. For more on the extended mind hypothesis, see Chapter 6 by Massimiliano Cappuccio.
12. Jake's total identification with his avatar might remind us of how gamers identify with their video game characters. When a video game character like Mario or Kratos is killed by a monster, the gamer will often shout: "It killed me!" There is usually no actual identification with the character – gamers usually don't actually believe they are Mario or Kratos – but rather just a loose association, because they control the character's actions. For more information on how this association comes about, check out Bob Rehak, "Playing at Being: Psychoanalysis and the Avatar," in Mark J. P. Wolf and Bernard Perron, eds., *The Video Game Theory Reader* (New York: Routledge, 2003), 103–128, or Espen Aarseth, "Nonlinearity and Literary Theory," in George P. Landow, ed., *Hyper/Text/Theory* (Baltimore, MD: Johns Hopkins University Press, 1994), 51–86.

12

"See the World We Come From"

Spiritual versus Technological Transcendence in *Avatar*

Dan Dinello

Sparkling woodsprites flutter in the forest and bioluminescent willow tendrils illuminate the strange ritual that ends *Avatar*. Human Jake lies head to head with his human–Na'vi hybrid avatar. Fine hair-like organelle threads have emerged from the Tree of Souls, fusing both bodies with the forest floor and connecting them to each other. Concentric rings of blue-skinned Na'vi people are entangled with the tree. They merge with its roots. Covered in translucent silken shrouds of cilia, the two Jakes lie motionless. The Na'vi sway in unison and chant hypnotically. Through this biological–spiritual ritual, Jake's human mind is transferred to his Na'vi body. Neytiri, his mate, removes human Jake's exomask, which protects him from Pandora's poisonous (to human beings) atmosphere, and gently kisses his closed, now dead eyes. Embracing Na'vi culture, abandoning his human body, and rejecting the monstrous aspects of the human race, avatar Jake opens his Na'vi eyes.

Jake is resurrected as a superhuman, scientifically created "transgenic" – an artificially fashioned organism that contains genetic material from two different species. Some viewers might see *Avatar* as advocating science and biotechnology as the salvation of a doomed humanity. If this view is correct, the movie would be reflecting the techno-utopian philosophy known as transhumanism.[1]

Avatar and Philosophy: Learning to See, First Edition. Edited by George A. Dunn.
© 2014 John Wiley & Sons, Inc. Published 2014 by John Wiley & Sons, Inc.

Here's how philosopher Max More summarizes the transhumanist program:

> We challenge the inevitability of aging and death. We see humans as a transitional stage standing between our animal heritage and our posthuman future ... This technological transformation will be accelerated by genetic engineering, life extending biosciences, intelligence intensifiers, smarter interfaces to swifter computers, neural–computer integration, worldwide data networks, virtual reality, artificial intelligence, neuroscience, artificial life, off-planet migration, and molecular nanotechnology.[2]

Inspired by scientific materialism and tortured by the prospect of senescence and mortality, transhumanists profess a belief in the almost divine power of scientists to engineer a new, technologically enhanced species, which eventually will supersede humanity. "When technology allows us to reconstitute ourselves physiologically, genetically and neurologically," says More, "we will transform ourselves into posthumans – persons of unprecedented physical, intellectual and psychological capacity, self-programming, potentially immortal, unlimited individuals."[3]

Like transhumanism, though (as we will see) for different reasons, *Avatar* views the human species as corrupted and endangered. Moreover, both transhumanism and *Avatar* hold out the promise of some form of transcendence or salvation for the human race. And along with transhumanism, but unlike much contemporary science fiction, *Avatar* presents science in a positive light, dramatizing the development of a biologically enhanced posthuman creature that offers humankind hope for survival. Yet, at a deeper level, *Avatar* subverts and eclipses the transhumanist viewpoint and criticizes its implications. Exalting spiritualism, pantheism, and nature while sounding alarm bells about the dangers of technology and scientific materialism, *Avatar* ultimately endorses a positive philosophy, antithetical to transhumanism.

Not Mad Scientists

In *Avatar* human scientists genetically engineer human–Na'vi hybrid bodies – avatars – so incredibly sophisticated that they function naturally on the Na'vi's home, the moon Pandora. Grown *in vitro* from a genetic splice of human and Na'vi DNA, these transgenic creatures – "hum'vi," if you will – exist as mindless inanimate organic pods, floating in synthetic amniotic fluid until a human driver takes control. In accord with the transhumanist viewpoint, the film presents the scientists and the consequences of their cloning and genetic engineering positively. The human–Na'vi clones are a nonviolent way to smooth relations between the natives of Pandora and the human corporation that wants to mine their planet's valuable ore, unobtainium. The avatars also allow the scientists to interact with the Na'vi people in order to study them and their culture.

The scientists may work for a rapacious corporation, but they're a charming, likeable, empathetic, and pro-Na'vi group. They're a sharp contrast to the racist corporate administrator Parker Selfridge, his violent chief of security, Colonel Miles Quaritch, and their private army of "trigger happy morons," as Dr. Grace Augustine, head of the Avatar program, describes them. These scientists not only walk a moral high ground by comparison to most other human beings in *Avatar*, but they also differ markedly from the mad or misguided scientists who populate most science fiction. From *Frankenstein* in 1818 to the recent TV series *Orphan Black* (2014), science fiction often portrays scientists as hubristic zealots, eager tools of corporate and military profiteering, or reckless experimenters who are oblivious to the dangerous consequences of their deeds.[4] These unflattering depictions of scientists encourage us to think critically about the ethics of scientific research and the potentially negative effects of technology.

Avatar, on the other hand, is likely to affect viewers in the opposite way. By presenting the scientists so positively, especially in comparison with the extremely unlikeable corporate and military personnel, *Avatar* discourages any moral questions about the scientists' work. No one asks how or from whom the Na'vi DNA was harvested. No ethical qualms are raised about growing insentient bodies in a vat, as slaves or artificial zombies. No experimental failures are shown, such as mutations discarded as organic garbage, or artificially created organisms that had become conscious of their plight.

Aside from scientific investigations that led to a book deal for Dr. Augustine, the scientists' mission involved at one time building a school and teaching English to the Na'vi, who needed neither. There's no critique of cultural imperialism, since the intentions of the scientists are presented as benign. The Na'vi themselves express no negative feelings toward them. The only criticisms we hear of the scientists come from a morally compromised source: corporate administrator Selfridge. He disparages the Avatar program as a "puppet show" and points out the hypocrisy of Dr. Augustine, who criticizes the corporation's strong-arm tactics when it's the quest for unobtanium – at whatever price – that pays for her beloved science. But, however beholden Dr. Augustine may be to the corporate purse strings, in the end she and her colleagues act heroically to oppose the forceful corporate–military takeover of Pandora.

In its highly favorable depiction of scientists, cloning, and genetic engineering, Avatar trumpets the values of scientific materialism, even in its most extreme transhumanist version. Reflecting her belief in the supremacy of scientific knowledge, Dr. Augustine initially believes that Na'vi spiritualism can be completely explained in biological terms, without invoking any kind of "pagan voodoo." In many ways the movie seems to side with her exclusive veneration of science; in fact it seems to endorse a techno-utopian transhumanist philosophy that hopes for the day when human scientists will design a technologized, posthuman species to replace the flawed, disease-prone, death-susceptible one, which transhumanists believe is at an evolutionary dead end. The human–Na'vi hybrids possess greater strength, resistance, resilience, athleticism, and vision than normal human bodies. They are striking examples of how science can create a positive, posthuman, techno-enhanced species.

Science as Salvation: Über-Na'vi Messiah

Avatar initially seems to reinforce the transhumanist technological vision of posthuman salvation and to dramatize the amazing promise of biotechnology and neuroscience. Paraplegic former marine Jake Sully is drafted to "drive" an avatar because its human DNA had been derived from his dead twin brother. As Jake explains, every driver must be genetically matched to his own avatar, so that "their nervous systems are in tune." Once Jake is linked to his avatar, the results are spectacular. After a few comically clumsy missteps, he masters the avatar operation in short order, without any training other than reading a manual. He runs and jumps gracefully, makes elaborate facial expressions, and controls his tail – all complicated maneuvers. Even more astonishingly, Jake's long, braided "queue" – with its fiber optic-like hair follicles that writhe with their own life – interfaces perfectly with the planet's biota. Using his Na'vi queue to connect neurally with the antenna of his personal mountain banshee, he bonds without the slightest technical glitch. Of course, a native Na'vi does this naturally, but Jake's avatar is not a native Na'vi – it's a complex, manufactured, genetically designed, transgenic product: created on Earth, grown in a tank on a spaceship, and operated by a remote control "psionic link."

The planet's divine force, Eywa, even sanctifies this biotechnologically enabled Jake. His anointment occurs at a propitious point in the story, only minutes after he first meets Neytiri. Having just saved his life by killing several direwolves, she angrily blames him for the death of the animals and for failing to appreciate the sadness of their demise. She calls him "stupid! Ignorant like a child." Dismissing him with a flourish of her hand, she says: "You should not be here" – and turns to walk away. Suddenly feather-light woodsprites float down and, pulsing with purpose, alight on avatar Jake. They dance gently around his shoulders, then spread over his arms, legs, and head, imbuing him with grace. Neytiri identifies them as atokirina, "Seeds of the Sacred Tree. Very pure spirits." He becomes a glowing, sparkling mass of light, which Neytiri interprets as a sign from Eywa. That they should alight on Jake seems odd, since he's there as a spy for Colonel Quaritch. Apparently they recognize his courage, his capacity for compassion, and his potential to transcend his spiritual corruption as a deceptive spy and cultural interloper serving imperialistic interests. They see in him what Neytiri sees: "a strong heart. No fear." She brings him to her village, sheltered inside the giant Hometree, where smelly alien dreamwalkers are not allowed. There he meets Mo'at, the clan's *tsahìk* or spiritual leader, who decides to let him be instructed in Na'vi ways, confirming his worthiness by tasting his blood. This bioengineered human–Na'vi clone has become the chosen one after a single day on the planet.

Remarkably, he learns to ride a banshee and to hunt as skillfully as a native, despite being an artificial Na'vi. His physical abilities are a testament to the power of the biotechnology that created his body. "I have to trust my body to know what to do," he says, as he masters the Na'vi acrobatic style of running, climbing, and leaping, as well as more refined skills like recognizing the forest's tiniest scents and sounds. There doesn't appear to be anything a Na'vi body can do that

Jake's avatar body wouldn't do just as well. Even the avatar body of nerdy, unathletic scientist Norm Spellman performs impressively, riding and handily controlling a direhorse during the battle with the SecOps forces.

Jake becomes a super-Na'vi, a Toruk Makto, rider of the last shadow, earning the respect of his romantic rival Tsu'tey, who salutes him with grudging admiration. Controlling the toruk, the gigantic red aerial predator that the human scientists call the great leonopteryx, Jake vindicates Eywa's endorsement by duplicating the legendary deed of Neytiri's "grandfather's grandfather" and by successfully leading the Na'vi insurgency against the human invaders. Human Jake becomes avatar Jake, the messiah, reflecting the original meaning of "avatar" as an incarnate deity who descends to Earth – or, in this case, Pandora. His ability to fulfill this role results from a combination of his human virtues, his rapidly maturing Na'vi identity, and a first-rate body that he owes to the power of human technology, specifically to genetic engineering, cloning, and the psionic link technology that knits it all together.

Transhumanist Mind Transfer and the Ghost in the Avatar

Belief in the inevitable development of mind-transfer technology – whereby our minds could be "uploaded" to another platform – is a central creed of the transhumanists, who see it as a means to life extension and possibly immortality, their ultimate goal. As transhumanist Ray Kurzweil explains:

> When our human hardware crashes, the software of our lives – our personal "mind file" – dies with it. However, this will not continue to be the case when we have the means to store and restore the thousands of trillions of bytes of information represented in the pattern that we call our brains. Ultimately software-based humans will be vastly extended beyond the severe limitations of humans as we know them today.[5]

Desiring escape from bodies they considered to be dead-meat relics of natural evolution, transhumanists hope that downloading our human identities into enhanced posthuman bodies will liberate us from the physical limitations of aging, disease, and death.

The concept of mind transfer addresses one of the most perplexing, persistent, and fascinating issues in the history of philosophy: the mind–body problem. What is the mind and how is it related to the brain and the body? The French philosopher René Descartes (1596–1650) offered an influential answer to this question through his doctrine of dualism. Famous for his dictum "I think therefore I am," Descartes divided the world into two different kinds of substance that can exist independently of each other: mental substances and physical substances, minds and bodies. As long as we live, our minds "drive" our bodies through a special "link" with the brain. Operating as part of the body's machinery, the brain is material. Operating beyond the laws of matter, without size or shape, the mind is immaterial and potentially immortal.

British philosopher Gilbert Ryle (1900–1976) attacked Descartes' distinction between mind and body as a "philosopher's myth." With what he admitted was "deliberate abusiveness," Ryle dubbed Descartes' dualism the "dogma of the ghost in the machine."[6] As an alternative, he endorsed materialism – the theory that the mind and the brain are the same thing rather than two separate substances. All that imaginative, smart, witty stuff we think up is nothing more than brain activity.

The transhumanist position occupies a peculiar middle ground between Descartes and Ryle. It proposes a quasi-dualistic materialism that fuses a belief in an immortal mind with a materialistic worldview. Simply put, the brain is a computer, the mind a software program. Viewing the brain as an information-processing meat machine while rejecting both classical materialism and ghost-in-the-machine spiritualism, transhumanism puts its faith in the notion of an independent mind whose patterns can be severed from our flawed flesh, transduced into a digital signal, and transferred into another – organic or silicon – brain.

This theory of digital mind transfer rests, however, on a shaky foundation of unproven and even fantastical assumptions. The theory assumes that mind or consciousness is a sort of "vaporous afterimage" – in the words of Erik Davis[7] – that emerges from complex patterns of electro-chemical machinations; that these complex neuronal patterns can be identified and precisely mapped; that they can then be replicated in a digital signal and coherently transferred into an artificial simulation of someone's brain or a cloned duplicate; and, finally, that these digitized patterns that constitute that person's mind will awake into consciousness, with its memories, personality, and identity intact.

Initially it appears that *Avatar* is endorsing the possibility of mind-transfer technology. When Jake links to his avatar, his brain is first scanned into a computer, digitized, and "phase-locked" with the brain of his hum'vi. As he sleeps, his identity – his personality, memories, and skills – streams through a pulsing tunnel of light and imprints the avatar brain. Jake's human mind animates his avatar body, controlling its movement and perceiving the world through its sense organs. His consciousness *seems* to be transferred between the avatar and his human body. Closer examination, however, shows this is not the case.

When Norm's avatar is mortally wounded, he immediately wakes up in his human body. But if his human mind had been really transferred into the avatar, killing his avatar would have killed him, just as destroying a computer destroys all the files it once contained. In fact the avatar link technology doesn't transfer a "mind file" from a human brain into the hum'vi, but allows the "driver" to operate the avatar by remote control – by using what is described as a "psionic link."[8] Somehow, perhaps by infrared, radio, or psychic signals, the wireless psionic interface extends the human mind into the avatar, receiving from its environment sensory stimulation that it feeds back to the driver's brain. The implication is that a human mind is linked to a particular human body, and yet also independently extendable to a second, avatar body. In a sense, a human ghost pilots the avatar.

Disappointing though it may be to the transhumanists, *Avatar*'s science can't accomplish complete mind transfer, as we learn when Dr. Augustine's human body is mortally wounded. Her fellow scientists make no attempt to save her through a mind link to her avatar, since the hum'vi works only if a living human mind operates it. When her human body dies, there's no more mind to be linked or transferred to her avatar. In *Avatar*'s 2154 vision of human science, a mind cannot be severed and transferred out of its original organic substrate.

"Through the Eye of Eywa"

Of course, as we saw at the beginning of this chapter, Jake is able to achieve a complete and permanent transfer of his mind "though the eye of Eywa" and into his avatar body. But this differs from the transhumanist version of mind transfer, since it's not accomplished through technology but through a biological–spiritual–religious ritual. More specifically, Na'vi mind transfer involves the cooperation of the natural world and the intercession of a divine force, two things that tend to be disregarded or even repudiated by transhumanists.

Listen to Dr. Augustine explain to Parker Selfridge the natural or biological aspect of Na'vi spiritualism:

> What we think we know is that there is some kind of electrochemical communication between the roots of the trees, like the synapses between neurons. And each tree has ten-to-the-fourth connections to the trees around it. And there are ten-to-the twelfth trees on Pandora. ... It's more connections than the human brain. Get it? It's a network. It's a global network, and the Na'vi can access it. They can upload and download data. Memories.

If they can upload and download memories, presumably they can do the same thing with whole minds. The Na'vi's biological communion with nature – their access to this "global network" – is made possible by a convenient plug – their neural queue – through which they can physically and neurally unite with trees and other animals, as well with one another.

But the mind transfer we witness at the end of the film involves more than just biology. It's ritualistically mediated by a religious ceremony, replete with chanted prayers, rhythmic music, and Na'vi bodies swaying in unison – all beckoning Ewya to facilitate Jake's rebirth as a Na'vi. If the interconnected system of roots is like Pandora's brain, then Ewya is its global mind, an independent spiritual force that is more than the sum of her biological parts. Dr. Augustine's dying words speak of her encounter with this reality, which express a spiritual vision rather than a scientific observation: "I'm with her, Jake. She's real!"

With the Na'vi on the brink of annihilation caused by the technologically advanced human beings, Eywa responds to a prayer from Jake with a unified attack from Pandora's fauna. Swarms of mountain banshees darken the sky with their gigantic leathery wings and ram the airships; a wall of hammerheads – the six-legged shark-like rhinoceroses with sledgehammer skulls – and vicious viperwolves, with flashing teeth and monkey-like agility, crash out of the foliage and stampede in human-crushing waves. Emerging out of the smoke, a bellowing thanator, a glistening three-ton black demon with an armored head, kills with razor claws and nightmare jaws. This attack reveals Eywa as a powerful, unifying, global intelligence with an independent volition, connecting and integrating Pandora's many life forms.

Through this depiction of Eywa, *Avatar* expresses the theme that nature is sacred. The Na'vi reverence for their mother goddess is in striking contrast with the attitude of the human beings, who we're told have poisoned their planet through greed, selfishness, and arrogance. Recall how Jake prays to Eywa, warning her about the "sky people" who are preparing to attack: "See the world we come from. There's no green there. They killed their Mother. And they're gonna do the same here."

Transhumanism does not view the natural world as sacred, but only as a resource to be exploited and then abandoned. "Humanity will become largely de-coupled from terrestrial nature," predict transhumanists Gregory Paul and Earl Cox. "No need to worry about floods, drought, disease, and pest-causing famines."[9] In the future envisioned by the transhumanists, technology will eventually free us from our dependence on the natural world. But if we regard nature as irrelevant to our future, we will see the world as merely something to be used and discarded. *Avatar*'s Resources Development Administration (RDA) corporation offers a picture of what British Petroleum (BP) or Halliburton might be like if they could operate on an interplanetary scale. Having done its part to ravage the environment of Earth, the RDA still hungers for profit, growth, and power. It employs its monstrous technology to rape Pandora's virgin rainforest, leaving lifeless craters and slaughtering the forest's inhabitants. They are sacrificed as collateral damage in the RDA's drive to extract Pandora's valuable unobtanium deposits. As Selfridge says: "Killing the indigenous looks bad, but there's one thing shareholders hate more than bad press, and that's a bad quarterly statement."

If the actions of the RDA and of its private military force bring to mind examples of American imperialism and environmental exploitation, perhaps it's because our own world is poisoned by similarly perverse values. The RDA's attempt to wipe out an indigenous population to clear a path to exploitable natural resources looks a lot like our genocide of Native Americans, as well as like our ongoing decimation of the rain forest. At times, the RDA's attempt to suppress the Na'vi insurgents evokes the jungle war in Vietnam. "Look, you're supposed to be winning the hearts and minds of the natives," says Selfridge to Dr. Augustine, repeating a phrase often used during the Vietnam War to describe efforts by the military to win the support of the local population. At other times the RDA's ruthless lust for the natural resources buried beneath the Na'vi's feet – not to mention its seamless integration of economic interest and armed aggression – serves as a barely veiled allegory for the US-led invasion and occupation of Iraq. "Our only security lies in pre-emptive attack," says Colonel Quaritch, echoing the argument made by President George W. Bush during the run-up to war. And, just in case we miss that clear allusion to Iraq, Max Patel further underscores the comparison when he refers to the attack as a "shock and awe campaign."

Spiritual Evolution: Transcending the Human

Contemporary philosopher Richard Tarnas could have been offering a summary of *Avatar*'s critique of transhumanism and scientific materialism when he wrote:

> The soul of the world has been extinguished: Ancient trees and forests can then be seen as nothing but potential lumber; mountains nothing but mineral deposits; seashores and deserts are oil reserves; lakes and rivers, engineering tools. Animals are perceived as harvestable commodities, indigenous tribes as obstructing relics of an outmoded past. At the all-important cosmological level, the spiritual dimension of the empirical universe has been entirely negated.[10]

Avatar shares with transhumanism a dark vision of the human future, but for very different reasons. Transhumanism places the blame for humanity's woes on organic flaws such as aging, disease, and death, while *Avatar* points to spiritual degeneracy as the cause of our troubles. Both respond with visions of human transcendence. *Avatar*'s hope for the apotheosis of humanity rests on social evolution and spiritual transformation. In contrast, transhumanism desires to perfect each of us in isolation from our social matrix, and eventually to secure our liberation in a postbiological form of existence. Emphasizing technology as salvation, transhumanists propose to enhance or replace our individual organic bodies, all the while denying or ignoring our pressing spiritual, ecological, and social problems. In short, they envision a technological utopia outside the world of nature.

Avatar dramatizes an alternative worldview. Jake's transformation may initially be enabled by genetic engineering and cloning, but its consummation is brought about by Na'vi spirituality, with its emphasis on community and its reverence for nature. In his prayer to Eywa, Jake voices his concern that human beings as a species are engineering not their enhancement, but rather their extinction – through their destruction of the natural world. Though somewhat stereotypical in its presentation of a peaceful, primitive people uncorrupted by literacy, cell phones, and civilization, *Avatar* rightly stresses the importance of community, empathy, and respect for nature – values that much of humanity ignores. Rejecting the anarchic capitalism, racism, and militarism of the RDA corporation along with the transhumanist plan for technological transcendence, Jake transcends humanity by embracing the spiritual salvation that comes from loving the natural Pandoran world.

Acknowledgments

Thanks to Maureen Musker for her criticism of earlier version of this chapter.

Notes

1. The central theorist of transhumanism is Ray Kurzweil; see his *The Age of Spiritual Machines* (New York: Viking, 1999). See also Gregory Stock, *Redesigning Humans* (New York: Houghton Mifflin, 2002); Lee Silver, *Remaking Eden* (New York: Avon, 1996); Ramez Naam, *More Than Human* (New York: Broadway, 2005). For a history and critical summary of transhumanism, see Daniel Dinello, *Technophobia! Science Fiction Visions of Posthuman Technology* (Austin: University of Texas Press, 2006); Francis Fukuyama, *Our Posthuman Future* (New York: Farrar, Straus and Giroux, 2002); Bill McKibben, *Enough* (New York: Henry Holt, 2003).
2. Max More, "Extropian Principles 3.0," http://www.maxmore.com/ extprn3.htm (accessed June, 2010).
3. More, "Extropian Principles 3.0."

4. For a fascinating history of mad scientists, see David Skal, *Screams of Reason: Mad Science and Modern Culture* (New York: W. W. Norton, 1998).

5. Ray Kurzweil, *The Singularity is Near* (New York: Viking, 2005), 325.

6. Gilbert Ryle, *The Concept of Mind* (Chicago, IL: University of Chicago Press, 1949), 15–16.

7. Eric Davis, *Techngnosis* (New York: Crown, 1998), 135.

8. Psi or psionic refers to psychic phenomena such as telepathy, clairvoyance, and psychokinesis. Psionic or psi phenomena appear in several other science fiction and fantasy worlds, for instance in *Stranger in a Strange Land*, by Robert Heinlein; *Ubik*, by Philip K. Dick; *Akira* (the anime and manga series); the *Star Trek* universe; and the *Starcraft* video game series.

9. Gregory S. Paul and Earl D. Cox, *Beyond Humanity: CyberEvolution and Future Minds* (Rockland, MA: Charles River Media, 1996), 298.

10. Richard Tarnas, *Cosmos and Psyche: Intimations of a New World View* (New York: Viking, 2006), 32.

Part V

SEEING OUR POLITICAL COMMUNITIES
"SKY PEOPLE CANNOT SEE"

13

"We Will Fight Terror with Terror"
Avatar and Just War Theory

Joseph J. Foy

"You are not in Kansas anymore." So begins Colonel Miles Quaritch's security briefing to the new arrivals on Pandora, a moon of the planet Polyphemus that Quaritch describes as brimming with countless threats and enemies. "Every living thing that crawls, flies, or squats in the mud wants to kill you and eat your eyes for jujubes," he warns the Resources Development Administration (RDA) corporation's new SecOps forces. Pandora, he explains, is unlike anything they've ever experienced before: a place where life and death hang in the balance of every decision they make. In such a world, he suggests, ordinary rules of justice and morality don't apply.

"They Attacked Me! How Am I the Bad Guy?"

Quaritch's depiction of Pandora is reminiscent of the writings of Thomas Hobbes (1588–1679), an English philosopher whose political treatise *Leviathan* has been an important influence on many modern theories of human nature, the state, and the causes of human conflict. Hobbes begins his examination of politics with a "thought experiment" or exercise in imagination that asks us to envision what human life would be like if there were no political authorities with the power to impose regulations and order. The most important feature of the "state of nature," as Hobbes called this imaginary pre-political

Avatar and Philosophy: Learning to See, First Edition. Edited by George A. Dunn.
© 2014 John Wiley & Sons, Inc. Published 2014 by John Wiley & Sons, Inc.

condition, is that everyone would be roughly equal in power. Some may be physically stronger, others more wily and cunning, but no one would have such a great advantage over others that he or she would have nothing to fear from enemies. And, according to Hobbes, in this state of nature we would all end up as enemies of each other, due to our competition over scarce resources as well as to the human tendencies to covet what others have and to pick fights just so we can enjoy the glory of trouncing someone.

Without any political authority to impose order, life in the state of nature as described by Hobbes is remarkably similar to Quaritch's depiction of life on Pandora: a state of universal conflict and a round-the-clock struggle for survival. Hobbes describes this state of nature as "such a war as is of every man against every man," in which there are no binding moral rules other than the overriding imperative to do whatever it takes to survive. Quaritch would probably agree with Hobbes that in such a state "nothing can be unjust. The notions of right and wrong, justice and injustice have there no place."[1] According to Hobbes, unless we have some guarantee that others will abide by the rules of justice, we have no good reason to do so ourselves, especially when engaging in fair play is likely to hasten the moment when someone takes advantage of our high-minded scruples to deliver a not so merciful *coup de grâce*. If our prime directive is to keep ourselves alive, then "force and fraud are in war the two cardinal virtues."[2]

According to Hobbes, the state of nature *is* a state of war, even when there are no open hostilities. This applies not only to individuals, but also to groups that confront each other in a setting where there is no higher authority recognized by all parties that could enforce the peace. That's why Hobbes believed that every sovereign state needed to regard itself as being in a state of nature in relation to all of its neighbors. Like later proponents of *Realpolitik* (political realism), he believed that all states are perpetually in conflict with each other and thus entitled to use any means whatsoever, no matter how cruel or underhanded, in pursuit of their national interests. This outlook also seems to define the perspective of Colonel Quaritch, for whom protecting the interests of the RDA corporation trumps any obligations to any other group, and specifically to the Na'vi of the Omaticaya clan. Without a higher authority on Pandora, the RDA and the Na'vi exist in a state of nature in which concerns about morality must take a backseat to the struggle for power. They're at war even before the first shot has been fired.

But, while Hobbes believes that anything goes in the state of nature and in times of war, he does not embrace a total moral nihilism that completely denies the existence of morality. As long as we live in a society with political authorities who are in position to enforce the rules, we have every reason to treat each other with fairness and respect. For, according to Hobbes, the existence of moral obligations toward others depends on our having entered into a "social contract" with them, an agreement to refrain from certain antisocial behaviors, like murder or theft, in return for the others' acceptance of the same restraints on their conduct. In short, morality is a bargain we strike with others so that we may live together in peace. But it would be foolish – and, in the state of nature, possibly fatal – to restrain ourselves unless we had some assurance that the others would live up to their side of the bargain. That's why Hobbes believes that we have no real moral obligations unless there is some "sovereign" or powerful political authority to enforce the "contract." But, since the contract applies only to individuals within a given society, outsiders are fair game.

Consider how Quaritch's attitude toward members of his own unit differs from how he regards the outside world. Toward the Na'vi he feels no obligations whatsoever; but he does recognize a duty to the soldiers under his command, as he tells the "fresh meat": "it is my job to keep you alive." When Jake agrees to supply Quaritch with inside information on the Omaticaya to help drive them from Hometree, the colonel assures the marine that "I take care of my own," promising to help him get back the use of his legs. Quaritch recognizes a contractual obligation to Jake. Later, when he berates Jake for siding with the Na'vi, he asks whether the marine had forgotten "what team you're playing for." Jake, in Quaritch's mind, is a betrayer who violated the social contract that required him to side with the RDA and the SecOps.

But, when it comes to warfare, Hobbes would insist that it makes no sense for us to label the actions of Quaritch and of the SecOps forces as ignoble or unjust. By the same token, the Na'vi resistance is neither right nor wrong. Because these groups remain within a state of nature with respect to each other, nothing they do to each other can be called just or unjust. They're merely two sides struggling for control over the same resources. On Hobbes's account, when one group feels threatened by another and they're not parties to a social contract enforced by a higher authority, any action taken for defense and security is acceptable. Even a preemptive strike is justified if one group so much as fears that the enemy *might* pose a threat.

"There Was a Sign from Eywa"

Quaritch's outlook seems to be in accord with Hobbes's view of the state of nature, but does the belief that nature is indifferent to morality and justice really reflect the viewpoint of *Avatar*? No, the claim that there's no justice in nature seems to be contradicted by several events in the film. For example, Eywa answers Jake's prayers by unleashing the animals of Pandora to defend against the RDA's attack on the Tree of Souls. In this way the Pandoran deity who is emblematic of the natural world directly refutes Hobbes's notion that nature cares nothing for justice. When Neytiri overhears Jake making his plea to Eywa at the Tree of Souls on the eve of battle, she tells him: "Our Great Mother does not take sides, Jake. She protects only the balance of life." Neytiri's sentiment seems to agree with Hobbes's position that, from nature's point of view, there is only the ongoing struggle of life, with no absolute right or wrong. If so, then are Jake and Neytiri no more "right" than Colonel Quaritch and Parker Selfridge? Condemning the RDA would be like judging a thanator for asserting its dominion over a certain territory, or a toruk for feasting on a banshee. Morality has nothing to do with it. But it turns out that Eywa sees things differently. The goddess *does* answer Jake's prayer, sending scores of hammerhead titanotheres and thanators in a ground attack and legions of banshees to rain down terror from the skies. Eywa embodies both the natural and the divine, so her support for the Na'vi in their resistance to the RDA's assault on the Tree of Souls is a clear sign that there are objective principles of right and wrong.

Of course, Eywa's intervention might only mean that the goddess is defending *herself* against a hostile invader. Jake's prayer provides fodder for this view. "See the world we come from," he warns Eywa. "There's no green there. They've killed their Mother. And they're gonna do the same thing here." When Eywa responds, she may simply be fighting for her own survival rather than exhibiting a morality. This might be a fair conclusion to draw about the will of Eywa, if it were the only evidence we had to go by. But it isn't, since the will of

Eywa is often cited by the Omaticaya as a reason for engaging in particular actions or as an explanation for the outcome of some event. Eywa plays an active role in the life of the Na'vi, as we see in several important events in the film. First, Eywa directly intervenes to prevent Neytiri from killing Jake when she first discovers him wandering in the forest. She sends a woodsprite that lands on Neytiri's arrow and stops her from releasing it. Soon after, Eywa sends another sign in the form of dozens of woodsprites alighting on Jake. This display of Eywa's interest in Jake persuades Neytiri to bring him to Hometree, where her mother Mo'at, the *tsahìk* "who interprets the will of Eywa" for the Omaticaya, spares his life and determines that the goddess wants him to be trained in the ways of "the people."

That there is a "will of Eywa" suggests that there is an objective right and wrong outside of the contractual obligations between individuals within a state. This objective right and wrong is reflected in the prayers of respect the Na'vi say over animals they have hunted for food: "I see you, brother. Thank you. Your spirit will now be with Eywa, but your body will remain for the People." Hobbes may argue that religion is manufactured by the state as a tool for maintaining order and that there is no divine will beyond the state, but the "will of Eywa" suggests that there are principles beyond the contract to which individuals ought to conform.

"I Was a Warrior Who Dreamed He Could Bring Peace"

But, even if we dismiss the moral implications of Eywa's will, *Avatar* presents us with many other examples of individuals who feel an obligation to others apart from anything imposed by a social contract. Jake's transformation from a soldier who follows orders – because he cares about his duty, or maybe just about the good pay or Quaritch's promise to restore his legs – to a resistance fighter who defends the Omaticaya is the result of his growing sense that the RDA's treatment of the Na'vi is wrong. Feeling bound by principles of honor and justice, he can't justify the forced dislocation of the Omaticaya. Trudy Chacón has a similar moment of self-awareness when she breaks ranks and flies back to base rather than participating in the destruction of Hometree. Grace Augustine and Norm Spellman also feel a sense of obligation to the Na'vi, even though they have no contract with them. All of them recognize moral obligations to others that extend further than Hobbes would allow, in his belief that all obligations are contractual.

Quaritch is the only main character who never displays a sense of remorse, uncertainty, or repentance. But he's such a crass, insensitive villain that we are left with the impression that his perspective is warped and harms his humanity. Quaritch's character is so perverse and vicious that you can see it in his face, his physical scars mimicking the inner scars his soul has suffered as a result of his deeds. His twisted sense of values even causes his own demise at the end of the film. Rather than recognize defeat and accept its terms, he sacrifices himself to his own vile nature: he tries to inflict as much pain and damage as possible, until Neytiri must kill him.

Clearly *Avatar* is making a moral statement about the nature of war and violent conflict rather than staging a nihilistic play in which neither side can be judged right or wrong. Far from sharing the "all's fair in war" outlook of Hobbes and Quaritch, the film offers insights into what makes the actions of the RDA indefensible and the actions of the Na'vi warranted.

"It'll Be Humane. More or Less"

Avatar is laden with images and themes of religion and spirituality. Theology also forms the base of "just war theory." The principles of just war theory were adapted by early Christian thinkers from the natural law theory developed by the Stoics – a group of ancient philosophers who believed that we could look to nature for guidance about what is right and good for human beings. The early Christians turned to just war theory to help resolve a quandary. On the one hand, Jesus, the founder of Christianity, advocated nonviolence and declared that "peacemakers" were blessed. On the other hand, once Christianity became a political force, it had to address society's need to defend itself against enemies. As political leaders sought legitimacy for waging war, Christian theologians were forced to wrestle with questions about when a nation could justly go to war and how a just war should be fought. One of the most prominent thinkers in this tradition, Saint Augustine of Hippo (354–430), shares his name with

Grace Augustine, the exobiologist who heads the Avatar program. Very much in the spirit of "peacemaking," Grace develops a bond with the Na'vi and makes numerous attempts to nudge Selfridge and Quaritch toward peaceful coexistence with the indigenous peoples – and other species – of Pandora.

Just war theory includes two related philosophical doctrines. *Ius ad bellum* is about when it's just to go to war, and *ius in bello* is about what it's just or unjust to do in the conduct of a war. Examining the actions of Selfridge and Quaritch in light of these doctrines helps us to see why they are unjust. *Ius ad bellum* shows us why Selfridge's authorization of force to displace the Omaticaya is wrong, while *ius in bello* exposes Quaritch's battlefield strategies and tactics as inhumane and indefensible.

"Find Me a Carrot That'll Get Them to Move, Otherwise It's Gonna Have to Be All Stick"

The principles of *ius ad bellum* permit the use of force only when certain conditions have been satisfied:

1. there is a *just cause* and *right intention*;
2. war has been declared by a *legitimate political authority*; and
3. violence is a *last resort*, used only after all reasonable attempts at resolving the conflict peacefully have been exhausted.[3]

Let's start by considering whether Selfridge had *just cause* to authorize the use of force against the Omaticaya. When vast deposits of unobtanium – a tremendous source of wealth and energy for human beings – were located under Hometree, was violence a justified response to the Omaticaya's refusal to move?

Ius ad bellum distinguishes between defensive and aggressive uses of force.[4] Wars of aggression are always unjust. Only defensive wars are waged for a just cause. Defending oneself against an aggressor, responding to a wrongful act, and protecting those who can't come to their own defense are all just causes, since they are attempts to prevent, stop, or correct some grave public evil. Using force for material and economic gain at the expense of one's neighbors, on the other hand, is *not* acting with a proper intention and so can't be justified.

The RDA's initial use of force against the Omaticaya was an offensive strike against Hometree, an attempt to clear them out of the way of the large deposits of unobtanium that rested in the ground under the Sacred Tree. The motivation was profit, pure and simple. As Selfridge explains to Jake: "Killing the indigenous looks bad, but there's one thing that shareholders hate more than bad press, and that's a bad quarterly statement."[5] But, from the perspective of just war theory, to attack the Omaticaya for the sake of a "little gray rock," even one that "sells for twenty million a kilo," is to act from an unjust intention and is therefore an unacceptable reason to use force.

Of course, later, after Jake establishes himself as the legendary Taruk Makto ("rider of the taruk") and begins assembling Na'vi clans all across Pandora to defend against the RDA, Quaritch attempts to spin the conflict in terms of security, as though unprovoked Na'vi clans were gathering to attack the RDA facilities for no reason.[6] In the face of this alleged threat, he can claim that a "preemptive attack" is justified as the only means of security. But this argument ignores the fact that the first act of war between the SecOps and the Na'vi came at Quaritch's orders.[7] His actions were aggressively hostile, while the Omaticaya warriors were engaging in a justified resistance to defend Hometree. When the actions of the two parties are compared, it's clear that the use of aggressive force by the RDA was unjustified, while the Na'vi acted acceptably, in self-defense.

A second issue to consider is whether the use of force was justly authorized. In just war theory, a war can be declared only by the proper legal authorities, as specified in a country's laws or constitution.[8] The RDA corporation is a privately held mining firm accountable to its directors and shareholders, not a government entity. Even the security forces of SecOps are nonstate actors, former marines who are now "just hired guns, taking the money, working for the company." Though the RDA would have the right to defend itself against any attack initiated by the Na'vi, they have no right to authorize a first strike. Since Selfridge, as the head of the mining operation, did not have the proper authority to use force against the Na'vi, the RDA's actions were not only unlawful but also unjust.

Finally, a just use of force must always come as a last resort. Superficially, it may seem that Selfridge and Quaritch have their bases covered on this score, since the RDA did make attempts at diplomacy to "negotiate the terms of [the Omaticaya's] resettlement." Selfridge reports that he offered the Na'vi "education, medicine, and roads," adding, in disgust, "they like mud." But, however much he would like to portray himself as a generous benefactor, his philanthropy was just a transparent attempt to manipulate the Na'vi for his own ends – an attempt doomed to failure, since he has nothing the Na'vi want. As Jake sums it up in his video log: "They're not gonna give up their home. They're not gonna make a deal. For what? Lite beer? And blue jeans?" Selfridge had viewed the Avatar program as only a "little puppet show" to "win the hearts and minds of the natives," so that they would begin to trust the RDA corporation and give it access to their sacred lands for mining. Quaritch expressed similar sentiments to Jake when he encouraged him to use his inside track with the Omaticaya to learn "how to force their cooperation or hammer them hard if they won't." Clearly neither Selfridge nor Quaritch were ever interested in "negotiating" with the Na'vi respectfully, as equals.

The insincerity of the RDA's "negotiations" is apparent in the fact that Jake is given only one hour to negotiate the Omaticaya's resettlement before the strike on Hometree. One hour is not enough time to negotiate anything, so the offer is obviously a sham, not a serious attempt at peaceful coexistence. Selfridge is merely paying lip service to the principle of using force only as a last resort. But his token offer does tell us that even he recognizes this principle as legitimate. Similarly, when Quaritch sees Jake and Grace bound as prisoners of the Omaticaya after their plea for relocation is rebuffed, he happily concludes: "Diplomacy has failed." It's clear that this "diplomacy" was a charade that was never supposed to work, but was undertaken only in order to make the subsequent resort to force *seem* more legitimate. War, not peace, was the real aim of their false diplomacy.

"I Was Hoping for Some Sort of Tactical Plan that Didn't Involve Martyrdom"

On all counts, the RDA's attack on the Na'vi fails to satisfy the principles of *ius ad bellum*, which specify when the use of force is acceptable. As we turn now to examine the tactics employed by Quaritch in carrying out the attack, it becomes even more obvious that this war deserves to be condemned as unjust.

Ius in bello is the part of just war theory that dictates what actions are permissible when fighting a war. It contains two broad principles: the principle of discrimination and the principle of proportionality. The principle of discrimination forbids targeting noncombatants and, most importantly, civilians. Only those who are directly engaged in waging hostilities – that is, only military personnel – are legitimate targets. The theory of proportionality begins with a recognition that the "destruction of life and property [is] inherently bad" and proceeds to the conclusion that "military forces should cause no more destruction than strictly necessary to achieve their objectives."[9] In short, gratuitous violence and destruction is wrong, so we shouldn't use military force whenever there are alternative means that would cause less damage but would have similar chances of success. We should always employ the least destructive tactics and weapons that can get the job done.

Did the RDA honor the principle of discrimination? No. In their attack on Hometree, they made no distinction between acceptable and unacceptable targets. Instead the SecOps defined the enemy as the entire Omaticaya clan – and, later, as all the clans of the Na'vi – just because they stood in the way of their procuring the large unobtanium deposits under Hometree. Because the Na'vi identified so closely with the land the RDA sought to conquer, the RDA defined its objective as displacing the entire population. Every member of the tribe was designated as a target, in defiance of the *ius in bello* principle of sparing the noncombatants. Quaritch put in his crosshair the entire Omaticaya population – male and female, young and old, healthy and infirm – when he turned his weapons on the base structure of Hometree.

One might respond that civilian casualties are a regrettable but inevitable part of every war. But the principle of discrimination says that civilian deaths are acceptable only as an indirect result of some legitimate use of force. You should never deliberately set out to kill noncombatants as a military tactic. But that's exactly what Quaritch did by first targeting Hometree and then the Tree of Souls at a time when it was surrounded by countless displaced refugees and noncombatants engaged in a religious ceremony. Given the aim of breaking the Na'vi's spirit and of destroying the basis of their culture, the killing of civilians was part of a deliberately chosen strategy, as important to Quaritch as waging war on the segment of the population that carried arms. Such an act is a violation of the principle of discrimination.

How about the principle of proportionality? Quaritch assures Selfridge that he'll limit the amount of force he'll use. "I'll do it with minimal casualties to the indigenous," he pledges. "I'll drive them out with gas first. It'll be humane. More or less." That's what he says; but his actions belie his words. In reality, the amount of force used by Quaritch is not only disproportionate, but downright gratuitous. Even his rhetoric soon changes from a "humane" concern with minimizing casualties to an eager anticipation of wanton destruction. "We will fight terror with terror," he tells his rallied troops. "The hostiles believe that this mountain stronghold of theirs is protected by their deity. And when we destroy it, we will blast a crater in their racial memory so deep, that they won't come within 1,000 klicks of this place ever again." As part of his terror campaign, he orders his well-armored gunships to open fire with high-tech weaponry on unarmored warriors who are equipped with little more than animal mounts, bows, spears, and knives. Through such a disproportionate use of force, he turns the war into a lopsided slaughter. He also runs roughshod over the principle of proportionality in his planned "shock and awe" campaign, in which a large shuttle was to be rigged with pallets full of explosives to destroy the Tree of Souls. The aim of this carnage was to decimate the Na'vi and to clear a path to the largest unobtanium deposits on Pandora, in the process completely annihilating the basis of Na'vi culture and religion.

The two principles of *ius in bello* make it clear that Quaritch's tactics fall well outside the bounds of justice. Only the *deus ex machina* intervention of Eywa saved the Na'vi from making a noble stand that would have ended in their being slaughtered by the vastly superior arms, armor, and technology of the RDA. The only possible outcome of an RDA victory would have been the complete destruction of the Na'vi way of life for the sake of corporate profit.

"We Will See If Your Insanity Can Be Cured"

From the perspective of the RDA corporation and its representatives, Colonel Miles Quaritch and Parker Selfridge, the use of force is acceptable whenever it's the most efficient means to their ends. Like Hobbes, they recognize no ethical obligations other than those that arise from a contract that binds them to other members of their own society. Outsiders like the Na'vi can be treated however one likes. Removing the Na'vi from their sacred land, destroying the basis of their religion and culture, and even slaughtering them wholesale are actions acceptable to Quaritch and Selfridge, if that's what it takes to access the rich natural resources of their land.

However, when we view their actions in light of the principles of *ius ad bellum* and *ius in bello*, we see that their use of force against the Na'vi was unjust and their tactics were immoral even in the context of warfare. Quaritch and Selfridge may delude themselves into believing that morality has no place in decisions about waging war; but, as we are reminded throughout the movie, "sooner or later you have to wake up."

Notes

1. Thomas Hobbes, *The Leviathan* (London: Penguin Classics, 1968), 188 (Part 1, ch. 13). Hobbes's prose has been adjusted to modern style.
2. Ibid., 188.
3. There are additional principles, often applied to the criteria of *ius ad bellum*, which, while relevant to the events in the film, are not as critical to this evaluation as the rest. The first posits that force is justified only when there is reasonable chance of success without resorting to disproportional tactics. It is possible to imagine that, even with their superior weaponry, the RDA would not be able to repel the fully amassed Na'vi forces. In that case, Quaritch's decision to use offensive force would have been futile and an unjust sacrifice of his soldiers. The colonel even expresses fears about the amassing tribes of the Na'vi assembling under the call of the Toruk Makto, because in "a week's time there might be twenty thousand of them," which would enable them to "overrun [the RDA's] perimeter." His strategic response is a preemptive strike on the Tree of Souls, an unconventional use of massive force in transforming a shuttle into a weapon of mass destruction, which suggests that conventional means of attack have a low, if not unreasonable, probability of success. Likewise, the other principle of *ius ad bellum* is that of proportionality, which considers the benefits of waging war and weighs them against the anticipated harms to all the affected parties (civilians and combatants). Like the concern about right intention and just cause, the benefits that gaining access to resources might bring to the RDA would have to be weighed against the complete annihilation of the spiritual and cultural way of life of the Na'vi – not to mention the countless deaths on both sides and the displacement of the entire Omaticaya clan. It is clear that the harm inflicted is not proportional to the material gain achieved through unfettered access to unobtanium.
4. It is worth noting that the distinction between just and unjust wars along the lines of defensive versus aggressive motivation has been codified in international law in the form of the Charter of the United Nations.

The only internationally sanctioned reason that would make a war just and legal is self-defense.

5. Lest anyone suggest that such motivations are beyond the actual reasons why people wage war, we need only look at the brutal history of colonization and of our contemporary world, in which scholars like Michael T. Klare have documented countless conflicts between states and groups that are over access to oil, water, mineral, and timber resources. Michael T. Klare, *Resource Wars: The New Landscape of Global Conflict* (New York: Henry Holt and Co., 2001). As Jake expressed it, with simple but righteous indignation: "This is how it is done. When people are sitting on shit that you want, you make them your enemy."

6. There are clear parallels here with the war in Iraq, which began in 2003. The US invaded Iraq on the pretext that otherwise Iraq might attack us, or that it might supply weapons of mass destruction to forces like al-Qaeda, which are hostile to the United States. Although there was no connection between the regime of Saddam Hussein and al-Qaeda, nor any weapons of mass destruction found, such arguments were the basis of the perceived threat that served as a pretext to war.

7. Presumably there were other instances of violence between the RDA forces and the Na'vi prior to Jake Sully's arrival. At one point, Selfridge tells Dr. Augustine that her whole program is designed to find a way to allow the RDA to mine unobtanium: "Isn't that the whole point of your little puppet show? You walk like them, you talk like them. We build them a school, teach them English, but after how many years the relations with the indigenous are only getting worse." Her response is to dismiss Selfridge by claiming: "Yeah, well that tends to happen when you use machine guns on them." This dialogue suggests that violence had occurred at some point prior to Jake's arrival, and that it was initiated by the RDA for an undisclosed reason.

8. The rationale for granting to duly appointed public officials the sole power to declare war stems from a certain conception of what constitutes a state and state authority. According to the German sociologist and philosopher Max Weber (1864–1920), a state is "a human community that (successfully) claims the *monopoly of the legitimate use of physical force within a given territory*." If corporate entities or private associations were to lay claim to this right, that would not only undermine the legitimacy of the state to create and enforce rules and establish social order, it would cause a possible breakdown of the social order that would come from those organizations that seek to defy the will of the state through force. See Max Weber, "Politics as a Vocation," in Max Weber, *From Max Weber: Essays in Sociology*, trans. H. H. Gerth and C. Wright Mills (New York: Oxford University Press, 1946), 77–128.

9. Douglas P. Lackey, *The Ethics of War and Peace* (New Jersey: Prentice Hall, 1989), 31.

The Community and the Individual in *Avatar*

Dale Murray

Avatar is many things: high-styled entertainment, a nature narrative, an environmental allegory, a reflection on religion and spirituality, a global warning, a love story, and more. But *Avatar* also illustrates two very different general views on how we should govern ourselves.

The first view is *individualism*. Individualists think that the primary function of the state is to protect individual rights and, in this way, to open up the moral space we need if we are to make meaningful lives for ourselves. This is roughly the goal of the liberal political tradition – which is called "liberal" because it emphasizes the importance of individual liberties, not because its adherents necessarily fall on the left side of the contemporary political spectrum on every issue. In contrast to individualism, *communitarianism* believes that the state ought to help us preserve our traditions, debate the meaning of the good, and shape ourselves into virtuous citizens. Communitarians hold that it "takes a village" to cultivate good citizens and virtuous people. Thus communitarians often accuse individualists of devaluing the community and of neglecting its role in shaping the identity, moral principles, and politics of individuals.

"We'd Like to Talk to You about Taking Over His Contract"

The philosopher Thomas Hobbes (1588–1679) falls in the individualist camp. He argued that human beings were by nature free and equal, originally under no authority except for their own individual

Avatar and Philosophy: Learning to See, First Edition. Edited by George A. Dunn.
© 2014 John Wiley & Sons, Inc. Published 2014 by John Wiley & Sons, Inc.

consciences. But, without some kind of state authority, human existence is far too perilous, given how prone we are to get embroiled in conflicts that always run the risk of escalating into violence. This "state of nature" – our original condition before the establishment of a central government – rather than being the peaceful idyll imagined by some, quickly devolves into a "war of all against all" in which, as Hobbes famously put it, our lives are "solitary, poor, nasty, brutish, and short," not unlike the description of life on Pandora "beyond those fences" that Colonel Miles Quaritch presents in his "old school safety brief" for the new arrivals.[1] Consequently the imperative of self-preservation makes it rational for us to organize politically and to surrender some of our natural freedoms in exchange for a more secure existence.

According to Hobbes, governments come into existence when rational individuals enter into a contract (or "covenant," as he put it) with each other to avoid the terrible chaos of the state of nature. Essentially, the contract says that I promise not to stab you in the back on condition that you promise not to do the same thing to me. Extending this idea to include everyone, each one of us gives up our originally unlimited right to do whatever we want and agrees to abide by the rules of society. The role of the government is to enforce this "social contract" and to protect us from each other, permitting us to build the trust necessary for social cooperation, cultural advancement, and economic enterprise. This idea of a social contract has been very important to the liberal political tradition. After all, if we start from the primacy of individual rights, a voluntary contract seems to be the *only* thing that can give legitimacy to state authority.[2]

John Locke (1632–1704), another important philosopher in the liberal political tradition, agreed with many of the essentials of Hobbes's account of the social contract but added a new emphasis on the importance of protecting private property.[3] Addressing the question of how an individual could gain an exclusive right to some item like a parcel of land when all the Earth was originally our common possession, Locke formulated what has come to be known as the labor theory of property. Since we "own" ourselves and, by extension, our own labor, we acquire property by mixing our labor with a piece of nature, such as a plot of land, to produce something of value. As the fruit of our own labor, that product is rightfully our own. Such an argument could be made by the Resources Development Administration (RDA) corporation to assert their ownership of that corner of Pandora on which they erected Hell's Gate, the facility that houses their spaceport and headquarters. Were they to succeed in mining the unobtanium deposits on Pandora, they might also appeal to Locke's theory to defend their ownership of the extracted ore that, in their minds at least, would otherwise have gone to waste. Putting land to use and not wasting resources are morally commendable goals according to Locke.

With the invention of money, it became possible for people to accumulate large stores of property and to enter into profitable commercial transactions with others, which Locke believed we should be free to do as long as those transactions remain voluntary. For this reason many people regard Locke as an early theorist of free market capitalism. Corporations like the RDA provide an opportunity for shareholders to pool their finances and to further their own interests by making a profit. In many places, including the United States, corporations can be regarded as "persons" under the law and be granted many of the same rights as individuals, such as the right to sue and enter into contracts. In this way even corporations can be individual economic and political actors with rights that the government is bound to protect. For Locke, one of the most important of these rights – coming in third place, after the rights to life and liberty – is the right to own private property and to dispose of it as one sees fit. In fact many of Locke's intellectual descendants believe that protecting private property is the cornerstone of liberal politics.[4]

Contracts and investments are important catalysts for the action of *Avatar*. The former marine Jake Sully is brought to Pandora as a replacement for his twin brother Tommy, a scientist who had been training for a mission as an avatar pilot for Dr. Grace Augustine's research team on Pandora but was murdered in a robbery before he could ship out to join the others. Agents of the RDA approach Jake as his brother's mortal remains – all that's left of the corporation's "significant investment" in him – are ushered into an incinerator. "We'd like to talk to you about taking over his contract," one of them tells the grieving marine – who, as his brother's genetic match, is the only suitable substitute to pilot his avatar. Jake is promised a "fresh start on a new world" and offered pay described as "*very* good."

"Think You Can Do That for Me, Son?"

For individualistic philosophers like Hobbes and Locke, the primary way in which we come to have duties to others is by entering into contracts with them. Consider the relationship between Quaritch and Jake. Quaritch, needing "intel" on the Na'vi, presents Jake with "an opportunity both timely and unique": the prospect of being the colonel's own "recon gyrene in an avatar body," of winning the Na'vi's trust, and of gathering information on them "right in the hostile's camp." Jake is a paraplegic, so in return Quaritch makes this promise: "You get me what I need, I'll see to it you get your legs back when you rotate home." In essence, they enter into a verbal contract. Later in the film, when Quaritch realizes that Jake has cast his lot with the Omaticaya and is actively working against the SecOps, the Colonel is furious. For Jake has not only violated the terms of his personal and professional agreement with Quaritch; he has done something much worse. "Hey, Sully," Quaritch taunts his opponent in the middle of the climactic single combat scene, "how's it feel to betray your own race?" (Jake responds by baring his teeth and hissing at the colonel, Na'vi style.) In Quaritch's mind, Jake has broken with the social contract, reverted to the "state of nature," and made himself fair game for attack.

Quaritch and his SecOps have also struck a deal with the RDA corporation. The SecOps provides security for the RDA and, when more peaceful measures fail, are on hand to drive the Omaticaya from Hometree, under which lie the rich unobtanium deposits that brought the RDA to Pandora in the first place. In return, the RDA pays their salaries. The Avatar program also owes its existence on Pandora to what comes down to a contractual arrangement with the RDA in which both the scientists and the corporation get something they want. Dr. Grace Augustine and her team get to study Pandora's flora, fauna, and indigenous people up close. In return, they provide the RDA with information that might be useful in negotiations with the Na'vi over access to Pandora's mineral resources. When Grace complains to RDA administrator Parker Selfridge about his interference with her department, he reminds her of the bargain she struck with the RDA in return for funding her research. "Look, aren't you supposed to be winning the hearts and minds of the natives?" he admonishes her. "Isn't that the whole point of your little puppet show?"

But, for a contract to happen, each party has to have something to offer, something the other party wants. In the case of the social contract, Hobbes thought that everyone involved would recognize the value of exchanging at least some of his or her freedoms for enhanced security. But, as Jake learns from his experience of living among the Na'vi, not everyone sees his or her relationships with others primarily in contractual terms, nor does everyone want the things that a wealthy and powerful corporation like the RDA has to offer.[5] "They're not gonna make a deal," he reports in his video log about the Na'vi. "For what? Lite beer? And blue jeans? There's nothing that we have that they want." Quaritch draws an ominous conclusion from Jake's assessment of the situation. "Since a deal can't be made," he reasons, "I guess things get real simple."

Anyone who has watched *Avatar* knows that we're supposed to sympathize with the Na'vi. The motives of most of the human beings on Pandora have nothing to do with establishing community with the Na'vi. Their aims are exploitative – to get access to the unobtanium beneath their village, by peaceful means if possible, by force if necessary. Without a social contract between itself and the Na'vi to restrain its actions, the RDA corporation has no good Hobbesian, individualistic, or self-interested reason to abstain from violence when negotiations fail. This is one unfortunate consequence of a philosophy that encourages us to think that we, as individuals, ought to strive first and foremost for our own benefit, regardless of whether the "individual" in question is an ordinary person or an impersonal corporation. When self-interest is taken too far, the result can be domination, the legitimate interests of others being a prime casualty.

On Pandora we see imperialism in its most basic form: grabbing the resources of a colonized people right out from under them and using them solely for the benefit of the more powerful occupiers. The SecOps are there to protect the interests of the RDA corporation and to enforce their dominance over their vastly outmatched foes, who won't be harmed so long as they move off the rich bed of unobtanium that lies below Hometree. While individualism may not *always* lead to the ruthless forms of capitalism and imperialism depicted in the film, it is nonetheless a real danger.

"Protect the People"

When Neytiri finds her mortally wounded father, Eytukan, crumpled on the burning forest floor after the SecOps attack on Hometree, he hands her his bow and utters his dying words: "Protect the People." "The people" is, in his mind, something greater than himself, greater than any individual. This emphasis on protecting the community and not merely furthering the private interests of individuals is one of several striking differences between communitarian political philosophy and classical contractarian liberalism. Communitarians don't dismiss individuals as unimportant, but they do tend to regard the individual and the community as inseparable. Most communitarians would argue that the individual is in large part defined by his or her relationship to some wider community and its traditions, so that we can't even really understand who a given individual is outside of the cultural context that gives his or her life its content.

Consider, for example, Neytiri's mother Mo'at. Can we really understand who she is in separation from her role as the *tsahik* and spiritual leader of the Omaticaya clan? And can we understand that role without also appreciating her significance as the interpreter of the will of Eywa, or the singular importance of Eywa within the traditions of the Na'vi? As communitarian philosopher Michael Sandel has observed, we don't normally think of ourselves as isolated individuals, but "as members of this family or community or nation or people, as bearers of this history, as sons or daughters of that revolution, as citizens of this republic."[6] In this respect, we are all like Jake, whose identity comes to be defined by his status as "a son of the Omaticaya."

Communitarians take tradition seriously, for the communities that shape and define us have both a history and a future, tradition being the bright thread that connects us across time. The Omaticaya remind us of the importance of maintaining our bond with past and future generations. After Jake's initiation into the Omaticaya clan, Neytiri takes him to Utraya Mokri – "the Tree of Voices, the voices of our ancestors" – telling him: "This is a place where prayers are heard. And sometimes answered." As Jake entwines his neural queue with one of the vines of the tree, he hears the songs, conversations, and laughter of past generations of Omaticaya. "They live, Jake, within Eywa," Neytiri tells him. "You are Omaticaya now," she adds, indicating that he is now part of a tradition that connects him with the voices he hears. To break that link with the past would mean the end of the Omaticaya people. As Norm Spellman remarks while Quaritch's SecOps team prepares for what they hope will be a decisive assault on the Na'vi: "If they [the SecOps] get to the Tree of Souls, it's over. That's their direct line to Eywa, their ancestors. It'll destroy them." It will destroy them not just in the sense of inflicting a profound psychological trauma, but in the even more literal sense of obliterating an essential component of their identity.

Communitarians also care deeply about communities of memory and about preserving a shared history – but not because they're compulsive archivists. They want to keep alive the memory of the past as a source of ideals that the community should strive to preserve and carry forward into the future, for the good of all its members. These ideals – along with the stories, rituals, and celebrations that convey them – bring hope and meaning to our lives. We see in the example of the Toruk Macto an illustration of how these ideals may work. On Pandora, the "baddest cat in the sky" is the fierce, pterodactyl-like toruk or "last shadow" – so called because it attacks from above, making its shadow the last thing that its unfortunate prey will ever see. Neytiri recounts to Jake the story, well known among the Na'vi, of how her "grandfather's grandfather" was chosen by a toruk to become "Toruk Macto, rider of last shadow," something that "has happened only five times since the time of the First Songs." The mighty Toruk Macto is celebrated by the Na'vi for having "brought the clans together in a time of great sorrow." This memory resonates so deeply with the Omaticaya that, when Jake appears from out of the sky on the back of a toruk, he becomes a powerful emblem of hope for the beleaguered clan, inspiring them to unite with the other Na'vi once again in fighting to defend their way of life.

Bio-Communitarianism

A communitarian outlook is thoroughly embedded in the political and social structure of the Omaticaya. But, beyond that, they're communitarian in an even deeper sense, which we could call *bio-communitarianism*. The Omaticaya are a uniquely communitarian society, whose communal bonds link them not only to each other, but also to the flora and fauna of the forest where they live. Teaching Jake the ways of her people, Neytiri introduces him to the dangerous rite of passage whereby a hunter bonds with an ikran – another aerial predator, known to the "sky people" as a "mountain banshee." As she explains, once a hunter and his or her ikran choose each other, the *tsaheylu* – the bond between them – is made for life and the ikran will never bond with another hunter. The ikran becomes, in effect, an extension of the hunter, who reaches out to include another part of the Pandoran biosphere into his or her own identity.

The Omaticaya also stage elaborate religious ceremonies in which the entire clan appears to participate, in a trance-like state. We witness one such ritual when a mortally wounded Grace is brought to the Tree of Souls, in hopes that Eywa will allow her to pass permanently into her avatar body. While praying to Eywa, the members of the clan join hands, sway vigorously in unison, and literally reach into the ground through their neural queues, joining themselves to the roots of the sacred tree. Meanwhile, brightly glowing fibers reach up out of the ground to embrace Grace and her avatar. This extraordinary image evokes how intensely – and literally – the Omaticaya are rooted in their forest home. The spiritual connection between the Omaticaya and their home is so strong and intimate that it creates an exceptionally holistic communitarian entity with a biologically diverse membership – what we could call *a bio-communitarian homeland*.

While most traditional communities aren't attached to the land quite as literally as the Omaticaya, the communitarian political tradition has also stressed the importance of *place*. The attachment to a certain geographical location, with its unique terrain and history – a *homeland* – has more than some mawkish sentimental value. Indeed, for many traditional communities, there's a rich connection between the people and the land they inhabit – a connection that shapes their way of making a living, their daily practices, and even their outlook on the world. This is expressed sometimes in romantic anthems and nationalistic slogans that pay homage to geographical features that are laden with meaning (like "purple mountains majesty"). Unfortunately the Nazis have poisoned the expression "blood and soil"; nonetheless, it does reflect the belief of many traditional communities that their identity is bound up with shared descent ("blood") and a shared homeland ("soil"). Communitarians don't necessarily treat ethnicity as the social glue, though this has been its role for many historical communities. But the more important insight is that an individual can come to feel like part of a greater whole not only through interpersonal bonds, but also through attachment to a particular place.[7] By and large, the "sky people" find it hard to understand why the Omaticaya are so attached to Hometree – "I don't know about you, but I see a lot of trees! They can move!" cries Selfridge – failing to see that displacing the Omaticaya from their land is tantamount to dislodging them from their identity, so intimately bound together are the two. *The Omaticaya simply can't be the people they are in any other location.* As Norm correctly observes, to destroy their home is to destroy *them*.

A Cautionary Tale

Avatar offers us a cautionary tale to remind us that a selfish individualist ethics can blind us to the importance of other people, of our communities, and of the living world of which we are a part, even to the point of threatening their (and our) very survival. *Avatar* also reminds us that the moral community need not be restricted to a single race – or even to a single species. The Omaticaya see themselves as part of an extended community that comprises not only "the people" but the natural world as well. They care about all the members of their community (whether these walk on two legs or on six) and they criticize the "sky people" for caring only about themselves. The "sky people" think of themselves and others as isolated atoms, competing for scarce resources and always trying to negotiate the best deal for themselves. They don't *see* the deep interconnections we have with each other, with the past, and with the environment and the "network of energy that flows through all living things."

In the end, all of this has more than just otherworldly significance. Indigenous groups here on Earth have tried to explain to generations of colonizers the significance of their rituals, their spirituality, and their sense of belonging to a place. *Avatar* brings home the importance of those values in a powerful and memorable way.

Acknowledgments

I thank George Dunn for his thorough editing job. I have incorporated many of his suggestions into this chapter.

Notes

1. Thomas Hobbes, *Leviathan*, ed. C. B. Macpherson (New York: Penguin, 1968), 186.
2. For more on Hobbes, see Chapter 13 by Joseph J. Foy.
3. John Locke, *The Second Treatise of Government*, in his *Two Treatises of Government*, ed. Peter Laslett (Cambridge: Cambridge University Press, 1960), 287–288.
4. Locke is also famous for his influential theory of personal identity. See Chapter 10 by Kevin S. Decker.
5. In Chapter 1 of this book, George A. Dunn and Nicolas Michaud contrast the contract-based approaches to ethics with the feminine care ethic of the Na'vi.
6. Michael Sandel, *Liberalism and the Limits of Justice* (Cambridge: Cambridge University Press, 1981), 179.
7. The notable exception to this is the Jewish people. Their "rootlessness" is one of the things that made them anathema to the Nazis. This example reminds us that the tie to a specific piece of real estate is not a necessary condition for cultivating a communitarian ethos. I thank George Dunn for reminding me about this example.

15

Avatar and Colonialism

Nathan Eckstrand

The thrill of victory washed through the audience as we watched the Na'vi finally repelling the human invaders. At last the greedy administrator Parker Selfridge and the menacing Colonel Miles Quaritch would be deported from the world of Pandora, their machinations no longer threatening its indigenous inhabitants. Jake Sully had repelled the forces of the "sky people."

When we first met the former marine, he was hardly a peacenik or a lover of exploited peoples. But by the end of the movie he had changed, thanks to a lesson in the horrors that colonization visits upon colonized peoples. Jake saw up close how the human colonizers ravaged the local environment, tortured and killed the animals, and treated with contempt the cares and beliefs of the Na'vi people – just to acquire the precious mineral unobtanium. With Neytiri's help, Jake developed a moral compass that refused to accept the destruction that the colonization of Pandora brought and that led him to take up arms against the corporate and military forces sent to Pandora from Earth. Viewed from the perspective of Jake's transformation over the course of the film, *Avatar* looks like a film that advocates for the little guy.

But what about the other perspectives found in the movie? Is *Avatar* opposed to colonialism in all its forms? Or does colonialism subtly creep its way back in, even as Jake, Neytiri, Grace Augustine, Norm Spellman, and the Na'vi courageously fend off the technological prowess of the colonizers? To answer these questions we'll need to examine colonialism, how it functions, and what philosophers mean when they argue that a form of colonialism persists to this day, even after most colonized countries have officially regained their national sovereignty.

Avatar and Philosophy: Learning to See, First Edition. Edited by George A. Dunn.
© 2014 John Wiley & Sons, Inc. Published 2014 by John Wiley & Sons, Inc.

Cutting Pandora into Two

Franz Fanon (1925–1961) knew from personal experience the anguish of colonization. His experience of living in colonial Martinique, Algeria, Tunisia, and elsewhere is not unlike the experiences of the Na'vi during their fight for independence. As a trained psychiatrist and journalist who worked in French hospitals as well as among revolutionaries, Fanon – like Jake – was able to straddle the divide between colonizers and colonized, seeing the conflict from both sides. Just as Jake's acceptance by both Quaritch and the Na'vi allows him to reveal Quaritch's fighting methods to the Na'vi so they can plan their counterattack, Fanon's experience as he grew up in a French colony and his subsequent revolutionary activities provided him with enough perspective to develop a handbook on the effects of colonialism – one that included possible countermeasures to combat those effects. But what specific problems did Fanon see in colonialism that led him to become such a prominent advocate for its abolition?

In *The Wretched of the Earth* Fanon discusses the most familiar and visible element of colonialism: direct military control of lands, resources, and peoples. For Fanon, the colonial world is split into two, one half being occupied by the colonized, the other by the colonizers. The line between these two worlds is the military, which keeps the colonized peoples in their place and prevents them from reaching the colonizers. In turn, the colonizers never venture directly to the place of the colonized, preferring instead to send policemen and soldiers. As Fanon explains:

> The colonial world is cut in two. The dividing line, the frontiers are shown by barracks and police stations. In the colonies it is the policeman and the soldier who are the official, instituted, go-betweens, the spokesperson of the settler and his rule of oppression … [T]he policeman and the soldier, by their immediate presence and their frequent and direct action maintain contact with the native and advise him by means of the rifle butts and napalm not to budge. It is obvious here that the agents of government speak the language of pure force.[1]

Avatar portrays this aspect of colonialism well, as Selfridge never engages with the Na'vi himself, preferring instead to send Quaritch and his SecOp forces. Aside from Jake and the scientists who appear to have been the Na'vi's primary human contacts in the past, the only contact the Na'vi have with the "sky people" is through the SecOps. These mercenaries don't use reason or dialogue to engage the Na'vi but rather gunships, rockets, and bulldozers. Hell's Gate and the Na'vi's world are sharply segregated from each other – by the available technology and building materials, by the relative material luxury that the "sky people" enjoy, and, finally, by the very biology that allows the Na'vi to survive on Pandora in areas where human beings cannot. Speaking metaphorically of the colonial world, Fanon says that "this world cut in two is inhabited by two different species."[2] His statement is literally true of colonized Pandora.

Within such a sundered world, what type of response is possible from those seeking to tear down the dividing wall that separates the colonizers from the colonized? Since diplomacy seems doomed to failure, Fanon argues for the importance of communal struggles for liberation – struggles that will most likely involve violence and that he felt were valuable for helping the colonized to reject colonial values and to develop a shared history.[3] The Na'vi are never fully colonized in the way Fanon experienced in the French colonies, although the Na'vi have been unsuccessfully targeted for colonization. Nonetheless, in the Na'vi's fight against the corporate and military forces we can hear echoes of the struggle that Fanon advocates. Recognizing that negotiation with the "sky people" is not an option, Jake, Neytiri, and the other Na'vi come together to oppose the invaders violently and, in so doing, they develop a sense of solidarity in opposition to the colonizing forces.

In response to the violence visited upon colonized peoples, Fanon believed the natives were within their rights to respond with their own form of positive, *constructive* violence – that is, violence that builds a community instead of tearing it apart.

> But it so happens that for the colonized people this violence, because it constitutes their only work, invests their character with positive and creative qualities. The practice of violence binds them together as a whole, since each individual forms a violent link in the great chain, a part of the great organism of violence which has surged upward in reaction to the settler's violence in the beginning.[4]

The Na'vi already have a well-developed sense of community when the movie starts – in this way they are distinct from Fanon's colonized. However, the struggle within the movie certainly reaffirms that sense of community, while at the same time incorporating Jake within it. In fact, since Jake was able to involve various Na'vi tribes in the struggle, it is even possible that some tribal animosities were resolved and a global sense of solidarity newly created. While violence is not always the optimal tactic given the tragic loss of life it produces on both sides, both Fanon and the Na'vi recognize its potential cleansing power and its ability to organically generate a new, more unified world in its aftermath.

Building Roads for "Blue Monkeys"

Yet the mechanisms that enact and perpetuate colonialism involve more than just direct military control, as Fanon pointed out in an earlier book, *Black Skin, White Masks.* One of Fanon's major contributions to philosophical thought was to reveal how colonizers are able to affect the shared identity of a colonized people through something as simple as linguistic practices. Language is used every day in multiple contexts and situations, so it's an excellent way to reassert control over a population by instilling in it a sense of inferiority or enslavement. Everyone is familiar with racial slurs; but the harm done by these words goes beyond the disrespect they show. Racial slurs compel the person at whom they're aimed to accept a damaging conception of who that person is supposed to be. Were Selfridge's portrayal's of the Na'vi as "blue monkeys" and "fly-bitten savages that live in a tree" to be heard by the Na'vi, it would indicate to them that they're meant to live out in the jungle, in squalor and ignorance. Even if the Na'vi were to hear and reject this claim, suffering such comparisons constantly would surely take a toll upon their confidence.[5] The barrier separating people like Selfridge from the Na'vi keeps the latter from having to endure the verbal slings and arrows that are the everyday experience of colonized people on our planet.

A final element of colonialism that we need to consider is often construed by those in favor of colonialism as a justification of it, namely the idea that the colonizers are helping the colonized through their good deeds and services. In *Avatar* this appears most prominently in Selfridge's attempt to justify his violent actions toward the Na'vi by arguing that the presence of the "sky people" is a good thing because of the roads they've built, the schools they've staffed, the medicine they've provided, and the overall improvement in the quality of life they've offered. In a rationalization resembling the arguments used by real colonizers, Selfridge implies that the unobtanium the "sky people" want is rightfully theirs due to the ways in which they've benefited the Na'vi. (In Selfridge's first onscreen interaction with Grace, he talks about "winning the hearts and minds of the natives" so as to be able to access the unobtanium.) While there's something to be said for helping another people by constructing schools, roads, and hospitals (assuming the people in question *wants* them), Fanon points out the negative side to it that's not being addressed: the dependency and inferiority complex that it creates.

The colonization of a society, even if it includes providing new goods and services, does not enrich that society, as the colonizers often claim. Rather colonization erases the old society, replacing it with a new one that makes the natives dependent on the settlers for these new goods and services to which they've become accustomed. The colonized may even become dependent upon the colonizer for their sense of self. The colonizer claims superiority, while forcing the colonized into continued subjugation. As Fanon writes:

> I start suffering from not being a white man insofar as the white man discriminates against me; turns me into a colonized subject; robs me of any value or originality; tells me I am a parasite in the world, that I should toe the line of the white world as quickly as possible, and "that we are brute beasts; that we are a walking manure, a hideous forerunner of tender cane and silky cotton, that I have no place in the world." ... As we have seen, the white man is governed by a complex of authority, a complex of leadership, whereas the [colonized] is governed by a complex of dependency.[6]

The Resources Development Administration (RDA) corporation obviously hopes that the Na'vi will become so dependent on them that it will be possible to bribe the Na'vi off their unobtanium-rich land. While the Na'vi had allowed the "sky people" to provide at least one service for them in the past – namely Grace's school, where some of them have learned English – and are in due course persuaded to allow human beings back into their camp, they never fall into the dependency trap that Fanon warns against. Receiving goods and services from the colonizers may be helpful in the short run, but it becomes dangerous over time as it robs a people of its independence and makes it reliant on the help of outsiders. True freedom and independence requires not taking the goods and services – or even too many of the ideas – of the colonizers, but learning instead how to subsist, survive, and excel on one's own.

Refusing to accept the colonizers' values, the Na'vi reject the crass consumerism and exploitation of nature embodied by the human lust for unobtanium, reaffirming their respect for Eywa and for the interconnection of all its life. The horrors visited upon colonized peoples can't be papered over with empty promises about how a better world will be possible if only the natives will accept colonial rule. Selfridge's cheap rationalization of why his meddling is justified – "I mean, we try to give them medicine, education, roads. But no, no, no, they like mud" – is seen by the Na'vi for exactly what it is: a crass attempt to bribe them, so that the corporation can reap the benefits of stealing Pandora's natural wealth.

Concluding *The Wretched of the Earth* with a call to action, Fanon describes the task of those who fight colonialism:

> The human condition, plans for mankind, and collaboration between men in those tasks which increase the sum total of humanity are new problems, which demand true inventions. Let us decide not to imitate Europe; let us combine our muscles and our brains in a new direction.[7]

When the Na'vi realize the true intentions of the corporate and military powers, they're able to oppose the colonialist influence on their world. By the time the credits roll, they have removed the corrupting human influence without succumbing to the various pitfalls of Fanon's colonialism.

"I'd Say We Understand Them Just Fine, Thanks to Jake Here"

Fanon's analysis of the psychological effects of colonialism influenced many thinkers, who have expanded his critique to investigate other ways in which colonialism can manifest itself – apart from direct colonial rule or military control. These ways – which may involve economic, social, or other forms of domination – are termed "neocolonialist." One of the most important thinkers of neocolonialism is Edward Said (1935–2003), whose major work *Orientalism* catalogues how Western knowledge about the history and culture of the East (the "Orient") has allowed – and continues to allow – colonialism to occur.

Said (pronounced Sa-yeed) described his work as "close textual readings whose goal was to reveal the dialectic between individual text or writer and the complex collective formation to which his work is a contribution";[8] and as an "intellectual genealogy."[9] In layman terms, he analyzes the writings of a number of different authors in a given historical period to show how the knowledge they collectively produce contains certain biases, which in turn create and sustain prejudices within their society. In particular, he looks at how nineteenth- and twentieth-century Western explorers, intellectuals, and politicians have discussed the history and culture of the Far and Near East. According to Said, before we can really understand Western attitudes and actions toward the East, we must discard the idea that knowledge is always dispassionate and neutral. Instead we need to appreciate how so-called "facts" and concepts can play a political role, even if their originators don't realize that they do.[10] Consequently his chief criticism of Western explorers, intellectuals, and politicians isn't that they're deliberately untruthful or inaccurate. Rather Said is mainly interested in how their various statements about the East have helped to enable colonial practices.[11]

We can explore this idea that knowledge has political implications by looking at some of the ways in which knowledge is generated and used in *Avatar*. Consider the use that Quaritch and Selfridge make of the scientific observations Jake recorded at Grace's behest: They conclude that no diplomatic solution is possible and that military action is necessary. But Quaritch and Selfridge are both on record with derogatory statements about the Na'vi. Moreover, they both work for a capitalist corporation that seeks to acquire Pandora's unobtanium and, as a result, they view the mineral primarily as a commodity and anything standing in their way as an obstacle. Their worldview is necessitated by their roles within a capitalist enterprise. So when they hear in Jake's video log that the Na'vi will never leave Hometree, they do what their role in the system require and send in the bulldozers. Neither Quaritch nor Selfridge is acting solely on solid, unbiased knowledge; both their concepts – that the Na'vi are "savage" or "fly-bitten" – and their facts – that the Na'vi do not want any human goods – are put to service of a larger economic system.

It's obvious that Quaritch and Selfridge are biased – they are the major colonial figures in the movie. But can we see biased knowledge at work in any of the other major characters? Let's take Grace, a scientist who's made her career by developing and testing knowledge about the Na'vi and Pandora's wildlife. Grace works for the RDA, so she's part of the same capitalist system as Quaritch and Selfridge. But she's also closely wedded to a scientific worldview reflected in the scientific language that laces her descriptions of Pandora. For example, instead of describing the neural connections under the forest floor as "bonds" with "Eywa," she describes them as a "global network" that the Na'vi can "access" in order to "upload and download data." Both descriptions are accurate, but the difference in vocabulary and meta phors reflects the different purposes they serve. One way of speaking allows the Na'vi to see themselves as part of a larger entity that includes all life on Pandora, while the other suggests a more impersonal understanding, which sees the planet more like a computer. Despite Grace's intentions, her description of Pandora as computer-like might even make it easier for decision makers to rationalize the destruction of the planet, since it's really just a piece of hardware, a mere thing.

More distressing is how Grace's "knowledge" leads her to view the Na'vi as objects to be studied and evaluated. It is true that Grace and her colleagues have benevolent intentions toward the Na'vi, but they still display attitudes that indicate that they don't see the Na'vi as equal partners – either in the study of Pandora or in its future development. In her role as an exobiologist, Grace is not required to consider how the human occupation of Pandora might affect the well-being of the Na'vi. Her task is simply to observe, quantify, and analyze data about the flora and fauna of Pandora. As a result, some of her interactions with the Na'vi suggest that she sees them as mere objects of study and not subjects with unique capabilities, desires, and interests. Said believes that Western investigators of Eastern history and culture, so-called "Orientalists," have adopted a similar perspective toward the "Oriental" people they study:

> The Oriental is given as fixed, stable, in need of investigation, in need even of knowledge about himself. No dialectic is either desired or allowed. There is a source of information (the Oriental) and a source of knowledge (the Orientalist), in short, a writer and a subject matter otherwise inert.[12]

Grace, luckily, is shaken loose from this worldview and thrown into action by her horror at the atrocities that Quaritch and Selfridge commit against the Na'vi. Although a scientist by profession, she transcends the worldview imposed by her job, to become a fighter against the colonial powers.[13]

Leaving Pandora

Quaritch, Selfridge, and Grace all generate knowledge that contains prejudices. This happens not because – or, in the case of Quaritch and Selfridge, not *only* because – they're malevolent, but because of how their jobs, environments, and socioeconomic backgrounds shape their outlook. But, if we accept Said's claim that everyone operates from a context that could prejudice or skew our perceptions, then there is always a danger that our "knowledge" might contain some biases. This can help us understand the phenomenon of "neocolonialism," as it is possible for a biased knowledge to perpetuate a colonial situation long after colonizing forces have left. Said gives many examples, but I will choose just one to illustrate this point.

According to Said, one of the most insidious myths – often presented as knowledge – about the East is the claim that people from the area are ignorant, violent, or impotent. This myth was used by the British and the French in the 1800s to justify their occupation of much of the East for the purposes of exploiting local resources, establishing schools for native children to raise them as Christians, and instituting Western legal and justice systems. More recently, it has been used by those Americans who mouth the refrain that Islam is a violent religion whose influence in the Middle East must be destroyed.[14] Thoroughly biased knowledge about the East is used to justify discriminatory economic systems, social structures, and individual perceptions, which can result in the restoration of second-class citizenship for former colonial subjects even after direct rule and military domination by the West has ended.

Imagine, for example, what would've happened had the "sky people" not been forced off Pandora at the end of the movie, but allowed to stay instead. Imagine how their capitalist and scientific worldviews might have determined their relationship with the Na'vi. Economic, social, and political structures could have easily developed that treated the Na'vi and their world as commodities (as dictated by capitalism) or as objects for scientific research (as dictated by a scientific methodology). These "neocolonial" structures could be established without any of the gunfire that normally accompanies colonization, but they could be just as effective in ensuring the continued domination of the Na'vi by the "sky people."

"White Savior" in a Blue Body

In the end, what lessons about colonialism does *Avatar* offer? Director James Cameron is on record stating that the movie "asks us to open our eyes and truly see others, respecting them even though they are different, in the hope that we may find a way to prevent conflict and live more harmoniously on this world."[15] There's no doubt that such a message is conveyed by the movie. In the end, those "sky people" who are outwardly dismissive or violent toward the Na'vi are forcibly ejected from Pandora. Those who have opened their eyes to the evils of imperialism and corporate greed are allowed to stay. The Na'vi continue their idyllic existence in communion with Eywa. All this adds up to a strong message against exploitation and discrimination. But is that the only message about colonialism the movie sends?

While I applaud *Avatar* for the outward message of anti-colonialism, I think that beneath the surface of the movie a subtle colonialist message goes unnoticed. For, while we can all agree that to stereotype an entire people as ignorant or vulgar is wrong, it's equally problematic to stereotype them by using bucolic or idyllic images. In both cases they're marginalized in a way that makes an actual dialogue across cultures impossible. For all their nobility and grace, the Na'vi perpetuate old stereotypes about native peoples: they live a primitive lifestyle in harmony with nature, they sport outlandish jewelry and hairstyles, they're uninterested in learning about others or venturing beyond their own borders, and they worship the spirits of plants and animals. The difference is that, whereas colonizers saw these traits as symptoms of ignorance, *Avatar* idolizes them as signs of wisdom and goodness. The Na'vi are admired for these traits; but they are not depicted as capable of fully understanding or interpreting them by themselves. So, while within the movie the Na'vi have an intuitive grasp of the planetary ecosystem that we can envy, only the "sky people" – specifically, the scientists – are able to comprehend properly what Na'vi intuition reveals. Standing outside the human community of rational knowers, the Na'vi are still seen as *other* and the sundered colonial world remains, albeit in a different form.

In addition, *Avatar*'s narrative shows the Na'vi as incapable of saving themselves: it takes Jake's knowledge, ingenuity, and bravery to convince them to form an effective plan of attack against the colonizing forces on Pandora. No other Na'vi tries to unify the various tribes by attempting to ride the toruk, even though they were all

facing the same threat to their very existence. No other Na'vi offers
the prayer to Eywa that moves her to rally all the planet's living creatures
in defense of Pandora. Finally, it is Jake rather than an experienced
Na'vi who is found worthy of leading the tribe. The second half of
Avatar is pervaded by the idea that a white man – in this case, Jake – is
the one most capable of saving the natives. The Na'vi, while capable
of mounting some defense on their own, become effective only
when Jake takes the reins of power. In short, the Na'vi are capable
of communing with nature and of coexisting with the "sky people,"
but only Jake (aided by the scientists and by one or two deserters
from the SecOps) is able to master nature and defeat the "sky people."
This is the narrative of the "white savior," which both Fanon and Said
believe lurks at the heart of colonialism and makes the natives appear
impotent. Despite the many negative characteristics of colonialism
that *Avatar* helps us to identify and critique, by the end of the movie
the specter of colonialism unfortunately still remains.

Notes

1. Frantz Fanon, *Wretched of the Earth* (New York: Grove Press, 1963), 38.
2. Ibid., 40.
3. Ibid., 45–46.
4. Ibid., 93.
5. Frantz Fanon, *Black Skins, White Masks* (New York: Grove Press, 1952), 14–15.
6. Ibid., 79.
7. Fanon, *Wretched of the Earth*, 313.
8. Edward Said, *Orientalism* (New York: Vintage Books, 1978), 24.
9. Ibid., 24.
10. Ibid., 10.
11. Ibid., 6.
12. Ibid., 308.
13. For more on how scientific objectivity gives us only a partial picture of reality, see Chapter 4 by Stephanie Adair.
14. For a good example of this, see "Censorship in Pashto and Arabic," in the *New York Times* of October 10, 2001, A18.
15. Quoted in Gary Susman, "Is 'Avatar' Racist?" (2010), http://insidemovies. moviefone.com/2010/01/11/is-avatar-racist/ (accessed on August 2, 2010).

Part VI

SEEING OUR ETHICAL
RESPONSIBILITIES
"SOMETIMES YOUR ENTIRE LIFE BOILS DOWN TO ONE INSANE MOVE"

16

"All That Cheddar"
Lessons in Business Ethics from the RDA Corporation

Matthew Brophy

One moral of *Avatar* pops from the screen as vividly as any 3D graphic: greedy corporations show no mercy on the warpath to profits. "Killing the indigenous looks bad," says Parker Selfridge, "but there's one thing shareholders hate more than bad press – and that's a bad quarterly statement." Selfridge is a corporate administrator for the Resources Development Administration (RDA) corporation. His mission is to boldly maximize profits for shareholders in a galaxy far, far away. Selfridge doesn't twirl a long handlebar mustache or wear a black cape and a top hat, but he clearly has a villainous agenda: maximize profits *at any cost*. Hometree is decimated, families are displaced, lives are lost – all to feed the corporate beast.

Selfridges's dastardly deeds on behalf of RDA shareholders would be denounced by a variety of ethical umpires, religious and secular. But maybe such denunciations are beside the point. Business is business, after all. As the Nobel Prize-winning economist Milton Friedman (1912–2006) declared:

> There is one and only one social responsibility of business – to use its resources and engage in activities designed to increase its profits so long as it ... engages in open and free competition without deception or fraud.[1]

But perhaps the ethical practice of business requires keeping one's eye on something more than just the "quarterly statement."

Avatar and Philosophy: Learning to See, First Edition. Edited by George A. Dunn.
© 2014 John Wiley & Sons, Inc. Published 2014 by John Wiley & Sons, Inc.

Business as Boxing

The RDA unleashes torrential firepower on Hometree to gain access to unobtanium, a priceless mineral. This destruction of a culture for profits screams immorality. But should business really be judged by the tenets of ordinary morality?

Religious ethics, for instance, promotes moral commandments such as "do unto others as you would have them do unto you." But perhaps in the competitive "game" of business a better dictum might be "get the better of others before they have a chance to get the better of you." To thrive, businesses must be competitive, aggressive, and self-interested. That is what makes a free enterprise system work and, on the whole, engenders prosperity. As Adam Smith (1723–1790), the Scottish philosopher and father of modern economics, argued: "It is not from the benevolence of the butcher, the brewer, or the baker, that we can expect our dinner, but from their regard to their own interest."[2] Business *should* be self-interested, not burdened with moral weights that impede economic and social progress. Or so the argument goes.

The contemporary philosopher Albert Carr compares business to a game of poker, where the rules of everyday morality don't apply.[3] Carr explains that, while lying in ordinary life tends to be immoral, in poker it's what a player *ought* to do. "Bluffing" is likewise an integral part of the business game. Business is also often compared to boxing. A boxer shouldn't enter the ring with a "golden rule" mentality and refrain from hitting his opponent. Rather he should hit him hard, with all he's got. There's nothing unjust about pummeling your opponent. It's what a boxer *ought* to do. Likewise, it might be argued that, if the RDA pummeled the Na'vi people for profit, it was just doing what businesses do.

The problem with these sport and game analogies is that, in boxing and in poker, all players enter the competition voluntarily. They're also relatively equal in capability (in their weight class or in other ranking) and fully informed of the rules. The Na'vi didn't enter the ring with the RDA freely, nor were they informed or equal participants. The RDA's attack on Hometree was more like a mugging than a boxing match.

"I Didn't Make Up the Rules"

Selfridge accepts his prime directive to be the maximization of RDA profits by any means necessary. As a corporate administrator, he has a "fiduciary duty" to the shareholders, that is, a duty to act in their best interest. This fiduciary duty is famously expressed by Milton Friedman, who calls it a direct responsibility "to conduct the business in accordance with [shareholder] desires, which generally will be to make as much money as possible while conforming to the basic rules of the society."[4] The manager is an agent for the shareholders. It's their money, which is entrusted with him so he can turn a profit with it.

But maximizing profits must be conducted within certain moral and legal boundaries. In particular, Friedman maintains that a business must "use its resources and engage in activities designed to increase its profits without deception or fraud."[5] To illustrate this moral requirement, consider the infamous Pinto case, which was big news in 1977. The Ford Motor Company knowingly sold its Pinto coupe to consumers without informing them of a deadly defect – an explosive gas tank. Ford was acquitted of all criminal charges, since the company's corporate actions were deemed legal. But, from the perspective of traditional business ethics, Ford was still guilty of deception or fraud, as consumers had a reasonable expectation that the Pinto would *not* explode during a fender-bender. At the very least, customers should have been informed of this potentially lethal "bug" before deciding whether to buy the Pinto.

For the RDA's corporate actions to pass moral muster, RDA members would need to follow the law while not engaging in any deception, fraud, or direct coercion. In 2154, the year when *Avatar* is set, there would surely be laws that regulate interplanetary business practices such as the Pandoran mining operation, just as there presently are laws regulating international business. For the sake of argument, let's suppose that the RDA follows the letter of the law. Selfridge certainly seems interested in shrouding the RDA's conduct in at least the *appearance* of legality. The Avatar project, for instance, is cited as essential to demonstrate that the RDA made a good faith effort at nonviolent cooperation ("winning the hearts and minds of the natives") before it brought the hammer down. The RDA can claim that it tried diplomacy first, but then had to defend itself after the natives attacked. This disingenuous "just war" strategy seems cleverly engineered to pass legal examination. The idea is to provoke an attack from the Na'vi, and then claim self-defense.[6]

Who Owns Hometree?

"Their damn village happens to be resting on the richest unobtanium deposit within 200 klicks in any direction," grumbles Selfridge, who wants the priceless rocks underneath Hometree. The Na'vi tribe won't abandon their sacred home, so Selfridge has Colonel Miles Quaritch blow it up.

Isn't this *coercive*? If so, then the RDA is in violation of *entitlement theory*, the predominant moral theory in business ethics today. According to this theory, individuals are entitled to their property unless they acquired it through fraud, deception, or force. To deprive others of their property through any of these three illicit means is to violate their property rights. Imagine some construction company knocking on your door to inform you that, since a wrecking ball is about to destroy your house to make way for a new private toll road, it would be a good idea for you to evacuate. That would be a violation of your property rights. And it doesn't seem to differ much from what the RDA corporation does to the Na'vi.

Of course, the RDA might counter that this home-wrecking analogy doesn't match up, since the Na'vi don't claim to "own" Hometree the way a homeowner claims to own her house. The Na'vi are more like squatters in some abandoned shack on unowned land. And if a corporation wants to evacuate squatters and then bulldoze the shack in order to utilize the resources underneath, that's no violation of the squatters' property rights.

But this squatting analogy, too, gets it wrong. The reason why the Na'vi don't "own" Hometree is that their culture refuses to treat living things as private property. But the RDA can take advantage of this loophole. Since the Na'vi don't claim any property rights to Hometree, the RDA might argue that it's free territory.

Such an argument is wrongheaded. Even if the Na'vi make no formal proprietary claim to Hometree, they still ought to be recognized as having de facto property rights to their home. There are several criteria traditionally acknowledged as sufficient for property rights and the Na'vi satisfy them all: (1) they initially claimed that parcel of land; (2) they have occupied it for generations; (3) they have threaded it into their lives, creed, and culture; and (4) they have mixed their labor with the materials supplied by Hometree to turn it into their dwelling.[7] For these reasons, the Na'vi possess an entitlement right to Hometree, even if this entitlement isn't cashed out in terms of property. Even the Na'vi appear to recognize such a right, as they decry the injustice of being forced from their home. Thus it would be disingenuous to suggest that the Na'vi have somehow forfeited their right to Hometree. The RDA's destruction of Hometree is in clear violation of entitlement theory.

"Are You Gonna Kill Children?"

Quaritch assures Selfridge that he can carry out the attack on Hometree with "minimal casualties to the indigenous. I'll drive them out with gas first," he says. "It'll be humane. More or less." But Grace Augustine knows what this "more or less" really means. "There are families in there," she reminds Selfridge. "There are children. Babies. Are you gonna kill children?" Selfridge understands that innocent Na'vi children will be likely casualties of the RDA's attack. He even appears to have some twinges of moral conscience. Nonetheless, he sees an assault on Hometree as the only way to maximize profits. His hands are tied by his fiduciary duty.

Perhaps Selfridge believes that imposing his own moral scruples on the rest of the shareholders would be tantamount to acting as their ruler rather than their agent. A corporate administrator is a person in his own right, with his own moral values and responsibilities, but he can't impose his *own* morality on the shareholders. If his own personal values conflict irreconcilably with those of the corporation, he's free to resign. But if he doesn't resign, then refusing to maximize profits on account of some personal moral qualms would be in breach of contract.

On the other hand, Selfridge's fiduciary duty needn't be exclusively to maximize profits. Milton Friedman points out that an agent might have a fiduciary duty to produce some social good if, for example, her employer were a hospital or school. For a hospital administrator to maximize profits by charging needlessly exorbitant fees for care would violate her fiduciary duty to promote the social good of health. One's fiduciary duty depends on the objectives and wishes of the principal or of the shareholders. While you're unlikely to a find a corporation that makes charity its number one priority, many corporations have mission statements, codified in their policies and implicit in their practices, which commit them to certain values. A manager for a corporation, then, can and should defer to the corporation's moral values, which are presumed to be reflective of the shareholders' values.

But what of corporations with no moral values? There's no such corporation. Even if it espouses no moral values in its statements or practices, a corporation such as the RDA is owned by shareholders, all of whom are individuals who share some basic moral values. Selfridge is acting on their behalf, so he must act as they would act in that situation. Would the shareholders, acting as individuals, be willing to cause the death of babies just to make some money?

An influential example from the contemporary philosopher Peter Singer poses a similar question.[8] Imagine you're walking near an ornamental pond and see a drowning child who has fallen in. Should you wade in and pull the child to safety? Saving the child might cause you some inconvenience and might even ruin the expensive clothes you're wearing. Still, if you were facing this hypothetical situation as an individual, wouldn't you – and virtually everyone else – acknowledge that it would be immoral not to save the child?

The RDA corporation's attack on Hometree is more egregious than failing to save the drowning child, since it actively imperils the lives of many children. And, while Friedman might rightly assert that Selfridge shouldn't foist his *own* moral values on the shareholders, this is a case where the vast majority of shareholders, were they in his situation, would probably refuse to cause the death of children in order to pad their wallets. By refusing to attack Hometree, Selfridge would not be imposing his own moral values upon RDA shareholders but deferring instead to the moral values the shareholders already have as individuals.

"Blue Monkeys" and "Fly-Bitten Savages"

When Grace protests the attack on Hometree, Selfridge dismisses her belief that the Na'vi are "people," saying: "They're fly-bitten savages that live in a tree!" Selfridge often dehumanizes the Na'vi, at one point referring to them as "blue monkeys" who "like mud" rather than civilized things. If the Na'vi are not moral persons – that is, if they aren't beings worthy of the same moral consideration as human beings – then they would have no legitimate entitlement claims. After all, monkeys don't "own" their trees.

But perhaps we should take Selfridge's dehumanizing hyperbole with a grain of salt. He may vent his frustration by heaping scorn on the Na'vi, but in his more emotionally sober moments he seems to regard them as moral persons who are capable of rationality. For instance, when he cheekily reminds Grace of her mission to win over the Na'vi's "hearts and minds," he betrays his belief that they have minds that can be persuaded. His pejoratives may not represent his own heart and mind, as he is privy to certain morally relevant facts about the Na'vi. From Grace he's learned about the sophistication, sensitivity, and richness of Na'vi culture. He's also sure to be aware of the sophisticated cognitive powers of the Na'vi brain, as these are made evident by the Avatar program.

But, even if Selfridge would grant moral rights to the Na'vi, perhaps his shareholders would not. Perhaps he's right that they care only about bad profits and bad press, in that order. If so, would his fiduciary duty require him to violate the rights of the Na'vi in order to maximize corporate profits? While fiduciary duties carry significant moral weight, those duties are circumscribed by prior moral considerations. Traditional business ethics recognizes the priority of natural rights as a set of "ground floor" ethical constraints in business. The underpinning of a free market economic system is, after all, the natural right to property. Even if Selfridge were directed by a shareholder vote to maximize profits by violating someone's natural rights, he would be morally obligated to refuse, regardless of whether the action in question were legal. Here's the bottom line: if the Na'vi have natural rights comparable to human beings, then Selfridge can have no fiduciary duty to do anything that would violate them.

Philosophers generally think that a being has natural rights by virtue of possessing certain traits, such as consciousness, self-aware-ness, creativity, willfulness, or rationality. From our intimate window upon the Na'vi culture as moviegoers, it's obvious that they possess such traits in spades. If shareholders clamor that the Na'vi have no rights, Selfridge must dismiss their objections as predicated upon nonsense, just as he would have to dismiss similar objections from misogynist or white supremacist shareholders who wished to deny the natural rights of women or people of color.

Ethical Sleight of Hand

Traditional business ethics provides two clear reasons why it's wrong for Selfridge to authorize the attack on Hometree. First, the attack violates the natural rights of the Na'vi; and, second, it doesn't keep faith with his shareholders' actual values.

So why is Selfridge, like many corporate managers, morally confused? One reason is that it's easy for moral responsibility to fall through the cracks when a corporate representative acts in the interest of shareholders. In the attack on Hometree, for example, Selfridge can say that he was just following orders. He can cite a fiduciary duty to maximize profits, despite any moral misgivings he may have. Each shareholder can also deny moral responsibility: after all, it was not the shareholder's decision to launch the attack. They just receive the checks. One dirty hand washes the other.

But you can't "contract out" of moral responsibility. For example, if I hire a car thief to steal my neighbor's car, I can't claim that I am innocent of wrongdoing on the grounds that I am not the one who stole her car. Nor can the thief claim that he was contractually obligated to steal the car on the grounds that I paid him upfront, in exchange for his solemn promise that he'd do it.

Nonetheless, "moral values" in the corporate world often disappear like a silver dollar in the hands of a magician. But business cannot really extinguish morality – not any more than a parlor trick can make a coin really vanish from the world. It's merely obfuscated as a result of misdirecting the human mind. Indeed the human mind has a number of tricks to escape moral restraints.

Rationalizing in a Galaxy Far, Far Away

Psychology has exposed a menagerie of rationalizations available to the human mind for evading a sense of moral responsibility. Consider the phenomenon called "diffusion of responsibility," the tendency of the individual members of a large group to feel less responsibility to help someone in need than they ordinarily would if they were alone. One such case occurred in 2007, in an apartment building in St. Paul, Minnesota, where none of the numerous witnesses to a woman being beaten and raped even called the police. As the woman screamed, five to ten people – men and women – "peeked out their apartment doors to see what was happening or started walking down the hallway and retreated after witnessing the assault," reports Commander Shari Gray, who reviewed the video tape of the assault.[9] Surprisingly, such "bystander apathy" turns out to be the rule rather than exception, in part because it's easy for us to assume that someone else will respond if we don't.

In a business context, diffusion of responsibility manifests itself in three primary ways. First, each shareholder takes her moral cues from other shareholders. Second, each shareholder feels insulated from personal moral responsibility, as she is just one among many. And, third, each shareholder complacently presumes that others have already made appropriate moral objections to any questionable business practices, so she doesn't need to take any action herself.

Another psychological phenomenon is known as "moral distance," colloquially captured in the phrase "out of sight, ought of mind," which means that it becomes easier for us to commit or allow immoral acts as our "distance – physical, temporal, or psychological – from the victim increases." In the case of *Avatar*, the moral distance is maximal: the RDA shareholders are five light-years away from the Na'vi and have no contact with them. Perhaps the shareholders have seen video footage of the indigenous people, but it would be easy to dehumanize them, as Selfridge does, as "fly-bitten savages that live in a tree!" To avoid the distorting effects of moral distance, we need to consider what the shareholder or Selfridge would endorse or condemn, were they in same position as Jake, directly encountering and interacting with the Na'vi people. The less moral distance between them and the Na'vi, the less they would be prone to complicity in the devastation of the Na'vi culture.

"You Don't Want That Kind of Blood on Your Hands"

As Selfridge green-lights Quaritch to decimate Hometree, his unsettled demeanor betrays his own moral misgivings. Yet his moral justification is, in effect, that he's "just following orders," just fulfilling his fiduciary duty to maximize profits for RDA shareholders. He suspends his own moral agency in order to serve the greater authority of the corporation. German soldiers during World War II offered this same excuse for gassing Jewish concentration camp prisoners. They, too, were just following orders.

In a landmark experiment, psychologist Stanley Milgram (1933–1984) revealed that this rationalization is prevalent among ordinary people.[10] He divided test subjects by giving them two roles: one was the "teacher," the other was the "learner." The "learner" was locked in a room and hooked up to electric shocks. Seated at a console, the "teacher" was required to ask memorization questions of the "learner" and to punish him with an electric shock for each wrong answer he gave. The voltage increased with each wrong answer until the "learner" would yelp in pain, plead to be freed, and would finally fall eerily silent, as if he had passed out or were dead. At one point during the experiment, a "learner" claimed to suffer from a heart condition, crying, "Get me out of here! I told you I had heart trouble!" But if at any point the "teacher" protested against administering the shocks, the scientist supervising the experiment would command him to go on, saying: "The responsibility is mine."

You should know that the "learner" in these experiments was just an actor pretending to be shocked. The only real test subject was the "teacher." Milgram wanted to see how far an ordinary person would go in harming another person if told to do so by someone in authority. The results of Milgram's experiments were remarkably constant. A proportion of 61 to 65 percent of the "teachers" were willing to shock "learners" to the point of death, as long as there was an authority figure instructing them to do so.

There are two psychological explanations for this type of immoral behavior, both relevant to Selfridge's predicament. First, people tend to leave decision making to the group and its hierarchy. As a corporate administrator, Selfridge answers to the shareholders, the CEO, and various corporate executives higher up on the food chain. When he authorizes the assault on Hometree, he's only doing what he thinks they expect of him. Second, a person may perceive himself as a mere instrument carrying out the wishes of higher ups and as no longer responsible for his own actions. Deferring to the authority of the shareholders, Selfridge sees himself as just a tool they use to maximize their profits on Pandora. In an attempt to dissuade Selfridge from attacking Hometree, Jake adjures: "You don't want that kind of blood on your hands." But, just as Milgram's subjects rationalized, Selfridge may believe that the blood is not on his hands if he's merely a good solider following orders.

Humanity, Inc.

As a morality tale, *Avatar* might be mistakenly taken as a sweeping indictment of corporations in general. After all, if a corporation has license to destroy a native culture so as to maximize its profits, doesn't that expose corporations as sociopathic by their very nature?

But this conception of corporations as devoid of moral values is too simplistic. At a bare minimum, a corporation must follow the moral code of shareholder theory, which permits it to maximize profits within the boundaries of the law, as long as it avoids deception, coercion, or fraud. Even this minimal conception of morality is sufficient to denounce the actions of the RDA when it engages in clear coercion by violating the liberty and entitlement rights of the Na'vi.

Still, the film rightly dramatizes how the corporate imperative to maximize profit can become dangerously misguided. Corporate managers must recognize that fiduciary duties include not only deferring to the law and respecting natural rights, but also keeping moral fidelity with their shareholders' values. Such fidelity means not engaging in actions that the shareholders would not themselves take in the full light of day.

Tragically, human beings can drift from their moral values, especially when they act as members of groups. *Avatar* luridly reminds us that our humanity can often get lost when it becomes "incorporated." Whenever that happens, whether on Pandora or on Earth, our first responsibility is to find it again.

Notes

1. Milton Friedman, "The Social Responsibility of Business is to Increase its Profits," *The New York Times Magazine*, September 13, 1970.
2. Adam Smith, *The Wealth of Nations* (Scotts Valley, CA: Create Space, 2009), 11–12.

3. Albert Carr, "Is Business Bluffing Ethical?" *Harvard Business Review* 46 (1968), 143–153.

4. Friedman, "Social Responsibility of Business."

5. Ibid.

6. For more on just war theory and the insincerity of the RDA's diplomacy, see Chapter 13 by Joseph J. Foy.

7. The philosopher John Locke (1632–1704) held that one way to acquire property rights is through mixing our labor with previously unclaimed natural resources. For more on Locke's labor theory of value, see Chapter 14 by Dale Murray.

8. Peter Singer, "Famine, Affluence and Morality," *Philosophy and Public Affairs* 1.3 (1972), 229–244.

9. Mara H. Gottfried, "A Rape Witnessed, a Rape Ignored," *Pioneer Press*, August 23, 2007.

10. Stanley Milgram, *Obedience to Authority: An Experimental View* (New York: Harper & Row, 1974).

"We Have an Indigenous Population of Humanoids Called the Na'vi"
Native American Philosophy in *Avatar*

Dennis Knepp

Before my wife and I went to see *Avatar*, our precocious 12-year-old babysitter told us: "It's just like *Dances with Wolves*." Others have compared it to *Pocahontas*, or even to *Fern Gully: The Last Rainforest*. Like these movies and others, *Avatar* is a new type of "cowboy and Indian" story in which an outsider grows close with the natives: learns their ways, starts to question his own assumptions, and in many cases is forced to choose between the natives and his own people.

The Na'vi, of course, bear a strong resemblance to our traditional image of Native Americans. The word "Na'vi" even looks like a contraction of "Native." The Na'vi wear face paint. They fight with bows and arrows. They have a deep personal connection with Eywa, their Mother Earth goddess. They scorn concepts like private property and don't accumulate material forms of wealth. They have sacred trees. They mourn the deaths of other living creatures. They're fighting for their survival against a technologically superior foreign invasion, just like in an old western movie. And they lose their home because it's sitting on top of unobtanium, just as Native Americans lost their lands because of the gold and other treasures buried underneath.

Colonel Miles Quaritch, on the other hand, has "cowboy" written all over him. He swaggers. He pumps iron. He carries a big gun. He has nothing but scorn for Pandora. "If there is a hell," he tells the new

Avatar and Philosophy: Learning to See, First Edition. Edited by George A. Dunn.
© 2014 John Wiley & Sons, Inc. Published 2014 by John Wiley & Sons, Inc.

arrivals, "you might want to go there for some R&R after a tour on Pandora." He even speaks with a Texas drawl. The big scar above his right eye might even remind us of the eye patch that John Wayne wore as US Marshal Rooster Cogburn in *True Grit*.

But the similarities between Na'vi and Native Americans run deeper than face paint. The Na'vi way of life exhibits four deep Native American philosophical ideas: the principles of interaction, pluralism, community, and growth. These four principles run counter to the colonial mindset of the invading "sky people." But they are not the sole property of the Na'vi or Native Americans. Available to us all, they're found in the homegrown American philosophy known as pragmatism.

Scott Pratt's *Native Pragmatism*

A central question in the history of American philosophy is that of the origin of the pragmatist movement, a school of thought that emphasized the importance of testing our ideas in practice. The traditional view is that, when the American philosopher Charles Sanders Peirce (1839–1914) launched the pragmatist movement with his two essays "The Fixation of Belief" and "How to Make Our Ideas Clear,"[1] he was transplanting European philosophy into a largely philosophy-free American wilderness.[2] But Scott Pratt, author of the recent book *Native Pragmatism: Rethinking the Roots of American Philosophy*, presents a different theory, arguing that America was not philosophy-free before the arrival of Europeans, since a non-European philosophy was already present in Native American thought.[3] Pratt argues that pragmatism shows Native American influences. Peirce, who spent most of his time among the high society of New York, Boston, and Paris, probably never met a Native American.[4] But he did most likely read Benjamin Franklin (1706–1790) and other American writers who took an interest in Native Americans and were influenced by their ideas.[5]

Pratt identifies four Native American philosophical principles that he believes influenced Peirce's theory of pragmatism: interaction, pluralism, community, and growth. These principles belong to what he calls "the indigenous attitude" – represented in *Avatar* by the Na'vi – in contrast to "the colonial attitude" embraced by the Resources Development Administration (RDA) corporation and its employees. Someone with a colonial attitude regards himself as an autonomous self who can know the one true world in the one right way. He dismisses every other way of understanding the world as something "primitive" that should be corrected in the name of progress.[6] Parker Selfridge, the corporate administrator for the RDA, is an excellent example of this colonial attitude. He seems to believe that there's only one right way to view the world: through the lens of quarterly reports, the interests of stockholders, and the market price of unobtanium. As far as he's concerned, the Na'vi's holistic way of thinking is laughably primitive.

To better understand the object of Selfridge's scorn, let's look closer at these four principles of interaction, pluralism, community, and growth.

The Principle of Interaction

The principle of interaction holds that things get their meaning and value from the connections they have with other things. When he first developed pragmatism, Peirce proposed using this principle as a way to clarify our idea or *conception* of what any given thing is. If we want to form an adequate idea of something, we should

> consider what effects, which might conceivably have practical bearings, we conceive the object of our conception to have. Then, our conception of these effects is the whole of our conception of the object.[7]

This is the pragmatic maxim: an object is known by its interactions with other things. A diamond is hard because it can scratch glass. Glass is brittle because it will break when you drop it on a hard surface.

Other pragmatists have taken this idea further, expanding it to make it apply to abstract concepts. For instance, we can understand the concept of "loyalty" by looking at how Jake Sully interacts with other characters. At the outset of *Avatar*, we recognize that Jake is loyal to Colonel Miles Quaritch from how he interacts with him. In particular, we observe Jake sharing important intelligence with the colonel. By the end of *Avatar* we know that Jake is no longer loyal to Quaritch because their interactions have changed: Jake now attacks and kills the colonel!

According to Pratt, this principle was expressed by Native Americans and recorded by European Americans long before Peirce formulated his pragmatic maxim. Evidence of this can be found in the book *A Key into the Language of America*, written by the Protestant theologian Roger Williams (1603–1683) about the language of the Narragansett Indians, a tribe that welcomed him after he was exiled from the Puritan Massachusetts Bay colony.[8] About the Narragansett fire god he wrote:

> When I have argued with them about their Fire-God: can it, they say, be but this fire must be a God, or a Divine power, that out of a stone will arise a Sparke, and when a poore naked Indian is ready to starve with cold in the House, and especially in the Woods, often saves his life, doth dresse all our Food for us, and if it be angry will burne the House about us, yea if a spark fall into the drie wood, burnes up the Country?[9]

We can know the fire god by what the fire does: it creates sparks, saves lives, warms food, and burns the countryside. Consider how fire interacts with other things – that's the Narragansett's entire conception of their fire god. And that's the principle of interaction, recognizable in Narragansett philosophy more than two hundred years before Peirce recorded his maxim.

Like the Narragansett with their fire god, the Na'vi know their goddess Ewya by her interactions with them. Neytiri knows that Jake is special to Ewya because a seed from the Tree of Souls lands on her arrowhead just as she's aiming it at him. Later the seeds bless his whole body. Through this interaction Ewya is revealed. In the final battle with the "sky people," Neytiri knows that Ewya has heard Jake's prayers because the animals of Pandora rise up to defend the planet. Ewya is not an ineffable goddess beyond our understanding. Rather she can be known by how she interacts with life on Pandora.

The Principle of Pluralism

The principle of pluralism, which states that there can be many valid ways of knowing and living, follows from the principle of interaction. Since things are known by their interactions, people will come to know things differently as a result of interacting with them differently. Consequently, the Na'vi way of knowing is not the RDA way, because they interact so differently with the creatures of Pandora. They may be on the same planet, but they live in two different worlds. Jake struggles to understand this Na'vi world that is initially so alien to him, which shows that at some level he accepts pluralism and acknowledges that there's another world to know. By contrast, Selfridge denies pluralism, since he rejects the possibility of knowing Pandora in any other way.

While some philosophers have believed that there could be one surefire "scientific method," good for finding the right solution to every problem, Peirce disagreed. Arguing that there isn't just one scientific method, he held the pluralistic view that science advances by using a variety of methods to acquire knowledge.[10] But Pratt's thesis is that Native Americans were the first to express this principle of pluralism, which is written down by sympathetic European Americans and eventually used by pragmatists like Pierce.

There is an incredible plurality of languages and beliefs among Native Americans. Here's how Native American philosopher Maureen E. Smith describes this variety:

> With over 500 individual American Indian nations in the country today, each with its own culture, language, and spiritual traditions, there exists great diversity among the tribes in the United States. Additionally, each individual tribal member interprets his/her spirituality in his/her own way.[11]

Five hundred nations, each member of which finds his or her own spirituality – that's a lot of variety. Many European Americans believe in the "melting pot" idea, according to which cultural differences are left behind as one gets assimilated into the larger society. By the same token, some philosophers may hunt for similarities and continuities among these five hundred nations, so they can claim that they are all really just one. But Viola F. Cordova argues that Native American philosophers celebrate their variety, differences, and pluralism:

> True tolerance consists, not of ignoring differences, but in acknowledging them and acknowledging with equal weight that even small differences carry tremendous import. But true tolerance also requires a recognition that there may not be a vast, universal, absolute, Truth (with a capital T). It may be that diversity, which appears to be the identifying characteristic of Earth's creativity, may extend to how we organize and explain our diverse experiences of the world.[12]

While we're discussing pluralism, it should be noted that Pratt's thesis that there are four common principles is *not* an attempt to homogenize Native American philosophers, for it is also but one of many ways of telling this story.

There's a diversity of right ways, not just one right way, as Jake learns when he is he initiated into a way of life that's totally unimaginable to someone like Selfridge. And even among the Na'vi there's diversity. When Jake becomes the Omaticaya war leader after taming the toruk, he unites 15 different tribes: his own Omaticaya clan, the horse clans of the plains, the ikran people of the Eastern Sea, and more. Each tribe has its own way of life. There are pluralities of worlds on Pandora.

The Principle of Community

The principle of community holds that the community is more fundamental than the individual. Brian Yazzie Burkhart writes that Native American philosophers must reject the standard Western philosophical bias that treats the individual as primary and must embrace instead the Native community as foundational. Referring to an often quoted line from the French philosopher René Descartes (1596–1650), Burkhart writes: "The *cogito, ergo sum* tells us, 'I think, therefore I am.' But Native philosophy tells us, 'We are, therefore I am.'"[13]

Descartes stressed the ideal of the heroic seeker for truth who turns his back on society in order to go it alone. But Peirce rejected the model of a single philosopher using a single method to discover the truth all by himself. Instead he argued that scientific progress relies upon the community of scientists using a variety of methods. For the findings of an individual researcher to be considered scientific, they must be investigated and appraised by the scientific community. Because *community* is fundamental to science, one person's idiosyncratic beliefs can never be scientific.[14]

A community requires some basic norms. Since we're unlikely to listen to those whom we don't respect, the scientific community expects its members to have respect for each other – even for other scientists with whom they strongly disagree. That's tough to do! It's not easy to listen to someone whom you believe to be incorrect, especially since, as Pratt argues, true listening requires more than just tolerance. You can tolerate someone without necessarily *listening* to that person. Beyond tolerance, Pratt believes that we need to cultivate the virtue of hospitality, a striking example of which is given in Narragansett stories of the Mohowaúgsuck, man-eating monsters.[15] In these stories, instead of fighting the Mohowaúgsuck or fleeing from them in terror, the Narragansett welcomed and tamed them, believing that even monsters can be part of the community. Stories like these prepared the Narragansett to welcome Roger Williams into their community when he was banished from Massachusetts Bay.

The Na'vi also practice the principle of community. Not only do they eat, sleep, and pray to Ewya communally, but they also exhibit hospitality by welcoming Jake Sully into their midst – albeit with some understandable initial reluctance. Earlier they had welcomed Grace Augustine and, although some rupture seems to have occurred in their relationship, they eventually welcome her back. Like the Mohowaúgsuck to whom the Narragansett extended hospitality, Jake and Grace are monsters – "demons in false bodies" – whom the Na'vi have every reason to fear and dislike, given the past behavior of their people. The Na'vi welcome them nonetheless. Jake, in particular, is not just *tolerated*. The hospitality offered to him extends to showing him how to hunt, ride, sleep, eat, pray, and eventually love like a Na'vi. The Na'vi community is welcoming enough to accept even a "demon."

The colonial attitude of the RDA corporation, on the other hand, has nothing but contempt for outsiders. To Selfridge, the Na'vi are nothing but "a bunch of flea-bitten savages who live in a tree." His colonial attitude mirrors the Massachusetts Puritans who, believing that there was only one right way, exiled Roger Williams for dissenting. To be banished in November into the harsh Massachusetts wilderness was effectively a death sentence, but, thanks to the community spirit of the Narragansett people, Williams was welcomed and survived. Jake Sully experienced much the same thing when he became stranded in the wild forests of Pandora and survived only because the Na'vi community accepted him.

The Principle of Growth

The principle of growth affirms the value of change that takes place in a local environment and is nourished by the past. Growth is natural, not forced, gradual, not dramatic. It builds on previous growth without destroying what came before. Hometree is a spectacular example of growth. It grew naturally and gradually into a massive structure in one particular location. Its daily growth builds on previous growth. Nothing says "we live by the principle of growth" better than living in a huge tree!

We can contrast the principle of growth with the principle of progress embraced by Parker Selfridge. Progress and growth share a similar orientation toward the future, but they differ in how they view the past. The principle of growth affirms the past, for that's what nourishes our drive toward the future. But, for the principle of progress, the past is only something standing in the way. We must destroy the old to make way for the new. Selfridge doesn't care how old Hometree is or how long the Na'vi have lived there. Indifferent to what that ancient growth means to the Na'vi ("They're just goddamn trees!"), he sees in it only an obstacle to progress that must be cleared away to get to "all that cheddar" – the unobtanium deposits underneath. That's progress, not growth.

Some philosophers follow the principle of progress and think that we should get rid of all our old beliefs in order to make room for new and improved ones. But Peirce rejected the idea that the search for knowledge should always start from scratch, ignoring the accomplishment of those who came before us. Instead he believed in the principle of growth, arguing that we must begin our search for knowledge by building on what we've inherited from past thinkers. We must start where we are, using the resources and beliefs available.[16] That's the Native American principle of growth, which relies on gradual local changes and is nourished by the achievements of the past.[17]

In April 2010 *Avatar* director James Cameron visited with indigenous chiefs in Brazil.[18] A photo of their conference shows Cameron wearing orange-stripe warrior face paint as he listens to the chiefs describe a proposed hydroelectric dam that would destroy their villages. Chief Arara compared losing his village to the plight of *Avatar*'s Na'vi, observing: "What happens in the film is what is happening here."

But *Avatar* ends with the Na'vi triumphant over the technologically superior "sky people." The Dragon Assault Ship is knocked out of the sky before it destroys the Tree of Souls, Quaritch is killed, and the Na'vi take over the RDA base, sending all but a few of the surviving "sky people" home. Since we have been like the "sky people" to the native people of North America, let's hope that *Avatar* is not our future. Most of us can't follow Jake's lead and "go native."[19] But, if Pratt's thesis is correct, we can still create a better future for us all – more tolerant, healthy, and sustainable – by adopting the principles of interaction, pluralism, community, and growth.

Acknowledgments

Thank you to George Dunn and Ariadne Blayde for great editing. Thank you to Bill Irwin for suggesting the fascinating *American Indian Thought*. And thank you to my wife Jennifer McCarthy for commenting on multiple drafts.

Notes

1. These are the first in a series of six essays titled "Illustrations in the Logic of Science" and published by *Popular Science Monthly* in 1877 and 1878. They are Peirce's two most famous essays and are widely reprinted in pragmatism anthologies. His name is pronounced like "purse." I will be citing these two essays from the scholarly edition of *The Writings of Charles S. Peirce: A Chronological Edition*, Vol. 3: *1872–1878*, ed. Christian J. W. Kloesel (Bloomington: Indiana University Press, 1986), 242–276. The index to that volume has no entries for "Indian" or "Native American," by the way.

2. A great book about the origins of pragmatism is Louis Menand's *The Metaphysical Club: A Story of Ideas in America* (New York: Farrar, Straus and Giroux, 2001). Menand presents pragmatism as a continuation of European philosophy on a philosophy-free American continent. His index has no entries for "Indian" or "Native American."

3. Scott Pratt, *Native Pragmatism: Rethinking the Roots of American Philosophy* (Bloomington: Indiana University Press, 2002). For some scholarly reaction to Pratt's book, see Neil Schmitz's review "A Symposium on *Native Pragmatism: Rethinking the Roots of American Philosophy* by Scott L. Pratt," in *Transactions of the Charles S. Peirce Society: A Quarterly Journal in American Philosophy* 39.4 (2003), 557–616. Of the six scholars who provide critical commentary for the symposium, I agree the most with John Carlos Rowe's assessment on p. 582 that, despite scholarly "quibbles," we must applaud Pratt's

attempt to broaden the scope of our study of pragmatism. I benefited from Pratt's quick summary of the colonial attitude and of the four principles of interaction, community, pluralism, and growth in "Philosophy in the 'Middle Ground': A Reply to My Critics," 591–616 (in the same issue of the *Transactions*).

4. Peirce was both an eccentric genius and a spoiled dandy. A great biography is Joseph Brent's *Charles Sanders Peirce: A Life* (Bloomington: Indiana University Press, 1993). Brent's index has no entries for "Indian" or "Native American."

5. In addition to being an important philosopher and logician, Peirce was a practicing scientist and a historian of science. Franklin advocated scientific experimentation and technological advancement, as did Peirce.

6. Pratt connects "the colonial attitude" to what John Dewey (1859–1952) called "the quest for certainty"; see Pratt, *Native Pragmatism*, xiv.

7. Peirce, "How to Make Our Ideas Clear," 266.

8. Sarah Vowell's *The Wordy Shipmates* (New York: Riverhead Trade, 2009) tells the story of how Roger Williams was exiled from Puritan Massachusetts, was accepted by the Narragansett people, and ended up being an early advocate of religious tolerance and separation of church and state. Vowell connects the Puritans' desire to liberate the Indians from paganism to President Bush's decision to liberate Iraq.

9. Pratt quotes Williams in *Native Pragmatism*, 102.

10. Peirce, "How to Make Our Ideas Clear," 273. There are other nonscience approaches to knowledge (tenacity, authority, and the a priori method) that fail, in part, by not using a plurality of methods to acquire knowledge. See Peirce, "The Fixation of Belief," 248–253.

11. Maureen E. Smith, "Crippling the Spirit, Wounding the Soul: Native American Spiritual and Religious Suppression," in Anne Waters, ed., *American Indian Thought* (Malden, MA: Blackwell, 2004), 117. Waters writes (p. xv): "This is the first book to publish a collection of articles written by American Indians with a PhD in philosophy." Many contributors to this pioneering anthology were involved in founding an academic journal of Native American philosophy: *Ayaangwaami zin: The International Journal of Indigenous Philosophy*.

12. V. F. Cordova, "Approaches to Native American Philosophy," in Waters, *American Indian Thought*, 33.

13. Brian Yazzie Burkhart, "What Coyote and Thales Can Teach Us: An Outline of American Indian Epistemology," in Waters, *American Indian Thought*, 25.

14. Peirce, "How to Make Our Ideas Clear," 273.

15. Pratt, *Native Pragmatism*, 84–94.

16. Peirce, "The Fixation of Belief," 248.

17. Many Native American philosophers apply this principle to their philosophical research. Brian Yazzie Burkhart draws upon the Seneca nation's story of the three sisters, corn, beans, squash, in "What Coyote and Thales Can Teach Us: An Outline of American Indian Epistemology," in Waters, *American Indian Thought*, 21–22. Ted Jojola writes about traditional Pueblo migration symbols in "Notes on Identity, Time, Space, and Place," in Waters, *American Indian Thought*, 90–93. Thomas M. Norton-Smith uses traditional Shawnee and Ojibwa numerical thought to critically examine the Western conception of numbers in "Indigenous Numerical Thought in Two American Indian Tribes," in Waters, *American Indian Thought*, 61–66. These examples can be multiplied, but the point is made. Native American philosophers begin where they are and use the beliefs available. They don't destroy the old in the name of progress but are nourished by the past in their future growth.

18. Alexei Barrionuevo, "Tribes of Amazon Find an Ally out of 'Avatar,'" *New York Times* online, http://www.nytimes.com/2010/04/11/world/americas/11brazil.html (accessed October 6, 2010).

19. Cordova's observations about non-Native Americans doing Native American philosophy apply here: Cordova, "Approaches to Native American Philosophy," 31.

18

I See Animals
The Na'vi and Respect for Other Creatures

Wayne Yuen

With their organic neural queues, the Na'vi are able to communicate with other species in a way human beings cannot. Along with their insights into other minds, the Na'vi have a deep respect for the other animals of Pandora. But how about us? What can we know about the minds of other creatures? And how might that knowledge affect our treatment of them?

C-Fibers, Hammerheads, and Zoe Saldana

People tend to agree that animals can experience pain and suffering and that it's better to meet our needs without causing pain and suffering if we can. So, as moral people, we should look for ways to achieve our goals that do not needlessly contribute to the pain and suffering of other creatures. But how do we know when an animal is suffering or in pain?

There are two primary ways in which we human beings can infer what another creature is experiencing, including whether it is suffering. The first involves studying its physiology and drawing inferences from the activity of its nerves and brain. For example, we know that human beings possess a type of nerve known as C-fibers, which are responsible for dull long-lasting pains, such as the ache we feel after a sharp punch. We might therefore think that we can determine whether

Avatar and Philosophy: Learning to See, First Edition. Edited by George A. Dunn.
© 2014 John Wiley & Sons, Inc. Published 2014 by John Wiley & Sons, Inc.

another creature is experiencing dull pain by checking to see whether its C-fibers are activated. But it turns out that pain and suffering aren't something that we can determine simply by examining a creature's physiology.

To see why, let's imagine we have recruited a Na'vi volunteer who allows us to study her experience of pain. Scanning her body, we discover that she has no C-fibers. Instead she has an entirely different kind of nerve fiber, unique to creatures on Pandora. Let's call it the "Vi-fiber." Moreover, let's say that these Vi-fibers are activated when there's damage to the tissue to which they're connected, but in a way that's radically different than the way C-fibers are activated in human beings. Vi-fibers also send signals to a completely different part of the brain. Yet, whenever these Vi-fibers are activated, our Na'vi subject reports an experience of pain. What lesson should we draw from this? Assuming we can trust what our subject is telling us, we now know that C-fibers are not – or at least *may* not be – necessary for the experience pain.

Even so, can't we still make the weaker claim that any creature that does have C-fibers will experience pain whenever they're activated, even if we must look for some other indicator of pain in creatures who lack C-fibers? In other words, C-fibers may not be *necessary* for pain, but wouldn't they still be *sufficient*, so that activating them would be enough to produce the sensation of pain? Actually, no, we're not even entitled to this weaker conclusion, as a slight modification of our original example shows. Imagine that the Na'vi have *both* C-fibers and Vi-fibers, but it turns out that their C-fibers are just a vestigial, non-functioning part of their nervous system, superseded by the more complex Vi-fibers that allow their neural queues to function. The C-fibers still fire off signals to the brain, but the Na'vi's brains simply ignore them. It's the firing of the Vi-fibers that causes the experience of pain in the Na'vi. If such a scenario is possible, then the activation of C-fibers might tell us nothing at all about whether a creature is in pain.

And there's yet another problem with hoping to discover whether a creature is in pain by attending solely to her physiology: objective measurements aren't always reliable indicators of subjective experiences. Consider what happens physiologically to Jake Sully when facing down a hammerhead titanothere: his palms sweat, his heartbeat races, his adrenalin pumps, and the blood vessels supplying his skin constrict. In Jake, these physiological responses are a response to danger, but is that what they always mean? Not at all, since I might have a very similar physiological response if I were to come face to face with Zoe Saldana, the actress who plays Neytiri. It wouldn't be because of fear, though, but because I was overcome by her beauty. But you couldn't tell that by looking only at my objectively measurable physiological responses to the encounter.

In short, inferences about the pain and suffering of other creatures drawn solely on the basis of their physiology may not always be reliable. Physiological responses are just too far removed from the subjective experience of suffering.

Do Hexapedes Grieve? Should Prolemurises Vote?

The second way in which we infer the presence of pain in others is by analogy. I step on your toe and you let go a yelp. When I yelp, it's usually because of pain – and I know that in my case pain can result from someone stepping forcefully on my toe. By analogy, I conclude that you're also yelping out of pain. In the same way, we can detect the presence of pain in cats, dogs, Na'vi, and many other creatures. But not all animals yelp or, for that matter, give any obvious – to us, at least – behavioral indication that they're suffering. When I'm suffering from the dull constant pain of a headache, you'll know it because you'll hear me complain a lot. But there are other animals who typically try to hide their pain, in order not to appear weak and vulnerable to predators. Consequently, we may not be able to tell when a cat or a viperwolf is experiencing a headache or a sore back. But, just because we don't see evidence of pain and suffering, it doesn't follow that pain and suffering are not there.

As philosophers, it's helpful if we make a distinction here between pain and suffering. Pain is the sensation that a creature typically experiences when it suffers some sort of physical trauma. Suffering, on the other hand, is a subjective mental event that can exist independently of physical pain. For example, someone who's spent many hours reading existentialist philosophers might suffer profoundly from the thought that his ultimate destiny is to be swallowed up into the merciless maw of death, although at the moment he's comfortably ensconced in his armchair, feeling not the smallest scintilla of physical pain. Similarly, a social animal like an elephant or a hexapede might suffer terribly from grief – not in anticipation of its own death, but because of the loss of a beloved mate or offspring. Arguably, the number of things that can cause a creature to suffer increases with its mental complexity. Still, it seems likely that severe and prolonged physical pain is the sort of thing that would cause any creature to suffer, so we shouldn't casually assume that pain inflicted on so-called "lower" animals is inconsequential.

What causes a creature to suffer may depend on what it values. One of the reasons why Jake suffers so much from being confined in a wheelchair is that he enjoys running, as we learn from his reaction to finding himself suddenly with two working legs. I don't particularly like running, so I might not suffer quite as much as Jake if I were in a wheelchair. I do, however, enjoy watching movies, which I typically do sitting down. Grace Augustine, who values the self-directed and unimpeded pursuit of knowledge, suffers because she's under the watchful eye of Parker Selfridge, but Colonel Quaritch and his men don't seem to mind that nearly as much. So, to know what causes a creature to suffer, we need to have some idea of what the creature values or needs in order to live a satisfying and fulfilling life. Depriving a gorilla or a prolemuris of the opportunity to explore its environment freely and to interact with other creatures would likely cause it to suffer. Depriving it of the right to vote would not.

This Consent Is *Killing* Me

The Na'vi have yet another way to know the minds of other creatures, one that we lack. Through their *tsaheylu* or neural bond with other animals, the Na'vi can access the memories, thoughts, and perceptions of other animals. This access gives the Na'vi intimate knowledge of what these animals are experiencing and what causes them to suffer. The Na'vi are better positioned to empathize with the animals of Pandora than human beings could ever hope to be in relation to other animals here on Earth.[1] The Na'vi truly *see* animals, recognizing them as independent beings who have their own needs, desires, and perspectives on the world – and who are therefore worthy of our respect. We human beings often have trouble seeing other animals in this way. "It's *just* a dog" or "It's *just* a cow," someone might say, expressing either a deep-seated prejudice against other species or a belief that those creatures are incapable of suffering in ways that are morally relevant. The Na'vi know better, having inside knowledge that comes directly from the direhorse's mouth – um, better make that her antenna. What's more, the Na'vi understand themselves to be joined to every other being on Pandora, as parts of a much larger network. Regarding yourself as part of a greater whole is one way to foster respect for others, with whom you come to feel the sort of solidarity you would feel for your teammates or for fellow citizens of your country.

The Na'vi's first-hand acquaintance with the inner lives of other creatures validates their deep respect for animals. On the other hand, our need to rely on more indirect ways of knowing what goes on in the minds of cows, horses, chickens, and other animals may help to explain why we often lack such deep respect.[2] We're simply unable to communicate with other creatures with the same degree of clarity as we do with each other. That can make it difficult for human beings to *see* another animal's capacity for pain and suffering. That sort of blindness is at the heart of the conflict on Pandora between the Resources Development Administration (RDA) corporation and the Na'vi. Jake is able to empathize better with the Na'vi, since he's immersed in the Na'vi worldview through his avatar. The Na'vi, in turn, are able to empathize with other life forms on Pandora in a way in which human beings simply cannot, due to the access their neural queues afford them to the experience of those other creatures.

The Na'vi's deep respect for other animals is reflected in the relationship between a Na'vi hunter and his or her steed, whether it's a direhorse or a mountain banshee (ikran to the Na'vi). Through *tsaheylu*, the Na'vi can direct their companions mentally. These bonds are freely chosen, since the animals give their consent to be joined with the hunter, albeit in a somewhat peculiar way in the case of the ikran. Neytiri tells Jake how he will know when an ikran has chosen him: "He will try to kill you." Presumably the Na'vi know this through their bond with the ikran. With their neural queue, they can learn what the actions of other animals really mean, whereas without the bond we can only observe and make our best guess through the lens of human interpretation. But, even though it may begin with a great deal of struggling and thrashing about, the bond between the Na'vi and the ikran is ultimately based on partnership and cooperation, not dominance and slavery. It's difficult, maybe impossible, to have genuine and deep respect for a creature you've enslaved.

"Excuse Me. This Is My Video-Log Here"

Human beings, of course, don't have organic neural queues like the Na'vi, so we may be concerned that we will always experience some degree of uncertainty about what's going on in the mind of a creature who lacks the ability to communicate her thoughts to us in words. But there are some among us who believe that their own neurological design is different in a way that affords them a special understanding of the minds of nonhuman animals even without the benefit of a neural queue. One such person is Temple Grandin, professor of animal science and well-known animal welfare advocate. Grandin is a high-functioning autistic person who believes that her autism furnishes her with unique insights into how nonhuman animals think and perceive the world.[3] "As a person with autism," she writes, "it is easy for me to understand how animals think because my thinking processes are like an animal's."[4]

Human beings typically think in language, which makes it easier for them to form abstract concepts but also removes them somewhat from the immediate sensuous reality of experience. Grandin, on the other hand, reports: "I have no language-based thoughts at all. My thoughts are in pictures, like videotapes in my mind."[5] And this, she believes, is precisely what goes on in the minds of other intelligent animals who aren't endowed with language. Being visual thinkers, the other animals may be attuned to features of their environment that we linguistic thinkers miss. Intelligent, nonlinguistic animals "are like autistic savants."

> Animals have special talents normal people don't, the same way autistic people have special talents normal people don't; and at least some animals have special forms of genius normal people don't, the same way some autistic savants have special forms of genius. I think most of the time animal genius probably happens for the same reason autistic genius does: a difference in the brain autistic people share with animals.[6]

Because their brains work differently, some animals may have the "ability to *perceive things humans can't perceive* or to *remember highly detailed bits of information we can't remember.*"[7] But by the same token these animals may be highly sensitive to sources of pain and suffering that may go unrecognized by us linguistic thinkers, who experience the world very differently. Grandin's cognitive difference is like an invisible neural queue that gives her a special ability to empathize with nonhuman animals and to identify things in their surroundings that might cause them pain, fear, or distress.

Typical human brains lack the features that afford the Na'vi and Temple Grandin access to the minds of nonlinguistic creatures. Still, our lack of information doesn't exempt us from our moral responsibility to minimize unnecessary pain and suffering. So what would be a responsible way of making decisions in light of incomplete information? It may be helpful to draw an analogy from our legal system. In courtroom trials, we artificially put the burden of proof on the prosecution. As we like to say, the accused person is *presumed* innocent until the prosecutor has *proven* her to be guilty. The benefit of the doubt always goes to the accused, who never has to *prove* her innocence. We'd rather err on the side of letting a criminal go than punish an innocent person, inflicting pain and suffering on someone who has done nothing to deserve it. For the same reason, even if we don't know with *certainty* that the animals in our care are experiencing pain, as long as we have some reason to believe they are, we should err on the side of caution.

"Personally, I Don't Feel These Tree-Hugging Traitors Deserve Steak"

But if the Na'vi have such deep respect for the other animals of Pandora, why do they hunt and kill them? When we deeply respect something, we don't typically destroy it. For example, many people have a deep respect for old growth redwoods that would be inconsistent with cutting them down for hardwood furniture. By the same token, most animal rights activists believe that truly respecting animals means becoming a vegetarian or vegan. Shouldn't the Na'vi become vegetarians, then? Not necessarily. It is a distinct possibility that a vegetarian diet wouldn't fulfill their dietary needs. Unable to survive as vegetarians, they would have no moral obligation to adopt a diet that would kill them. There's an important moral principle at stake here: our only moral obligations are the ones that we are really capable of fulfilling. For example, a viperwolf has no obligation to adopt a vegetarian diet, since as a carnivore it needs meat to survive. Likewise, for tribes of human beings who inhabit the arctic tundra, living from the produce of their backyard gardens isn't really option. The Na'vi may be in one of those situations – be dependent on meat for sustenance either because of the design of their digestive system or because they are unable to obtain enough edible vegetable matter to cover all their dietary requirements. But neither of those circumstances applies to the average citizen in an industrialized nation.

One of the main objections that animal rights activists make against eating meat is the inhumane treatment of livestock on "factory farms," where, packed into confined spaces in order to produce meat at the lowest possible cost, animals live in continuous pain and suffering. Thus 97 percent of poultry, 97 percent of pigs, and 61 percent of cattle raised in the US are raised in factory farms. Animals are crowded into confinement facilities that afford them no opportunity for healthy exercise; they are rarely given access to the world outside; they are mutilated in order to prevent them from injuring each other in the fights that inevitably result from overcrowding; and they are given a constant supply of antibiotics designed to prevent infections caused by their atrocious living conditions.[8] Consider the plight of factory chickens, who have become some of the most abused animals due to the popularity of poultry as an alternative to red meat. Chickens are crowded 40–50,000 to a warehouse, with little or no room even to flap their wings. These crowded conditions would lead them to kill each other to make more space – just as we would, were that many human beings packed into such a small space – were they not debeaked soon after hatching. Crowding also causes a rapid spread of infections, which is controlled through overuse of antibiotics.

Even so-called "free-range" chickens are not free from suffering. By US law, a free-range chicken must have access to pastureland for at least a few months before it is slaughtered. But access can mean no more than a small opening in the warehouse, which may only frighten the chickens when opened, as they've never seen sunlight before in their lives. These "free-range" chickens may never venture outside the warehouse, because their unnatural living conditions have made them terrified of the natural world. So-called "organic" chickens can be raised in the same way as other factory chickens, as long as they receive no antibiotics. This means that even genuinely sick chickens who could benefit from antibiotics are not given them, since that would violate their "organic" status. Animal rights activists also object to the brutal and painful manner in which factory farm animals are slaughtered. Moreover, animals raised for human consumption are slaughtered at a fraction of the age to which they would live if granted a full lifespan.

Because most people are blissfully ignorant of where their dinners come from, animal rights activists try to educate people about how their food is produced in order to encourage empathy with these suffering creatures. As long as human beings can get all their essential nutrients from plant sources, buying meat from factory farming operations only helps sustain a system that causes unnecessary pain and suffering on an unimaginably horrendous scale. With their deep respect for other living creatures, the Na'vi would never take part in such a wantonly cruel system of food production.

And yet they hunt. Can the practice of hunting be consistent with respecting your prey?

"I See You, Brother" – And Kill You!

When Jake makes his first "clean kill" as a hunter, he recites a Na'vi prayer over the body of the hexapede as he takes its life with his knife: "I see you, Brother, and thank you. Your spirit goes with Eywa. Your body stays behind to become part of the People." This prayer can help us understand why the Na'vi might believe that their hunting practices are consistent with their respect for animals. In the prayer, there is a distinct assumption that the spirit of the animal continues on in some fashion after its physical death. Its body continues also, albeit transformed into energy, to sustain the Omaticaya clan. "All energy is only borrowed," Neytiri tells Jake, "and one day you have to give it back." The matter or energy of the hexapede will become part of "the people" on its way back to the soil. From there it might undergo a further transformation, into forest vegetation that will nourish other hexapedes. Of course, this may not be much consolation for the slain hexapede, who can no longer enjoy the pleasures of a fully embodied existence. In thanking the hexapede, though, the Na'vi prayer seems to recognize that a sacrifice has been made. A desire to minimize the suffering that accompanies this sacrifice is apparently what motivates Neytiri's praise of Jake for making a "clean kill." The hexapede's death was a swift one, leaving it little time to experience pain and suffering.

We don't know whether the Na'vi could survive on a vegetarian diet. Perhaps they could. Even so, their way of obtaining meat is clearly much more humane and respectful than factory farming. The brief moment of pain and fear that the hexapede experiences before its death is nothing compared to the horribly protracted suffering of an animal raised in a confinement unit. Most importantly, the Na'vi recognize that the hexapede is not just a machine for producing meat, but one of their brothers – a fellow creature whose existence is valuable and whose death is therefore regarded as a sacrifice, a genuine loss.

But supposing that the Na'vi must eat meat to survive, is it really necessary for them to hunt? Wouldn't it be more humane for them to domesticate hexapedes and other creatures, raise them on farms and ranches rather than hunting them down on ikran or direhorses? We naturally assume that the Na'vi would never subject their domesticated animals to the sort of horrible abuse inflicted on creatures who live out their mercifully short lives on our factory farms. That being the case, wouldn't animal husbandry – the controlled breeding of animals – be better than hunting?

Not necessarily. Choosing to hunt may be more respectful of animals than domestication, since husbandry divests them of their autonomy, their ability to govern themselves. That's no small loss, even if the animals themselves are not in a position to recognize what's been stolen from them. Consider what the lives of Jake, Grace, and Norm Spellman might have been like if Trudy Chacón hadn't busted them out of the brig. Imagine they were forced to spend the rest of their lives in prison as traitors. For the sake of argument, let's assume that they're sent to a prison that's not overcrowded (as most real prisons are) and where the prisoners are treated well and never abused. They get, among other amenities, free meals, free health care, an exercise yard, and access to computers and a library. But, however comfortable their existence may be, they've still been deprived of something precious – their ability to come and go as they please, without having their choices dictated to them by someone else. Our recognition of the value of autonomy explains why we find people like Colonel Quaritch and Parker Selfridge so despicable. They don't respect the Na'vi's autonomy but treat them instead as though they were mere things to be manipulated – as "humanely" as possible, as savagely as necessary – for the sake of satisfying human needs. This is not much different from the way farmers treat their livestock.

So, if autonomy is a real value and its loss a real deprivation, then even the most humane forms of husbandry – those that provide animals with the kind of food they evolved to eat, with access to open spaces on a regular basis, and with many opportunities to engage in activities natural to their species – may fail to show these animals sufficient respect. That's not to say that farmers don't have *any* respect for their livestock (although factory farmers would be hard pressed to show that they do), but their relationship with these domesticated creatures lacks the deep respect the Na'vi show their prey. Perhaps hunting also violates an animal's autonomy, at least at the moment when its life is taken from it without permission. But that's just a moment – not a disrespectful, dominating relationship that lasts a lifetime. We don't need a neural queue to recognize that we owe our fellow creatures much better than that.

Acknowledgments

I'd like to thank George Dunn for a great deal of assistance with this chapter.

Notes

1. But, though *tsaheylu* might put the Na'vi in a better position to empathize with the other animals of Pandora, *tsaheylu* itself might not really qualify as a form of empathy. For a discussion of *tsaheylu* and empathy, see Chapter 6 by Massimiliano Cappuccio.
2. This doesn't mean that knowing what is going on in the mind of another will automatically generate a kind of deep respect. I may understand

what is going on in the mind of a serial killer, but I don't think I could ever empathize with or respect him or her.

3. Temple Grandin is the author of several popular books on animals and autism, such as *Animals in Translation: Using the Mysteries of Autism to Decode Animal Behavior* (New York: Simon & Schuster, 2005) and *Animals Make Us Human: Creating the Best Life for Animals* (New York: Houghton Mifflin Harcourt, 2009), both co-written with Catherine Johnson. She's also the subject of an extraordinary HBO (Home Box Office) biopic, *Temple Grandin* (2010), starring Claire Danes.

4. Temple Grandin, "Thinking the Way Animals Do," http://www.grandin. com/references/thinking.animals.html (accessed November 6, 2010).

5. Grandin, "Thinking the Way Animals Do."

6. Grandin, *Animals in Translation*, 8.

7. Ibid.

8. There are many good sources of information about conditions on factory farms. One especially well-written book that strives to be balanced in its presentation is Jonathan Safran Foer's *Eating Animals* (New York: Little, Brown and Company, 2009).

Part VII

SEEING THE MOVIE
"YOU ARE NOT GONNA BELIEVE WHERE I AM"

19

The Digital Cabinet of Curiosities
Avatar and the Phenomenology of 3D Worlds

Robert Furze and Pat Brereton

Avatar draws us into the beautiful and exciting world of Pandora, with its fantastic locations and its exotic and dangerous creatures. As we watch the film, we become immersed in this world, amazed by special effects that seem all the more special as they create an environment that is genuinely alien and exotic. We can believe in Pandora as a planet unlike our world or any world we have ever seen before. But is this a good thing?

The Na'vi on Main Street

When we become immersed in a fictional world, especially one that's so obviously imaginary as *Avatar*'s, we suspend our disbelief. A combination of elements – such as our sympathies for the characters, our interest in the story, and the film's enticing images – allows us to "forget ourselves" and, in a manner of speaking, to step into the world of the film. In the case of *Avatar*, our willingness to suspend our disbelief is helped by the fact that the digital, computer-generated Pandoran life forms, including the Na'vi themselves, are as real to our eyes as the human actors. So, while we know we would never see a Na'vi walking down the main street of a city, for the duration of the film and in the context of the world of *Avatar* we

Avatar and Philosophy: Learning to See, First Edition. Edited by George A. Dunn.
© 2014 John Wiley & Sons, Inc. Published 2014 by John Wiley & Sons, Inc.

have absolutely no doubt that they exist. And if we watch *Avatar* in 3D there is a further level of immersion, as the added depth of the images creates an even greater sense that we are able to enter the world of Pandora.

The experience of watching *Avatar* in 3D is like looking into a cabinet of curiosities, a pastime that was particularly popular during the Victorian era. These glass-enclosed cabinets contained strange and exotic things – such as plant and animal specimens from far-flung corners of the world – the likes of which people had never seen before. The digital 3D creatures of Pandora are just as strange and exotic to us, and just as realistic and compelling to gaze upon.

But are the special effects in *Avatar too* immersive? What if the suspension of disbelief becomes so total that we enjoy watching life on Pandora without noticing how the struggles of the Na'vi are no different from struggles taking place in our own world? If the "wow" factor of the film consumes all other aspects – such as the message creator James Cameron wants the audience to take away – then the film is in danger of becoming nothing more than entertainment

For Cameron, *Avatar* is as much an ecological film as it is a special effects-driven action extravaganza. In other words, he sees the film as delivering a message about what human beings are doing to our planet.[1] Just as the Resources Development Administration (RDA) corporation in *Avatar* is intent on mining the precious resource unobtanium while completely disregarding how its actions will affect the Pandoran balance of nature, so does the mining of oil in deserts and oceans threaten the global climate and environmental well-being of Earth. But, when we accept the invitation offered by *Avatar's* tagline to "Enter the World," do we completely forget about the world in which we live and flee to Pandora as a place of escape from our individual and global problems?

Running with Jake in the Recreation Yard

When we watch *Avatar,* we're engaged by the characters and how they interact with each other and their environment. We're also impressed by the action and the special effects. We can call these things the "what" and the "who" of the movie: "what" and "who" meaning "*what* happens" and "*who* is involved," or "*who* does it."

To illustrate this point, consider the sequence in which Jake Sully is first linked to his avatar. Watching this scene, we can see both *what* is happening and *who* is involved. We understand *what* is happening because we heard the scientists in the Avatar program explain the process earlier in the film. We also know something about Jake: that he's a marine who currently uses a wheelchair because of injuries he incurred in a terrible battle that happened before the story begins. So, when we see Jake put into a state of deep sleep in what looks like a high-tech coffin, we know this is part of the process of connecting him to a new body through which he will experience the world.

We see the first shot of this sequence through Jake's new eyes, viewing what looks like a hospital ceiling and two doctors who look down at him and ask whether he can hear them. When the next shot shows Jake in his avatar body, we can see that he has indeed been relocated to the body of a Na'vi.[2] And, as the scene progresses, we get a full view of what the Na'vi look like. They're blue, with stripes, yellow eyes, and tails, and they're much, much taller than human beings. They're also very athletic, as we learn when Jake escapes into the recreation yard to test how fast he can run on his new legs. We can also see his first reactions to the sight of his new limbs and how groggy he is when he steps off the gurney. Finally, we see him laughing with delight at the newfound freedom of his restored physical wholeness. The "who" and "what" of this scene are very clear: Jake is escaping from a hospital ward and running through a recreation yard.

When we watch this sequence, we don't just take in passively what we are seeing and hearing. We also experience it vicariously. When Jake first wakes up in his new body, we see through his eyes, as the camera gives his perspective, looking up from the gurney. The image of the doctors looking at him is slightly distorted and their words are echoed and a bit muffled, giving us an idea of how woozy Jake feels. But we don't just get to see through his eyes. We also get to share in his emotions. We feel exhilarated when he's running through the recreation yard, in part because, like Jake, we're experiencing the rush of learning for the first time what this new, athletic Na'vi body can do. But, what's more, we empathize with Jake. We're not just thrilled by the physical sensation of him running; we also understand what this freedom of mobility must mean to him as someone whose human body is confined to a wheelchair.

These, then, are the "whats" of *Avatar*: what happens and what we feel about the things that happen. But linking these two "whats" is the "how" – specifically, how the movie is able to draw us into its world and its characters. Let's return to the notion of *Avatar* as a cabinet of curiosities in which we see, hear, and respond emotionally to wonderful things behind a glass. When we consider the "how" of *Avatar*, we're asking why we're not also aware of the shape of the cabinet and of the glass that separates us from this other world of Pandora. We are considering what makes it possible for us to lose ourselves in that spectacle in the first place.

The Na'vi on the Other Side of the Keyhole

When we explore how we watch *Avatar*, we're paying attention to our own consciousness and adopting a *phenomenological* approach to the movie. Founded by Edmund Husserl (1859–1938), phenomenology is a way of doing philosophy that focuses on our *awareness* of the world in order to investigate how we experience and make sense of the things we encounter.[3]

Consider, for example, that when Jake wakes up in his new body he's aware of how different this Na'vi body is from the one to which he is accustomed. He's especially conscious of how unsteady he is. Focused on his body, he's not very aware of the other things around him, such as the room and the objects and people in it. They're all less important to him at that moment than learning how to stand and move around. But when he becomes used to the way his new body moves, he becomes far less conscious of *it* than of the *world* he uses it to navigate. When he almost runs smack into a soldier in an amplified mobility platform (AMP) suit, his consciousness is focused first on the soldier and then on the place to which he leaps to avoid a collision. And when Dr. Grace Augustine throws him a piece of fruit, his full attention is given to the fruit, so that he can catch it.

Like Jake, we are not aware of everything happening in the world around us, but only of selected details. And this fact can help us understand our experience of a movie like *Avatar*, which entirely immerses us in another world.

Our captivation by the action of the film is similar to an experience described by perhaps the most famous phenomenologist, Jean-Paul

Sartre (1905–1980), in his book *Being and Nothingness*.[4] Sartre asks us to imagine a voyeur looking through a keyhole. As the voyeur watches what's happening on the other side of the door, he's so wrapped up in what he sees that he forgets everything else, even himself. More precisely, the voyeur forgets his own body, becoming for all intents and purposes a disembodied observer. It's only when someone else looks at him that the voyeur is brought back to himself and feels shame at having been caught spying through a keyhole.[5]

Likewise, we forget ourselves when we watch *Avatar*. While we are engaged with the film, we aren't aware of our own bodies sitting in a cinema seat or on the couch at home. We're lost in the action on the screen. Phenomenologically, it's like we really are on Pandora with the Na'vi. Only when something interrupts our viewing do we become conscious of the world and of our own existence outside the film.

We can compare this experience of forgetting ourselves with what happens to Jake when he awakens in his avatar body. He's so completely absorbed in the experience of his avatar body that he's oblivious to having another body that's presently enclosed in a coffin-like machine. As he races laughingly through the recreation yard, his attention is swallowed up in his immediate experience of enjoying the abilities of this wonderfully strange physical form. Of course, this doesn't mean he entirely forgets his humanity, just as we, as viewers of the film, don't entirely forget our bodies. In both cases we know at some level where we are. But, as our bodies aren't relevant to us in any way that requires our immediate and ongoing attention, we temporarily forget about them.

The Two Jakes

Avatar's incredible special effects make Pandora seem as believable and real as our everyday world. Most of the creatures and plants of Pandora, including the Na'vi, are designed using computers. These digital special effects deliver a level of detail far beyond what was possible before computers started creating alien worlds and their inhabitants. Part of the reason why we can get lost in *Avatar*'s landscapes and creatures is that the digital special effects make them look so real.

We can appreciate how detailed the digital special effects are when we compare Jake in his avatar form to his ordinary appearance as a human being. When first introduced to his avatar, Jake observes that the blue creature floating in the tank looks like his twin brother Tommy. "No," says Norm Spellman, "it looks like you." This computer-generated version of Jake is so perfect that we in the audience can see the resemblance too. It has his features, but they're combined with the strange and exotic appearance of a Na'vi. What's significant from a phenomenological viewpoint, though, is that we can't see the seam. The face of digital Jake is as realistic as the face of Sam Worthington, the actor. Even though Jake's avatar has blue skin, stripes, and yellow eyes, these alterations are made digitally, in a way that preserves all the details of his real face. In close-up, we can even see that the skin of his avatar has pores. We can see his bone structure under his blue skin and the muscles and veins of his body. Jake's avatar looks just as natural and lifelike as human Jake.

Digital Jake seems so real because he's created through a process called motion capture, which maps the details of the computer-generated Na'vi form onto the movements of the live actor.[6] This means that, while key aspects of the avatar's appearance may be digitally created, the performance still belongs to Sam Worthington. This process is now so advanced that we can read the expressions of digital Jake as easily as we can read those of the human actor. In fact Jake looks so convincing, both as a human being and as a Na'vi, that we don't ever doubt the reality of either while we're watching the film. And, because what we see in *Avatar* is so believable, we find it easy to forget our own world.

Compare this to how such effects would have been done in the past, before computers could make the transformation so realistic and vivid. Sam Worthington would have had to paint his face blue or wear a mask. If he wore a mask, his skin wouldn't be nearly as convincing, since it would be made of some material that doesn't share the look or texture of real skin. Although we may still get wrapped up in the film, we'd be aware that something is not right about the world we're looking at. It would be hard to ignore the fact that Jake's avatar is really just an actor wearing a mask.

On the whole, this pre-digital version of *Avatar* would be much less convincing to us because not only the faces of the Na'vi but all of

Pandora would have to be made of materials that are obviously fabricated. It would all look too artificial, not like something from a far-off galaxy, but like something constructed on a movie lot right here on our own planet. Of course, it's true that before digital effects audiences were capable of suspending their disbelief when watching science fiction films, even when the aliens were obviously actors wearing makeup. But now we expect special effects that depict otherworldly creatures to be not so obviously of *this* world. Digital effects have made possible what was inconceivable when computers were not nearly so powerful, creating a semblance of reality that enhances both our pleasure and the degree of our immersion when watching a film like *Avatar*. The advantage of creating the world of *Avatar* digitally is that computers can create anything the special effects designers can imagine. They're not restricted by the limitations of rubber, modeling clay, paint, or other materials that would have been used in the past.

Into the Third Dimension

Another way *Avatar* enables us to view Pandora as real is through its use of 3D, which was something James Cameron wanted to get exactly right.[7] 3D in films gives the impression that images on a flat screen have real physical depth, creating what's called a stereoscopic effect. The experience is akin to listening to music in stereo, where different sounds come from each speaker. Similarly, when we watch a movie in 3D, a slightly different image is presented to each eye due to the way each lens of our special glasses filters what we see on the screen. When we watch a movie in 2D, it's like looking through a single eye. But with 3D we're seeing with both eyes, just as we do in the real world.

The effect is stunning. Fleeing from a ferocious thanator, Jake runs blindly through the forest, narrowly escaping the monster's jaws by making a wild leap off a cliff next to a waterfall. We see him from above as he plunges downward, the stereoscopic effect giving us a powerful sense of the depth of the waterfall and of the distance he has to fall. Because we feel like we're looking down a real waterfall, our physical and emotional response is similar to what we would experience if it were really happening to us. Our heart rate accelerates and we may grip the edge of our seat (or the person sitting next to us). In this way the 3D experience, too, helps us to forget our surroundings and become immersed in the world of *Avatar*.

But Is *Avatar* Too Real?

Avatar's use of digital 3D allows us to forget our world and to enter a new world of fantastic but believable creatures. Can these digital and 3D effects be too good, however? Does forgetting about our world run the risk that Cameron's ecological message may be lost?

From the beginning, Cameron has said that *Avatar* is, above all else, a film with a message. It's his response to the things he believes are wrong with our world, such as our wars and the enormous dangers that our reckless patterns of consumption pose to the Earth's environment and climate. *Avatar* offers an ecological warning, telling us that something is going terribly wrong on planet Earth and encouraging us to be kind to our planet.

But, according to our phenomenological argument, all our attention when watching *Avatar* is swallowed up by the wonderful digital special effects and by the excitement of seeing this new world. And, because for the duration of the movie we forget about ourselves and the problems of *this* world, the movie's message might be forgotten too. It seems possible that we become so immersed in this breathtakingly beautiful digital reality that we miss the bigger message that Cameron wants to send through the medium of film.

But there's something else we need to consider. While we may concentrate on only certain *aspects* of our world at any given time, phenomenologists point out that we make sense of those aspects by relating them to what we already know of the world *as a whole*, that is, the world in which we conduct our daily lives. The upshot is that we can become lost in the world of *Avatar* only because there are certain aspects of that world that resemble our more familiar experiences here in the quotidian world of ordinary reality.

If *Avatar* were completely alien to our experience, it would in fact be unwatchable. We would be unable to follow the story or feel empathy for any of the characters. But this is not at all the case: impressed as we are by the film's special effects, we can also see in those effects something we recognize from our own experience.

Ecology and Special Effects

Imagine describing the appearance of the Na'vi to a friend who's neither watched the film nor seen any pictures from it. You might tell her that the Na'vi look human, except for certain differences, such as their blue skin, their very, *very* tall height, and their bright yellow eyes. You might also mention the tiger-like stripes on their arms and legs. You could also describe their braided hair and remark that they have an ancient "tribal" look. You might remind your friend of photographs or paintings she may have seen of other ancient tribal cultures, such as the Native Americans or the Zulu of southern Africa.

It's clear what is happening in this conversation. Because your friend has no idea what the Na'vi are like, you have to describe them using things she already knows. All your words are taken from her everyday experience, even if they're combined in some surprising ways ("blue skin"). You help your friend to understand something new by comparing it to something she already knows. And this is exactly how phenomenologists say that we make sense of new things we encounter: we compare them to the things we already know.

As you describe the Na'vi to your friend, you draw connections between the Na'vi and people in our world, such as indigenous tribes, whose lifestyle is similar to that of the Na'vi. Thinking about the importance of the ecological balance of Pandora to the Na'vi may then lead you to reflect on how those indigenous tribes in our world manage to live in harmony with the same environment that our modern civilization recklessly destroys. The comparisons that allow us to understand the movie – not just when we're describing it to a friend, but even as we sit watching it in the theatre – take us directly to the heart of Cameron's message.

The special effects actually help us to make these connections. Jake's avatar looks like Jake in his human form, except that it has the physical characteristics of a Na'vi. As we learn more about the freedom and wisdom of the Na'vi and we connect them with people who live close to nature on our planet, we may come to see them as better versions of ourselves. The message of the film gets through precisely because the digital effects that turn Jake into a full-fledged Na'vi – at first only in outward appearance, but later in spirit as well – offer a powerful visual allegory for the transformation we must all undergo as we learn to emulate the Na'vi's simpler and purer attitude toward nature.

Cameron, for his part, is also making sure that the real-life peoples who inspired the Na'vi way of life continue to be part of our experience. In 2010 he visited a tiny village in the Brazilian rainforest, where a project to build a huge hydroelectric dam threatens the Xingu tribe's way of life. By raising awareness about the plight of these rainforest dwellers, Cameron reminds us of how the Na'vi are not so very different from people who live on our own planet. As extensively reported in the press, Cameron has become a spokesperson and activist for the Xingu people, all the while comparing their way of life with the purity of Na'vi existence.[8]

A phenomenological view of *Avatar* allows us to see how its special effects can have a positive influence on how we view our own world. Rather than dismissing it as a film that only entertains us for a few hours, we can appreciate how its use of advanced, digital special effects to create a fantastic but believable alternative reality actually reinforces our ability to connect the events of *Avatar* to our own world. As dreamlike as *Avatar* may be, at its center is a message to which we all need to wake up. What's going on inside the digital cabinet may well hold our attention, but only because we recognize something of our own lives behind the glass.

Notes

1. James Cameron has campaigned extensively on "green issues." It is impossible to list here every magazine, newspaper, or online article written about his thoughts on our current global crisis. The pieces referred to in this chapter are only the tip of the iceberg. For an overview of his opinions, you might also want to read the online article "James Cameron Says Avatar a Message to Stop Damaging Environment," *The Telegraph* Online (2009), http://www.telegraph.co.uk/culture/film/film-news/6782339/James-Cameron-says-Avatar-a-message-to-stop-damaging-environment.html (accessed July 12, 2010).
2. Or, more accurately, a human–Na'vi hybrid.
3. Husserl's major exploration into phenomenology began in the early years of the 1900s, with a two-volume classic that's still in print. See Edmund Husserl, trans. J. N. Findlay, *Logical Investigations* (London: Routledge, 2001). For a discussion of Hussel's contribution to our understanding of empathy, see Chapter 6 by Massimiliano Cappuccio.

4. Jean-Paul Sartre, *Being and Nothingness*, trans. Hazel E. Barnes (London: Methuen, 1986). Sartre is famous for developing the concept of existentialism, which works with Husserl's original ideas to probe further into the relationship between human beings and their ways of experiencing the world.

5. Of course, we don't feel ashamed if we're caught watching *Avatar*. That's because Sartre's voyeur is doing something he shouldn't and we aren't. Even so, Sartre's example perfectly illustrates how we can become so wrapped up in another world when we watch a film that we forget for the moment that we're actually sitting watching that film. See Sartre, *Being and Nothingness*, 259–260.

6. For an excellent work on the techniques and meanings of digital acting, see Dan North, *Performing Illusions: Cinema, Special Effects and the Virtual Actor* (London: Wallflower, 2008). The book was written before *Avatar* but is a very interesting examination on this subject.

7. Cameron's love of the technology and the expanse of epic cinema is well documented. For a discussion of this topic with the director, see William Langley, "The Master of Epics – and Monster Budgets," *The Sunday Telegraph* (December 13, 2009), 19.

8. Tom Phillips, "Director Joins Real-Life Avatar Battle in the Amazon Forest," *The Observer* (April 18, 2010), 3.

Notes on Contributors
Our Avatar Drivers

Stephanie Adair is a philosophy PhD candidate at Duquesne University in Pittsburgh, and is currently teaching at the Universität Heidelberg in Germany. If it takes a journey to another world and a fight to the death against The Man to really *see* the truths of the universe, she's signing her whole class up for the next transport out of here.

Jeremy David Bendik-Keymer is the Beamer-Schneider Professor in Ethics at Case Western Reserve University in Cleveland, Ohio and author of *The Ecological Life: Discovering Citizenship and a Sense of Humanity* (2006). He is an old Boy Scout and grew up with farmers in his extended family, on whose farm he worked as a boy. When he saw *Avatar*, his love for sci-fi merged with echoes from his childhood and he felt right at home. An added twist is that his Grandpa Bendik was a miner for a quarter century in southern Ohio. The things of fantasy come from the things of our world.

Pat Brereton teaches at the School of Communications at Dublin City University. He is committed to promoting ecology and likes living in another world of science fiction. He believes that *Avatar* and its innovations in special effects have been a major development in film production and deserve to be examined in great detail. Furthermore, he believes that philosophy, which has informed much of his writing over the past few years, has become an important avenue for thinking

Avatar and Philosophy: Learning to See, First Edition. Edited by George A. Dunn.
© 2014 John Wiley & Sons, Inc. Published 2014 by John Wiley & Sons, Inc.

about film. If witnessing utopian spaces being ravaged on other worlds provides a useful means of teaching mass audiences about the ecological problems we are causing on this planet, then he's all for it.

Matthew Brophy teaches business ethics as Assistant Professor of Philosophy at High Point University, North Carolina, where he's paid in unobtanium. He resides with his beautiful wife and above-average child in Greensboro, North Carolina. In his free time he avidly champions equal rights for blue people everywhere, from Na'vi to Night Elves to Smurfs.

Kyle Burchett is a doctoral candidate in the Department of Philosophy at the University of Kentucky. His research aims at understanding how negative interactions between human beings and their environment are ultimately based on metaphysical assumptions that negate human life. He traces the cause of the current mass extinction event to anthropocentric notions that arbitrarily restrict the moral community to a small number of organisms, deemed to be "like us." He plans to conduct research into the minds of microorganisms on his next assignment to Pandora, preferably deep within the Flux Vortex.

Massimiliano Cappuccio is a postdoctoral researcher in philosophy whose previous research linked the philosophy of mind with cognitive neuroscience and phenomenology. His current work is focused on empathy, motor intentionality, gestures, and the origins of symbolic culture, employing a perspective that combines enactive and extended approaches to cognition. Having previously studied and worked in Italy, France, Holland, Scotland, and the United States, he's currently applying for a grant to travel to Pandora, where he plans to conduct research to determine whether the macaque-like prolemuris possesses mirror neurons.

Kevin S. Decker teaches philosophy of pop culture, ethics, and American philosophy at Eastern Washington University. He has been widely published in various philosophy and popular culture series and is the co-editor of *Star Wars and Philosophy* (2005), *Star Trek and Philosophy* (2008), and *Terminator and Philosophy* (Wiley Blackwell, 2009). His house in Spokane, Washington sits on the largest single remaining unobtanium deposit on Earth, and he expects to be evicted quite soon (and quite violently).

Dan Dinello is Professor Emeritus at Columbia College Chicago. Using only his queue, he wrote *Technophobia! Science Fiction Visions of Posthuman Technology* (2007) and *Finding Fela: My Strange Journey to Meet the Afrobeat King* (2012), while contributing chapters to *The Culture and Philosophy of Ridley Scott* (2013), *The Rolling Stones and Philosophy* (2012), and *Philip K. Dick and Philosophy* (2011). An amalgamation of human and Na'vi DNA, Dan operates the website Shockproductions.com via psionic link.

George A. Dunn teaches philosophy at the University of Indianapolis, the Ningbo Institute of Technology, Zhejiang University in China, and Indiana University–Purdue University at Indianapolis. He is the co-editor of *True Blood and Philosophy* (Wiley Blackwell, 2010), *The Hunger Games and Philosophy* (2012), and *Sons of Anarchy and Philosophy* (2013), and the editor of *Veronica Mars and Philosophy* (2014). Teaching on two continents, George flies regularly between the United States and China – but, alas, not on the back of a giant leonopteryx, which would certainly make the 14-hour flight much less tedious. He's often thought about how nice it would be to have an avatar on the other side of the world. But, until psionic link technology becomes available, he's asking the airlines to put him in cryo.

Jason T. Eberl is the Semler Endowed Chair for Medical Ethics at the Marian University College of Osteopathic Medicine in Indianapolis. He teaches and publishes in bioethics, medieval philosophy, and metaphysics. He's the editor of *Battlestar Galactica and Philosophy* (Wiley Blackwell, 2008) the co-editor, with Kevin Decker, of *Star Wars and Philosophy* (2005) and *Star Trek and Philosophy* (2008), and the co-editor, with George A. Dunn, of *Sons of Anarchy and Philosophy* (2013). He's contributed to similar volumes on Stanley Kubrick, *The Hunger Games*, Metallica, and other topics. Jason refuses to watch *Avatar* on Blu Ray until he's able to install a 3D IMAX projector and screen in his home so he can view it the way James Cameron intended.

Nathan Eckstrand is a graduate student at Duquesne University in Pittsburgh. Specializing in social and political philosophy, he is the co-editor of *Philosophy and the Return of Violence* (2011). Since childhood Nathan has been an avid fan of science fiction movies, but his dream of going into space and exploring new worlds had to be put on hold when he realized that Pandora had yet to be discovered and the avatar technology yet to be created.

Joseph J. Foy is Associate Professor of Political Science at the University of Wisconsin-Waukesha. Foy is the editor of the John G. Cawelti award-winning book *Homer Simpson Goes to Washington: American Politics through Popular Culture* (2008) and co-editor of the follow-up *Homer Simpson Marches on Washington: Dissent through American Popular Culture* (2010). Although Foy spends a lot of time in the world of politics, he continues to turn to philosophy in hopes that his insanity can be cured.

The late **Robert Furze** completed his PhD at Dublin City University where he taught film studies in the School of Communication. His research was focused on the incommunicable aspects of cinema and the visual language of new media, with a particular emphasis on video game theory. His book *The Visceral Screen: Between the Cinemas of John Cassavetes and David Cronenberg* is being published by Intellect Ltd. His spirit lives on in his writings.

Dennis Knepp teaches philosophy and religious studies at Big Bend Community College in Moses Lake, Washington. He has contributed essays to *Twilight and Philosophy* (Wiley Blackwell, 2009), *Alice in Wonderland and Philosophy* (Wiley Blackwell, 2009), *The Hobbit and Philosophy* (Wiley Blackwell, 2012), *Superman and Philosophy* (Wiley Blackwell, 2013), and others. Until Dennis makes *tsaheylu* with his own ikran, he will be chasing hexapedes in his wife's 1990 Toyota Corolla.

James Lawler teaches philosophy at SUNY/Buffalo and is the author of *The God Tube: Uncovering the Hidden Spiritual Message in Pop Culture* (2010), which explains the philosophical tradition from Plato, Kant, and Hegel through *The Simpsons*, *The Matrix*, *Star Wars*, *Buffy the Vampire Slayer*, and Woody Allen's *Crimes and Misdemeanors*. Look for his forthcoming book on pop culture and philosophy, *Jean Baudrillard's Impossible Exchange: Transliteration* *and Elaboration* (2014). His favorite human person is Sigourney Weaver, who braved the aliens on planet LV-426 to rescue little Newt, strapped down with more ammo than Neo and Trinity combined. Jim wishes to thank James Cameron for giving Sigourney a well-deserved respite on Pandora, so she can collect samples before passing through the eye of Eywa. Jim thinks about such things a lot.

Nicolas Michaud co-edited *The Hunger Games and Philosophy* (Wiley Blackwell, 2012) with George A. Dunn. Nick was encouraged to see *Avatar* by Powell Kriess, a woman far better suited to live among the beautiful things of Pandora than here on Earth. Having learned to "see" the film through her eyes, he has fallen deeply in love with it, the forest, the People, and her.

Dale Murray is Associate Professor of Philosophy and holds a joint appointment at the University of Wisconsin-Baraboo/Sauk County and University of Wisconsin-Richland. He is the author of the book *Nozick, Autonomy and Compensation* (2007), in addition to several articles and reviews. Dale's article "Making Mountains out of Heaps: Environmental Protection One Stone at a Time" was published in *Climbing: Because It's There (Philosophy for Everyone)*, edited by Stephen Schmid (Wiley Blackwell, 2010), a 2010 finalist for the Boardman Tasker Prize for Mountain Literature. Dale's research is mainly in social and political philosophy and applied ethics. When he is not engaged in academic pursuits, he tries to imagine he is nothing more than his avatar.

Asra Q. Nomani teaches journalism at Georgetown University. She is the author of *Tantrika: Traveling the Road of Divine Love* (2004), *Standing Alone: An American Woman's Struggle for the Soul of Islam* (2006), and *Milestones for a Spiritual Jihad: Toward an Islam of Grace* (2010). She is co-director of the Pearl Project, an investigation into the murder of Wall Street Journal reporter Daniel Pearl. Her activism for women's rights at her mosque in West Virginia is the subject of a PBS documentary: *The Mosque in Morgantown*. She channels Neytiri whenever she can.

Ryan Smock teaches philosophy and British literature at the Charles A. Tindley Accelerated School. His life's work is dedicated to applying video game design and theory to educational practice and to ushering in the upcoming era of human enhancement through genetic manipulation, biotechnology, electronics, and robotics. He regards the Avatar program, the development of the first fully functional AMP suit, and the successful integration of brain matter with microchips as fine examples of things to come. He is also awaiting corporate approval to replace his "deficient" eyes with advanced synthetic counterparts.

Andrew Terjesen has a PhD in philosophy from Duke University and a JD from the University of Virginia School of Law. Previously a visiting Assistant Professor at Austin College, Washington and Lee University, and Rhodes College, he will soon begin practicing law in New York City. He is especially interested in ethics and its intersections with psychology, biology, and economics. Andrew has contributed essays to other volumes in the Blackwell Philosophy and Pop Culture series that touch upon these interests, including *Battlestar Galactica and Philosophy* (Wiley Blackwell, 2008), *Iron Man and Philosophy* (Wiley Blackwell, 2010), and *Green Lantern and Philosophy* (2011). Although he loves his work, Andrew knows he has to put his money wisely in inflation-resistant investments. Hopefully he'll do a better job cornering the unobtanium market than he did with adamantium.

Wayne Yuen teaches philosophy at Ohlone College and is an avid geek of everything James Cameron. He has contributed essays to *Terminator and Philosophy* (Wiley Blackwell, 2009) and several other Philosophy and Pop Culture volumes. He was once immobile in a chair, but then realized that the movie was over and decided to leave before the clean-up crew thought he was a *skxawng*.

Index
My Last Video Log

Americans with Disabilities Act (1990), 144
analogy, empathy as process of, 76, 77
animal husbandry, 233–236
animal rights activism, 233, 234
anthropocentrism, 92, 96, 115–123
Aquinas, Thomas, 23, 25, 26, 27–28, 29, 31, 32
Aristotle, 127
  De anima, 92
  Politics, 92–93
Augustine of Hippo, Saint, 30, 31, 172–173
authenticity, 119, 120
autonomy, value of, 236

Baier, Annette, 15, 16
Balcombe, Jonathan: *Pleasurable Kingdom*, 93
beauty of God, 23, 26, 32
being
  hierarchy of, 27, 29
  property of, 23, 25, 26, 32
Bekoff, Marc, 97

Wild Justice (with Pierce), 95–96
Benedict XVI, Pope, 20
Bihar School of Yoga, 38
biocentrism, 118
bio-communitarian homeland, 187
bio-communitarianism, 186–188
biodiversity, Christian view of, 21
biophilia, 121
body image, 134
British Petroleum (BP), 116, 160
Buber, Martin, 121
Buddhism, 37, 46
Burkhart, Brian Yazzie, 220
Bush, George W., 161
business ethics, 203–213
bystander apathy, 211

Cameron, James, 1, 2, 3, 19, 30, 36, 123, 139, 199, 222, 242, 247–250
capitalism, 182
Capturing Avatar (documentary), 36
care ethics, 11–13, 14–15, 16–17
  feminine voice on, 9, 10

Avatar and Philosophy: Learning to See, First Edition. Edited by George A. Dunn.
© 2014 John Wiley & Sons, Inc. Published 2014 by John Wiley & Sons, Inc.

Carr, Albert, 204
Carson, Rachel: *Silent Spring*, 117
Catholic Church, anti-environmentalist
    stance of, 19
C-fibers, 226–227
Chalmers, David, 147, 148
Christianity, attitude toward nature,
    20, 21, 22–24, 28–33
Clark, Andy, 147, 148
cognitive empathy, 62, 64, 65, 66, 72
cognitive ethologists, 95
colonial attitude, 216–217
colonialism, 190–200
communitarianism, 180–188
community, principle of, 216,
    220–221
consciousness, 97
contractualism, 9, 11
Cordova, Viola F., 219
Cosmopolitanism, 41
Cox, Earl, 160
cruelty, 29, 30
cultural imperialism, 153
Cvek, Peter, 27

Dances with Wolves, 215
Darwin, Charles, 113
Davis, Erik, 157
deep humanity, 116–117
deism, 21
Descartes, René, 93, 97, 129,
    157, 220
dialectical logic, 106, 112
dialectical reason, 111
diffusion of responsibility,
    210–211
disability, 139–150
disciplines of normality, 141–142,
    144, 149
discrimination, principle of, 176
dualism, doctrine of, 157
duty, 53, 54

ecocentrism, 117, 118, 120
emotional engagement, caring
    and, 15
empathic distress, 70
empathy, 62–73, 229
    limits of, 74–85
empiricism, 104, 105, 107–109,
    110, 112
engrossment, 14, 16
entitlement theory, 206
environmental ethics, 117–118, 120
epistemic action, 148
essential self, 130, 131, 133, 135, 136
evolution, theory of, 24, 113
existential phenomenology, 132,
    135, 136
existentialism, 228
extended mind hypothesis, 81–82

factory farming, 233, 234, 235
Fanon, Franz, 191–193, 194, 200
    Black Skin, White Masks, 193
    Wretched of the Earth, The,
      191, 195
feminine ethical theories, 9, 17
Fern Gully: The Last Rainforest, 215
Feuerstein, Georg, 37, 41
fiduciary duty, 207–208, 209,
    210, 211
flight, as metaphor for freedom,
    39–40
folk theory of essences, 127–128,
    129, 135
Ford Motor Company, 205
Francis of Assisi, Saint, 23
Franklin, Benjamin, 216
free market capitalism, 182
Friedman, Milton, 203, 205, 207, 208

Gandhi, Mahatma, 117
Gates, Bill, 64
gender differences in ethics, 8–9

Genesis, Book of, 19, 22, 30–32
Gilligan, Carol, 13
  In a Different Voice, 8–9
goodness, property of, 23, 25,
  26–27, 32
Gorke, Martin: *Death of Our
  Planet's Species, The*, 91–92
grace of God, 31–32
Grandin, Temple, 231–232
gravity, 113
Gray, Commander Shari, 211
grief, 229
Griffin, Donald, 97
Griffin, Susan, 142
growth, principle of, 216, 221–223
Gyatso, Geshe Kelsang: *Guide to
  Dakini Land*, 43

habits, 132
Halliburton, 160
Hegel, Georg Wilhelm Friedrich,
  104–114
  Philosophy of Nature, 104, 105
Heraclitus, 54
Hill, Lenora Hatathlie, 134
Hinduism, 37, 45
Hobbes, Thomas, 168–169, 170, 171,
  172, 177, 180–181, 183, 184
  Leviathan, 167
homeland, 187
humanity, sense of, 116–118, 119,
  120, 121, 122, 123
hunting, 26, 33, 76, 106–107, 171,
  187, 230, 234–235
Husserl, Edmund, 76, 80, 244

identity, sense of, 128, 129
immanence of God, Christian
  view of, 21
imperialism, 184, 185
indigenous attitude, 216
individualism, 180–188
insanity, 90–92

intelligence of plants, 98–100
interaction, principle of, 216,
  217–218
interpersonal conflict, 10
ius ad bellum, 173, 175, 178
ius in bello, 173, 176, 177, 178

Jaggar, Alison, 55
Jerry Springer Show, The, 64
Johari, Harish, 40
Johnson, Mark, 135
  Philosophy in the Flesh
    (with Lakoff), 127, 128
just war theory, 167–177, 206
justice, 11, 12, 15, 16–17
  masculine voice on, 9

Kant, Immanuel, 109
Khajuraho, Indian village of, 44
Khanna, Madhu, 40
"Kingdom of God," 31, 32
kinship, 119
Kurzweil, Ray, 156

labor theory of property, 181
Lakoff, George, 135
  Philosophy in the Flesh
    (with Johnson), 127, 128
LeBlanc, Jill, 23
liberalism, 180
Lipps, Theodor, 75, 80
Locke, John, 129, 130–132, 133,
  135, 181–182, 183
  *An Essay concerning Human
    Understanding*, 129
loyalty, 217

macrocosm, 113
masculine ethical theories, 9–10, 17
materialism, 157
maternal work, 13–14
"melting pot" idea, 219
memory, 130

Merleau-Ponty, Maurice,
132–134, 135
microcosm, 113
Milgram, Stanley, 212–213
mind transfer, 156–158, 159
mind–body interaction, 132–133, 157
mirror neurons, 79–81
Mookerjee, Ajit, 40
moral distance, 211
More, Max, 152
mother, role of, 13–16
motivational displacement, 14, 16
motor reflexes, 132
Muktananda, Swami, 38
multiple realizability, 83–84

Narragansett philosophy, 218, 221
Native American philosophy,
215–223
Native American spirituality, 134
Navajo ceremony, 134
Nazism, 187–188
neocolonialism, 195, 198
Newton, Sir Isaac, 113
Nietzsche, Friedrich, 55, 58
Noddings, Nel, 13, 14, 15, 17
Noë, Alva, 96, 97

observation versus seeing, 55–56, 59
opacity, empathy and, 81, 84
Orientalists, 197
Osservatore Romano, L', 19, 21

pain
physical, 226–228
suffering versus, 228–229
pantheism, 21, 23
Paul, Gregory, 160
Peirce, Charles Sanders, 217, 218,
220, 222
"Fixation of Belief, The," 216
"How to Make Our Ideas
Clear," 216

personal identity, 129, 130,
131–132, 133
phenomenology, 241–250
Pierce, Jessica, 97
Wild Justice (with Bekoff), 95–96
pity, sense of, 29
Plato, 127
pluralism, principle of, 216,
218–220
Pocahontas, 215
pragmatism, 216–223
Pratt, Scott, 218, 220–221, 223
Native Pragmatism, 216–217
private property, 215
profit maximization, 207–208, 209,
210, 212–213
progress, principle of, 222
property, labor theory of, 181
property rights, 206–207
proportionality, principle of,
176–177
Punja, Shobita: Khajuraho: The First
Thousand Years, 44

Realpolitik, 168
reciprocal altruism, 95
reenactive empathy, 66, 67, 68, 70, 71
relational reason, 115–123
religious ethics, 204
respect, 53–54
for life and mind, 89–101
for other creatures, 226–236
Rinpoche, Sogyal, 46
Rizzolatti, Giacomo, 79
Ruddick, Sara, 13, 14
Ryle, Gilbert, 157

Said, Edward, 198, 200
Orientalism, 195–196, 197
Saldana, Zoe, 228
Sandel, Michael, 185
Sartre, Jean-Paul, 244–245
Being and Nothingness, 245

scientific materialism, 152, 154, 161
scientific method, 219
seeing, 51–61, 67, 92, 94–95,
        100–101, 134
    scientific manner of, 54–55
    observation versus, 55–56, 59
Shakespeare, William, 12
shareholder theory, 213
Shelley, Mary: *Frankenstein*, 153
Simard, Suzanne, 100
simulation theorists, 68
sin, 31
Singer, Peter, 208
Smith, Adam, 75, 204
    Theory of Moral Sentiments, 67
Smith, Maureen E., 219
social contract, 169, 171, 181,
        183–184
socially extended mind, 82–83, 85
Socrates, 129
Solomon, Robert, 132
Splice (2010), 142
squatters' property rights, 206
Star Trek, 77
Stein, Edith, 64, 76, 80
stigma, 139–150
Stoics, 172
stream of consciousness, 130, 132
suffering versus pain, 228–229
sympathy, 75

Tantra, 36–48
    ajna, 46
    anahata, 45
    atman (true self), 46
    bardo (transitional state) of
        dying, 46
    chakras, 40–41
    "experiencing nectar," principle
        of, 42–43
    manipura, 42
    muladhara, 41–42
    sahasrara, 46–47

    swadhisthana, 42
    vishuddha, 45
Tardiff, Andrew, 29
Tarnas, Richard, 161
technological transcendence, 151–162
theory theorists, 68
Thompson, Evan, 96, 97
three-dimensional effects, use of,
        247–248
Tibetan Book of the Dead, 46
transcendence of God, Christian
        view of, 21, 23
transhumanism, 151–152, 153,
        156–162
Trewavas, Anthony, 98–99
True Grit, 216

value of rational and nonrational
        creatures (Aquinas), 27–29
Vatican
    anti-environmentalist stance of, 19
    environmental principles of, 20
Vatican Radio, 21
vegetarianism, 31, 232–233, 235
Vietnam War, 160–161
violence, 11, 29, 31, 52–53, 192–193
    constructive, 192
    gratuitous, 176
    as last resort, 173
vivisection, 93, 111
voyeurism, 245

Wakeford, Tom, 99, 100
Wayne, John, 216
Wendell, Susan, 141, 142
    Rejected Body, The, 140
White, Lynn, Jr., 22, 23, 28
Wiliams, Roger, 221
    *Key into the Language of
        America, A*, 218
Worthington, Sam, 246

Yeshe, Lama, 38, 42

Printed and bound by CPI Group (UK) Ltd, Croydon, CR0 4YY

25/03/2025

14647350-0005